WHY NOT ME?

CRA

A000 000 000 8294

WHY NOT ME?

A Story of Love and Loss

BARBARA WANT

Weidenfeld & Nicolson

LONDON

First published in Great Britain in 2010
by Weidenfeld & Nicolson

1 3 5 7 9 10 8 6 4 2

Text © Barbara Want 2010

A CIP catalogue record for this book
is available from the British Library.

ISBN-13 978 0 297 85187 5

Typeset by Input Data Services Ltd,
Bridgwater, Somerset

Printed in Great Britain by
CPI Mackays, Chatham, Kent

Weidenfeld & Nicolson

The Orion Publishing Group Ltd
Orion House
5 Upper Saint Martin's Lane
London, WC2H 9EA
An Hachette UK Company
www.orionbooks.co.uk

The Orion Publishing Group's policy is to use papers
that are natural, renewable and recyclable products
and made from wood grown in sustainable forests.
The logging and manufacturing processes are expected
to conform to the environmental regulations of the
country of origin.

To Sarah Kershaw

Who helped me piece my life back together

I am staring at a photo taken in the summer of 2005. My husband Nick sits on a sofa in the drawing room of an elegant country house. Cupped in his arms, one on each side, are two slumbering three-year-olds, their heads drooping, their lips moist and slightly parted, their long brown eyelashes resting motionless on sun-kissed skin.

I can feel the heat of that day, smell the long, damp grass spattered wet from a waterslide down which twenty children have slithered and screamed, hear their peals of laughter drifting in from the garden and snaking down the hallway. It is late in the afternoon and the cool indoors provides a refuge as the long hot day begins to take its toll.

Nick's face glows from fresh air and sunshine, and from the love and pride he feels for those two sleeping boys, his sons, our children. His smile seems to lift itself out of the photo and plead with me to join him, and I so want to reach out — and find a way back into that glorious, precious day. It is still a recent memory, so recent that if I turn round and look into my past I feel as if I can touch it.

I want to be there next to him and stop the fun, end the day, quell the laughter and scream at Nick, 'You've got cancer. This is all going to stop. You're going to die.' Because looking at him now and knowing what was happening and what lay ahead for us, is unbearable.

ONE

I don't spend a lot of time thinking, 'Why me?' People always say that's what you must think, but I don't. If you're slightly fatalistic about cancer, as I am, then you always think 'why not me?'

NICK'S AUDIO DIARY, APRIL 2006

They say death announces itself. It did for me, but I misread the signs.

It knocked at the door long before I heard it. Like the rumble of a distant train, I knew it was out there somewhere but had no idea it was headed my way. A premonition, I thought, a strong and unfathomable premonition. But unlike premonitions I'd had before, this one was sinister: an uneasy, creeping discomfort which was as inexplicable as it was ridiculous and which my rational mind told me to ignore.

And I tried to. I began to talk glibly about death, but it was *my* death I talked about, *my* death I thought I heard calling. I even consulted the vicar at my local church about my funeral arrangements. 'Will you bury me?' I asked, somewhat to his surprise. My conversations became littered with morbid banter. 'I don't think I'm going to live that long,' I joked to a shopkeeper who was trying to sell me a Christmas stencilling kit which he promised would last me 'for years'. When I peered into the future it seemed to collapse in on itself, leaving a part-blank canvas; a sure sign, I thought, that my days were numbered.

3

Looking back now, I can see my intuition had picked up on something lurking in the wings of our lives that summer of 2005. It was our luck, and it was running out. But wrapped up with two young boys and the chaos of our daily domestic routine, I couldn't see it. I didn't spot that Nick was losing weight: a stone and a half over the course of a few months. Fifteen years of marriage and the easy familiarity that came in its wake meant my senses were no longer acute. Nick chose not to notice either. 'I realized my watch strap was getting looser and made a note to buy a new one,' he wrote later. At work people commented that he was pale and often tired. 'That's what happens when you have young children,' he said, and laughed it off. It seemed funny at the time.

What he did notice was a tightening sensation in his left buttock. It began to encroach on his walking. 'Maybe you should see an osteopath to ease it,' I suggested half-heartedly, knowing that Nick regarded any form of medical intervention as undesirable at best, suspect at worst. 'It feels like a muscle spasm. It'll go away in time,' he insisted, while noting in his diary:

> I constructed a diagnosis based on half-digested bits of medical information: a trapped nerve or muscle strain was causing me to walk awkwardly, and it was this that had caused a slight swelling. For a time, I even did exercises to try to relieve the pressure, reassured by the fact that the bump didn't seem to get any bigger. It didn't get any smaller, either.

It gave him no pain, but as that glorious hot summer spilled into a warm and mellow autumn, his mood changed. He started to get tetchy. 'You're so bloody grumpy at times,' I snapped irritably one day, and to my further irritation he said nothing but looked downcast and turned away from me. He began to get tired, so tired he couldn't push the boys' buggy and I had to take over. 'Oh, the perils of being an older father,' I muttered under my breath with yet more annoyance. For the first time in our eighteen years together he didn't buy me a birthday present that year and I wondered whether he was losing interest in me.

And then one day he couldn't walk down some steps. And that was when everything changed. For ever.

Death no longer knocked at the door. It entered our house. And was all around us.

That day was in September. Nick and I had travelled, as we'd often done in the past, to New York to visit Jane Cooke, widow of the broadcaster Alistair Cooke who had died the previous year. Nick had struck up a close relationship with Alistair over the years he had spent writing his biography and Jane now wanted to give Nick a memento from Alistair – some drawings by the British political cartoonist David Low – and she'd insisted that he collect them himself. Maybe, at the age of ninety-three, and knowing that Nick had little reason now to travel stateside, she wanted to see him for what she thought might be the last time.

I flew out ahead of Nick to spend some time idling and shopping with an old friend, but my stomach churned with fear. I tried to reason that all mothers, separated from small children, experience such churnings and I put them down to maternal angst. But my long-awaited break provided little respite.

I said nothing of this to Nick. And he said nothing to me of the onset of his own worries, which started around this time.

I think the closeness that had grown between us in what had become an exceptionally strong marriage had made us over-protective of each other.

At the weekend we joined Jane at the Cooke family retreat at Nassau Point on Long Island. It is a perfect spot, a spit of land on the northern shore with house and garden perched precariously above the waters of the Peconic Bay on the Long Island Sound. Summer was fading but the air was warm and the light luminescent. Nick grilled swordfish for dinner in the small kitchen with its ancient cooker, unchanged since the house was built back in the 1940s, and he and Jane dug the Low cartoons out of Alistair's study. We slept in the small single beds used by Cooke children and grandchildren over the years, and woke to a hypnotic stillness. Stepping out through the large glass doors, we watched the sun burning through the early-morning mist and reflecting harshly off the white clap-board walls. Across the bay nothing moved but the fishing boats, mere specks sending out ripples across a shiny glass surface. An osprey soared gently above.

But something was different that day. And it wasn't that, for the first time in many visits, Alistair wasn't there. There was a flight of wooden steps – nearly a hundred in all – from the cliff-top garden behind the house down to the beach below where we had stood together so often before, mesmerized by the empty expanse of silver-blue water and lulled by the sound of its gentle currents lapping on the shingle at our feet. 'Let's go down before breakfast and walk along the shore,' I suggested. To my surprise Nick hesitated. 'Can we leave it this time?' he replied. 'I'm quite tired.' It was an innocent enough remark which belied the horror of what was happening to him, and about to happen to us. His hip had become unbearably uncomfortable and he knew he would never manage to walk down those steps, let alone back up them.

What he didn't know was that in a matter of weeks he would discover that he would never walk anywhere again.

The following month we headed for Cheltenham, as we did every year. Nick, an established and respected journalist best known for presenting Radio 4's daily current affairs programme *The World at One*, was chairing two sessions at the annual Literature Festival and I was trailing along behind him for the fun of it.

The event was taking place at the conference centre by the racecourse, just outside town, in front of more than two thousand people. His star guests were Rory Bremner, who was talking about his career as an impressionist, and Stephen Fry, who had written a book on poetry. Nick's calm beforehand, I knew, concealed his excitement at meeting these two great figures, and I glowed with pride to see that each of them seemed equally thrilled to meet Nick: 'We listen to you every day as part of our research,' said Bremner, talking of his satirical television programme, *Bremner, Bird and Fortune*. 'I don't know how we'd put our show together without hearing you unpick the political stories.' And while I stood tongue-tied and shy in the charismatic presence of Fry, larger than life and dressed head to toe in purple velvet, Nick joked that his last brush with him had been listening to his audio recording of *Winnie the Pooh*. 'Ah yes, Tigger's such a fascinating character,' said Fry, 'a classic case of manic depression, up one minute and down the next. And I do love *The World at One*, Nick.'

I watched the show from the back of the hall. Nick handled

the audience and his stars with grace and humour, and found it hard to hide his delight when Bremner invited him to share a classic scene from his programme in which the hapless politician George Parr is grilled about his incompetence. 'It was like a dream come true,' Nick gushed afterwards. What I also saw that evening was something that had been staring me in the face for weeks but which I hadn't noticed until that night. Sitting on that stage was a man who was thinner than he should have been, paler than I had realized, and, as we headed out of the auditorium and along the brightly lit corridors to the exit, beginning, very slightly, to limp.

'You need to go to the GP and get this checked out,' I said crossly, because as soon as the words left my lips I could see they were falling on deaf ears. I tried again, and again, but to no avail. If only I had known. Known that the grumblings in Nick's mind about what was happening had switched by now from being niggles to deep concern. That the 'tightening' in his hip was not easing as he had hoped, and that as it started to swell its shape and form had planted the first seeds of fear. That the fear was soon so great he resigned himself to the worst and saw no point in bringing forward the moment of truth. Memories had begun to haunt him of his mother declining into a shadow of her former fit and active self when she went through treatment for, and died from, cancer. 'Even as I watched, I could not imagine that I would ever be able to go through the same process,' he wrote later.

I was in denial, a state compounded by a fear of doctors and disease, in roughly equal measure. Just occasionally the discomfort was too great to ignore, and I developed a daft philosophy to explain my inaction. It went something like this: if the problem was benign, it would disappear in its own good time – if not, going to the doctor would mean the end of life as I knew it. I would become a patient and probably a cancer patient at that. In my mind a patient was a pitiable figure, at the mercy of doctors, enduring unthinkable medical procedures (quite probably much worse than the condition itself) and transformed in the eyes of friends and acquaintances from somebody 'normal' into something much more complicated. 'Did you hear about Nick Clarke? Terrible, isn't it?' A patient.

Which is exactly what was about to happen.

As autumn turned to winter, fate signed, sealed and delivered its verdict. 'I finally realized the game was up,' said Nick. 'On a cold November afternoon I witnessed the end of a relatively easy and untroubled life: the day the luck ran out.'

On the GP's desk was a sheet of paper and at the top I could make out the words 'West London Urgent Suspected Cancer Referral Form'. The GP filled out the form but never spoke the word aloud. 'You need to get this checked out at once,' was all he said. And when Nick pressed him, he just added, 'I'd be lying if I said I wasn't worried.' We knew what the word was though, and it hung heavy in the air. Nick reached for my hand. 'I'm so sorry,' he said. 'I'm so very sorry.'

I had imagined that such moments would be like those you watch in a film: Nick would fall into my arms weeping and I would be strong and brave. But the truth was different. It was I who cried and Nick who was strong. In fact he was remarkable. He held me tight while I sobbed there in the surgery, and then as we walked back home through the chill grey streets. Nick later told me that he was thinking, 'I am now

9

a cancer victim, transformed by one brief bloody visit.' But all he said to me at the time was, 'I'd better call the office as soon as we get back to tell them I won't be there tomorrow.' His deep and sonorous voice, which had been his trademark as a broadcaster, seemed somehow diminished in its tone and authority.

In my hand was a piece of paper the G P had given us to take to the hospital the next morning, but I didn't look at it until we got back. There was still no sign of that unspoken word. Instead he had had written 'suspected tumour' and a word I didn't understand but which seemed less menacing than the big 'C'. It said 'sarcoma' and there was a question mark after it. In my ignorance the word gave me reassurance. How naïve I was.

It was the death sentence I'd been waiting for. It just wasn't the one I had expected.

TWO

Before I can go on, I have to go back eighteen years to a sunny afternoon in May 1987 when the trees were full of blossom and I was walking on air. That was when I first got to know Nick, the man who was to become my lover, my husband and my soul mate. But on that day my mind was on other things and I had no idea that I had stumbled upon love. I was twenty-six, a young assistant producer cutting my teeth in the hothouse of a major news and current affairs television programme, and I was on my first mission out of the office. I had been sent from the *Newsnight* studios to Wandsworth in south-west London, and I had to get a story on air.

Newsnight in the 1980s buzzed with ambition, determination and fear. It probably still does. The Lime Grove studios in Shepherds Bush were home to the BBC's main current affairs programmes of that era: *Panorama*, *Watchdog*, *That's Life* and *Nationwide*, to name but a few. The building was a labyrinth of staircases, fire escapes, hidden doors and lifts that from time to time would break down as a senior politician was being ferried to a grilling in the studios. Interviewees never saw the offices, which were strewn with the debris of manic activity: tapes, newspapers, coffee cups, scripts and discarded plates of half-eaten food, all exposed in the glare of fluorescent lighting which flickered constantly.

I had arrived at the BBC just three years earlier as a wide-eyed trainee, naïve about the world of work and utterly in awe of the brilliance of my fellow trainees – self-confident and accomplished graduates from top universities who had beaten off stiff competition from thousands of contenders to scoop one of the best jobs around. Now I had made it to the first rung on the *Newsnight* ladder, where yet more brilliance abounded among my high-flying, hard-working colleagues and my awe turned to a deep-seated fear that someone would discover that my presence there was a terrible mistake.

I started in the humble ranks of the 'daily desk' where producers and assistant producers assembled the reports that would appear in that night's programme, pulling together footage, editing material and churning out scripts on big clunking typewriters. Sweating blood to impress, we worked long days, rarely broke for lunch, and never ate dinner. As stories broke, developed or died during the day, so the running order for the items in the programme would be juggled, re-shaped, or simply abandoned for an entirely new one. We became jacks of all trades, masters of none, required to grasp the subtleties of the big stories of the 1980s: Cold War tensions, the decline of Labour, the rise of Thatcherism, Poll Tax riots, civil conflict in southern Africa or the interminable Middle East peace process – all within hours, sometimes minutes. I had little in-depth knowledge of any current issue, but developed a facility for turning my hand to almost anything, instantly. I tried to broaden my knowledge by poring over the *Economist* and the *New Statesman*, neither of which interested me as much as *Cosmopolitan*, but still it was hard to keep up with my peers.

As we went about our work we eyed each other up to see who was getting the big reports and how they were managing, feeling that frisson of competitiveness that has always stalked the television world, wondering how to stand out from the crowd. When Alex Thomson, now a Channel 4 news presenter, had a book published at the tender age of twenty-something he spread copies of it ostentatiously across his desk, telling anyone who passed, 'Yes, it's mine. It's out next month.' Were we jealous? Palpably so.

While we scurried around at the 'daily desk', the editor of the day sat on his throne at the 'top desk', flanked by a pair of bulky computers churning out news stories running on the wires, and two special assistants whose role it was to ensure that the programmes made it on air. The editors were talented young journalists, many of whom were to rise to the very top of the tree. Mark Damazer would become Controller of Radio 4, Jana Bennett Director of Television and Mark Thompson Director-General. Our presenters included some of the biggest names of that era, including Peter Snow and John Tusa. I would watch, spellbound, as Mark Thompson and Peter Snow debated the day's events and their significance head to head. It might be Margaret Thatcher's problems with disgruntled Cabinet members, or one of Peter's favourite subjects, the military build-up by the world's Superpowers. Some of those conversations are imprinted on my memory. 'We really should be doing something on Nimrods and AWACS,' Peter would urge. 'There are new rumours about the contract – but it's your call, Mark, your call.'

I produced more reports with Peter on the relative merits of British Aerospace's Nimrods and Boeing's AWACS – radar planes designed to give early warning of a Soviet missile attack – than on any other subject. I knew nothing about them at the outset, but Peter would talk me patiently through the issues. 'We need a good "explainer" for this story,' he'd say, meaning the background report that preceded a studio interview, invariably packed with Peter's much-loved graphics wizardry, 1980s-style. While I went off to draft the 'explainer', he'd rummage through his enormous address book before slipping away to the privacy of his office to ring a Whitehall contact for a briefing.

Many other great names in television journalism passed through *Newsnight* in that period: Charles Wheeler; Joan Bakewell; Vincent Hanna, who made his name with quirky by-election reports and was always attached to what looked like a small suitcase but was in fact one of the earliest mobile phones; Gavin Esler, now a regular *Newsnight* presenter; Will Hutton, who went on to edit the *Observer* and become a great friend of Nick's, as did programme editor Richard Tait, who went on to run ITN and later returned to the BBC as a governor.

It was a highly charged and daunting environment. At least, I found it so. Daily programme meetings filled me with dread. Each and every one of us had to suggest at least one item for the programme, expand on it, defend it, and wait to see whether it was accepted, passed over or, worse, shot down in flames. I once came up with an obscure idea for a piece on the Angolan Civil War, but was forced to retreat, red-faced at my ignorance, when I let slip that I thought Angola was on the east coast of Africa rather than the west. I was far too stressed in those early days, too busy trying to hold my own and keep up with those around me to take much notice of the quiet, balding reporter who sat in the corner. With an enigmatic and gentle smile on his face, he looked knowledgeable and confident. When he introduced himself as Nick Clarke and confessed that he often felt the same apprehension about those meetings as I did, I sighed with relief.

There was, of course, an upside to the stress and angst of

that job. The terror I felt while getting items on air, often against the odds and always against the clock, was tempered by the exhilaration that comes from working on a live news programme. It was enormously exciting and it taught me skills that have served me to this day. But, like all of us at the daily desk, what I wanted more than anything was to get out of the office to produce, direct and edit short filmed reports on location. The dream was to sling your bag over your shoulder, walk past colleagues still chained to their typewriters, knowing you had cast off your shackles and were part of a team of people who could be sent anywhere in the world at a moment's notice on the most extraordinary missions.

Finally I joined their ranks. And was sent all the way to Wandsworth. Where I spent the day with a cameraman, a sound recordist, and that quiet, balding reporter, Nick Clarke.

The story we were tackling that day was a tale of two schools, one state-run and the other in the private sector, located within a stone's throw of each other but separated by the gulf that money – or the lack of it – creates. Our report was a comparison of their respective facilities and in the grand history of television journalism it was a run-of-the-mill assignment, but it was a day that transformed my life.

It was to be a short item – around six minutes long, the type of report we called an 'on-the-day'. You started it, completed it, and it went out that evening. My job was to 'run' events – to make sure the crew turned up at the right place, to decide what we needed to film, to direct the cameraman, to discuss with Nick what questions he would ask and to listen to his interview to make sure it provided what we needed. He would write and record the script back at the studios while I fused words and pictures in the editing suite. Like most 'on-the-days' it was finished with minutes to go. On many occasions the minutes became seconds. In those days the technology was laborious and slow, frazzling everyone's nerves.

As Nick and I shared a taxi from Wandsworth back to Lime Grove, we chatted with an ease that startled me, so familiar did it feel to be talking to him. Where I'd thought I would be quizzed on world events or the latest Westminster gossip we slipped instead into talk of family life. 'How do you manage to combine it with all the travelling you do?' I asked, genuinely intrigued, and his unfussy reply – I expected bravado – touched me. 'It's give and take. Yes, I travel a lot, but I'm at home a lot in between and I try to make the best of both. I'm lucky to have such a great job.' We talked on and on, as if we had known each other for years, and by the time our meanderings were curtailed by our arrival at the studios, I knew I wanted to talk to this man again. And again. Little did I imagine that I would still be talking to him eighteen years later.

Nick was born in Godalming, Surrey, in 1948. His father John was a journalist who had been in Special Operations during the war. Nick had always assumed – and rather hoped – that he had been some sort of spy. His mother, Ruth, was a violinist but had worked as a nurse during the war and prided herself on being one of the first WRENS to enter the Italian town of Monte Cassino after its liberation by the Allies.

After the war John penned a weekly column in the *Evening Standard* called 'John Clarke's Casebook' in which he reported from the divorce courts in an age when attitudes to divorce were different and the fascination with the details, which were fully publishable, great. His passion, however, was cricket, and in time he became the paper's cricket correspondent, doing the

rounds of the county circuit in summer, then making the long
sea voyages to Australia, South Africa and India with the
England team on their winter tours. Ruth filled the absences
socializing and playing music. In time their separations and
divergent interests took a toll on the marriage. As small children often do, Nick blamed himself for their incessant arguing.

His father's journalism and his mother's music didn't bring
in a huge amount of money, but any surplus his parents did
earn went on Nick's and his sister Suzie's education. Nick was
sent to Westbourne House Prep School in Chichester at the
age of eight. His misery at being away from home and the
loneliness of boarding school stayed with him throughout his
childhood and dogged him like a nagging sore for the rest of
his life. He detested the bland food and the cold showers, and
counted the days to weekend *exeats*, always worried about the
tensions between his parents back home. At nights he lay in his
bed crying silently or humming Beethoven's violin concerto –
the first classical recording he had ever owned – to help him
get to sleep.

At eleven he won a scholarship to Bradfield College near
Reading, in Berkshire, where living away from home became
more routine, and where his beautiful and mellifluous voice
made him a star on the school stage. In his final year he became
Head of House, a privilege which brought with it the duty of
administering beatings to younger pupils. Nick simply refused
to follow suit. The school already had a resident sadist in the
form of headmaster Anthony Chenevix-Trench. He had been
a prisoner of war in Japan and was badly scarred by the experience. Like many pupils, Nick was often summoned to the
head's office where a spotlight was trained on his eyes and a
cane was swished menacingly about his ears. Nick's parents

neither knew nor guessed what was going on: Chenevix-Trench was a split personality, adept at concealing his dark side. He later moved on to Eton, then Fettes, the Edinburgh school which numbers Tony Blair amongst its old boys. His sadistic tendencies were exposed much later by Paul Foot in *Private Eye*.

As Nick's schooldays reached their close, tragedy struck. He was only seventeen when he was summoned to his house-master's study. 'Nicholas,' he was told, 'I'm afraid I've got some bad news. Your father is dead.' He had collapsed while reporting from Lord's and died just a few days later. His father, a heavy smoker, had been ill for some time with cancer of the oesophagus and hadn't even told Nick's mother how serious it was until the very late stages.

When the news reached Nick he was in the middle of the dress rehearsal of *Macbeth*, playing the lead, and it seemed unthinkable that he should drop out. So the show went on. Nick said later that it didn't feel wrong at the time: his father's death seemed unreal. The loss, however, was to haunt him. For years he had dreams about trying to meet his father again and then trying desperately to cling to him, only to watch him slip away from his grasp. I think it gave him a sense of foreboding, a fatalistic belief that the hour-glass that had counted down his father's life so quickly was already measuring his own days.

From school, Nick went to Cambridge, where he read French and German, and where he was soon reviving and writing for the university newspaper, *Broadsheet*. After Cambridge and a six-year spell at the *Yorkshire Evening Post* in Leeds, he applied for a job with BBC Television in Manchester. By now his hair was thinning on top and he had grown a beard to compensate. 'Would you be willing to shave it off?' he was asked at his interview. He was so desperate for the job he asked for a pair of scissors there and then, and a broadcasting career was born.

Nick was soon reporting for local and national television from Manchester, where the presenter Stuart Hall gave him the nickname Billy Buttocks after laughing at the way he walked. He also worked alongside Jenni Murray and Anna Ford. 'Manchester was buzzing in those days,' Nick once told me. 'It was a golden period. And it was the only time in my life that I was truly famous.' He was often asked to attend fêtes and open supermarkets, and for the rest of his life would bump into people who recognized him solely from that era. By the time the call came to go to London he had a young family in tow, having married Sue, a fellow journalist of whom he remained for ever fond. He later wrote: 'I acquired a lovely young wife who could cook better than my later wife and who was much more tolerant and easy to live with, and some children, the first two of whom arrived at once – a theme I was to return to later in life.' Twins Ali and Tom were followed three and a half years later by Pete.

Once in London, Nick joined *The Money Programme* working with Valerie Singleton and Brian Widlake, and then moved to *Newsnight*. His debut on the programme came early in 1986, some ten years after he'd joined the BBC, on the day the Space Shuttle *Challenger* exploded over the Atlantic shore of Florida. As one of the biggest stories of the decade engulfed an over-stretched *Newsnight* team, the editor Richard Tait decided it was time to 'call in the Bald Eagle!' as Nick was affectionately known. He was at home on a day off, but arrived forty minutes later, his hands covered in cement and what was left of his hair full of grey dust. 'Sorry,' he laughed. 'I was concreting the drive.'

My background was different from Nick's, but not markedly. I was born and brought up in the suburban outskirts of north-west London in Pinner, Middlesex, on a road of box-like, detached, 1960s houses which abutted the Metropolitan Green-belt. My father was a company manager and my mother a teacher, and like so many of their generation they loved their leafy suburbia. My abiding memory of our neighbours is of gin parties where everyone sang the hokey-cokey and tangoed round the living room, and of the Sunday ritual of car-washing in the drives. It was suburban heaven – or not, depending on your age, I suppose.

Right from the time I passed my eleven-plus and went to the local state grammar-turned-comprehensive, my father had ambitions for me to go to Oxford or Cambridge. I had no real idea what that meant at first, but in time it became my over-riding goal too. I could see how much it mattered to him. I think he secretly wished he could have had an Oxbridge education himself. To him, the hallowed courts and intellectual atmosphere of those ancient, stone-built colleges had an almost mystical allure.

I worked ferociously hard through my school years and won a conditional offer of a place at Gonville and Caius, Cambridge, to study Social and Political Science. When my A-level results came through, my dream became reality.

After working so hard in pursuit of my aims I decided, once I arrived at Cambridge, to have fun. Besides, I reasoned, the place was full of first-class students and there was absolutely no point in competing with them. I socialized, partied, and started working on the student newspaper. Having no idea what I wanted to do with my life, I concluded that journalism would be the best way forward.

Stop Press – the university newspaper (renamed since Nick's day) – was probably a good training ground for what lay ahead, being a viper's nest of untrammelled ambition. Everyone, but everyone, wanted to get a place on the coveted BBC journalist trainee scheme. I don't think we ever questioned why, nor indeed whether we really wanted to be broadcasters. I rather fancied being a newspaper journalist, ultimately a writer, but the BBC was where we all set our sights. In due course I applied and, much to my amazement, was short-listed for interview. I prepared for it with a vengeance.

We didn't have televisions in our rooms in those days, and besides, I'd been too busy over the past three years to sit around watching TV. But I needed one now. It was no good going to the Junior Common Room – it was always full of men watching football – so I went to Robert Sayle, Cambridge's version of John Lewis, and bought a black-and-white set for £47. Big money. I watched it solidly for ten days and then, after the interview, took it back and told them I couldn't get a signal because I lived near the gas works. I got a full refund. I also got the job.

I was just twenty-two when I moved back in with my parents and joined the BBC's News Trainee scheme. There were sixteen of us that year. We strutted and posed shamelessly to each other in a transparent attempt to hide the deep insecurities most of us felt as we did our stint in the classroom, learning about script-writing, tape-editing, and news evaluation. After that we went our separate ways, sent on three-month postings at various locations around the BBC News empire around the country to gain some on-the-job experience.

All trainees had to find a job within two years of joining the Beeb and often did so in the regions. I applied for, and got, a post as a Regional Television Journalist in Newcastle, working on the local evening news programme, *Look North*. The north-east was a strange new world to me. I struggled with the Geordie accent and was always having to ask people to repeat themselves, earning myself the nickname, 'Miss Middlesex'. As to the job, I was expected to turn my hand to whatever came along, which included writing the Saturday sports bulletin, on my own and knowing nothing about the subject. On one memorable occasion I composed a report on a match in which I'd got three teams playing. On another I forgot to give the final score. No one ever spoke to me about my cock-ups, so I carried on in blissful ignorance. Some time later I discovered that my bulletins had become required viewing for my colleagues, and the subject of much hilarity.

I must have been doing something right, however, because in 1987 I got a lucky break. I was at a regional election planning meeting and met the deputy editor from *Newsnight*, who suggested that I apply for a job as an assistant producer on his programme. I didn't need any encouragement. This was the big time, the sort of post that we'd all aspired to. I landed the job, and headed back south.

So here I was, twenty-six years old and working with hardcore professionals on a really, seriously, grown-up programme. I was no longer reporting on house fires and local sporting events, but on world affairs – my knowledge of which was not much better than my understanding of football. And I hadn't been there long when I met this man I now noticed every time he entered the room and whose eyes kept meeting mine.

In the weeks that followed our taxi trip back from Wandsworth, Nick and I waltzed round one other with studied indifference. His, I later discovered, was born of sheer disbelief that I might find him interesting, mine of bewilderment that I should be drawn to a man who was twelve years older than me, slightly overweight, slightly balding, with the rather careworn look of someone approaching middle age – and the beige trousers and checked jackets that went with it. I later discovered that he bought these outfits in a dreadful menswear chain called John England, from which I banned him, before, mercifully, it vanished from the high street.

It was all very tentative: a word or two here, a glance across the office or an occasional joke aimed at each other across the desk, once or twice a hurried BBC canteen lunch together. It was a slow-burning, drawn-out flirtation. It had to be. Our work filled every minute of our days, leaving little time for much else – let alone courtship. But finally, in late September, we found ourselves together in Blackpool as part of a *Newsnight* team covering one of the party political conferences.

We were still rushed off our feet, and the days remained inhumanly long. They started soon after eight in the morning when our team of half a dozen – production assistant, director, producers, reporter and presenter – would meet over breakfast, read the papers and plan the day before heading to our temporary office, usually a cramped Portakabin in the car park behind the conference centre. We worked flat out, watching the debates, interviewing politicians, filming short reports, and preparing to send the fruits of our labour for incorporation into the main programme. Throughout the day we wrangled over how big a chunk of the programme would be allocated to our story.

By the time we'd watched the broadcast and heard the usual cries of, 'They've cut our interview, the bastards!' it would be close to half past eleven, nearly sixteen hours since we'd started. We were invariably hungry, weary, grouchy, and generally desperate for a drink. We'd start our wind-down session in a local restaurant, arriving just as all the other journalists were heading to bed. We'd sit up well into the early hours, sharing the latest conference stories: the senior Labour politician who only agreed to be interviewed on condition that a bottle of best malt whisky was delivered to his hotel room; or the trade union leader who told our (female) editor of the day to 'run along, dear, and check this with your boss'. And then we might settle down to the luxury of general chat, usually spiced up by tales of life 'on the road' – told by those who had travelled the world, and listened to by those of us who yearned to follow in their footsteps.

On one of these nights I watched Nick in full flow. He was a great story-teller, often holding a group in rapt attention always self-deprecating and frequently funny. 'We were in Japan,' he said. 'We'd spent three weeks travelling around the Far East when we arrived in Osaka to interview some men in suits about the state of the economy. We checked into a rather wonderful hotel where the food was legendary. Just before dinner, the cameraman we were going to work with showed up. He'd spent a fortnight filming a golf tournament – lucky guy – and when I told him what we were doing next morning he threw a complete wobbly – and I had to try and calm him down. There I was, next door to the best sushi bar in Japan, buying one gin and tonic after another and trying to persuade him that a *Newsnight* report on the state of the Japanese yen would be just as much fun as a golf tournament . . .' Nick sat there basking in approval as everyone laughed. He was all set to elaborate when I butted in. 'Yes, that must be really tough,' I said, 'spending licence-payers' money on drinks in fancy hotels in faraway places . . .' My smiling interruption put an abrupt end to his story-telling and finally unleashed a passionate love affair.

I can't remember where the conversation went after that, but he and I were the last to leave at around two o'clock, and somewhere along the Blackpool seafront as we trudged back to our hotel through the rain, we finally *did* it. We held hands.

While the build-up to our getting together had been slow and measured, what followed was fast and furious. I fell in love with Nick deeply and passionately. He was funny, he was kind, he was gentle and he was clever. For the first time in my life I found someone who could brush away the layers I had used as a defence mechanism against everything I found hard to handle. With him, I no longer needed to hide. Many years later, I told him that I felt as if I had waited all my life to meet him. 'I know,' was all he said, and all he needed to say.

I was always myself with Nick. Nothing else intruded. It couldn't: he would have seen through it and past it. He never played games with my feelings, insisting that love deserved better. And he set the example. Once when I complained bitingly to a friend – in front of him – about something he had done, he said, 'You simply can't do that to me. I'm not perfect, but if you love me you have to take me as I am. That's what love is about.' And I never did it again. Falling in love with him was easy. He even laughed at my jokes.

As to why he fell in love with me, I have no idea. I don't recall that he ever put it into simple, easy to remember words. But he did tell me about two incidents when he *knew* it had happened. The first was the time we were in Germany together on a *Newsnight* assignment about the benefits available to workers under a social contract with the trade unions. It wasn't the stuff to make a journalist's pulse race, but what *was* exciting was that I had found a way to get the BBC, unknowingly, to hire us a powerful BMW. I was at the wheel, and with no speed limit on the *autobahns* here was a chance to see how fast it could go – and perhaps show Nick just what kind of woman he was tangled up with.

He told me afterwards that he knew he had fallen for me when the speedometer hit 200 kilometres an hour and he realized that he was feeling absolutely no fear.

Then there was the day he turned up at my flat in West London while I was decorating. He looked around the place, and asked who had drained all the radiators and lifted them off the walls. 'I did,' I said. 'But who helped you?' he asked. 'No one,' I said. 'I did it myself. It's not difficult.' He was, simply, awestruck.

Having an affair with a married man meant we had to be discreet, furtive, clandestine. It was uncomfortable. For a long time we lived a semi-secret and often angst-ridden existence to which there seemed no resolution. We thought our feelings were known only to ourselves, but colleagues later told us they knew very well what was happening between us. It was simple enough: Nick had suddenly given up meat. I'd been a vegetarian for years.

As time went by we stole more and more time together and found it harder than ever to be apart, yet there seemed no way forward. He had his family; I only had him. There were rows, of course, particularly over our separations. And as anyone who's been through this sort of thing knows, the worst time is Christmas, because that's when families come first and lovers a distant second. In 1988 I decided to go to India over the festive season – alone. Nick didn't want me to. We argued furiously, on one occasion so furiously that I tried to leap out of the car while we were driving along Acton High Street. I probably did it mainly for effect, but it certainly rattled him: as he tried to pull me back in he almost ripped my new coat in half.

I still made the trip to India, but that separation brought things to a head, for both of us. When I returned home he moved into my cramped little flat and our 'secret' was no more.

That was the year he gave me a Victorian pin brooch in the shape of a piece of heather, dotted with seed pearls. 'It's lucky heather,' he said. 'I feel lucky to have met you.' I felt blessed too. Yet as our passion unfolded it did seem that fortune was against us. We had met at the wrong time, or at least at a time when nothing was in our favour. I was in love with a man who had a family he adored and commitments he would always honour and which would always make claims on him. It threat-ened to tear his heart in two. I was of an age when I yearned for the sort of love that was unencumbered, that could be wild and reckless, could uproot and take flight, and I resented having found a love that came with so many complications. It saddened Nick, it confused me, and it nearly destroyed us. But neither could let the other go.

It took a long time for the situation to be resolved, for Nick to work out what he wanted, what he wanted to do about it, and how he could achieve that with the least damage to those he loved. I know that Nick had many agonies to deal with during this period and he kept them largely private even from me, telling only one close friend of the pain he was going through. I wish we had been able to talk more openly at that time, that I had been able to share his pain and spend less time struggling with my own conscience about how hard I found it to take on another person's family. For in truth I had no idea how to relate to three youngsters who had no reason to like me, and I was jealous that a piece of Nick's heart would forever be devoted to them. It would take years, and having children of my own, before I fully resolved those unwanted feelings.

Nick's divorce from Sue came through in 1991. Shortly afterwards, in a drab little pizza parlour in Amsterdam, three and a half years after we'd held hands on Blackpool Prom, he proposed to me.

It wasn't the most romantic moment in our time together. In fact the build-up had been so long that he didn't really need to say anything. He simply handed me a little box. I took it from him with my heart in my mouth, worried that I wouldn't like what I knew was inside. And I didn't. But I did manage to say, 'Yes', before handing the ring back. 'They assured me it could be exchanged,' he said, with a resigned smile.

We were married weeks later in Mauritius on a wind-swept beach with waves crashing behind us and menacing dark clouds building up over the sea. Our witnesses were a local policeman with very few teeth and a photographer who insisted he knew better than us and refused to take direction. We ended up with a set of photos so dull and lifeless that we never had the enthusiasm to put them on our mantelpiece.

On that same holiday, the longest we ever took together, Nick agreed to go on a wild, almost reckless adventure, just to please me. I wanted to travel across the Indian Ocean and through Madagascar, at that time more or less unknown to all but the more intrepid tourists, and just about impossible to penetrate without a four-wheel-drive vehicle and an experienced guide. But we found a travel agent who was willing to sort us out an itinerary, and set off.

It nearly ended in disaster. A general strike in protest against the rule of President Ratsiraka grounded the island's air network. We found ourselves stranded on a tropical island with nothing to eat but locally caught lobster. Nick loved the thrill and his excitement swept away my worries. We were eventually picked up by a local coaster carrying a cargo of chickens and a few abandoned tourists like ourselves, all of whom sat nauseous and silent while our smelly feathered friends clucked and crowed as the boat bobbed down the coast. Once back in the capital, Antananarivo, Nick was overjoyed to discover that one of the leaders of the revolutionary forces was our very own travel agent, who agreed to tap into his black-market supply of petrol to get us to the international airport where a rescue flight was allowed to land and take the tourists out.

Nick dined out on the story of our honeymoon for years. My main memory of the holiday, however, was of the night he fell ill in a small town, miles away from any source of medical help. Ihosy (pronounced Ee-osh) was a characterless staging-post on the thousand-kilometre 'highway' we were taking to the south-west coast of the island. After a full day's driving along a pitted and cratered road, engulfed in clouds of red dust which billowed up around the car, our throats were dry and our bones were aching. We reached our destination and clambered stiffly out of our seats, our every move greeted by squeals of laughter as a crowd of children gathered to watch this pair of aliens in strange clothes talking an incomprehensible language. I was exhausted and floppy; Nick was oddly lethargic.

Our 'motel', tucked away behind the main thoroughfare, was a group of low huts, the windows no more than gaps between the white building-blocks covered with mosquito netting. There was running water, but it was cold; there were beds, but they were hard; there was electricity – but it was only available until ten p.m. The uncertain political situation meant a guard was stationed outside our room. He cut a lackadaisical figure in his *lamba*, the traditional swathe of decorated sheeting wrapped round the body. But he was armed – with a long spear.

As we settled in, Nick's lethargy turned into a raging fever, with a soaring temperature and bouts of sickness, interspersed with clammy shivers. Our driver had left us for the night and we had no idea where he was. Since he doubled as our translator, we had no way of communicating with the guard, and the town was now cocooned in darkness, completely silent. Terrified that Nick might have contracted cerebral malaria, and racked with guilt at having dragged him to the back of beyond to satisfy my wanderlust, I sat through the night watching him, with no idea what to do should he take a turn for the worse, just willing him to pull through. In the end I fell asleep.

I woke up next morning to find that Nick was up and about, and hungry. Whatever it was that had come over him, he'd emerged unscathed. That night I had experienced the real pull of deep, deep love, heightened by the fear of losing it. Something, maybe intuition, maybe just fatalism, maybe one of those premonitions that have stalked me through my life or maybe

Nick's own fatalism about his life after his father's early death, seemed to be warning me that my time with Nick would be limited. I think I knew right there and then that he would be ripped, untimely, from me.

THREE

The honeymoon over, we settled down to life as Mr and Mrs Clarke. Well, sort of. I never took his name and Nick never expected me to. But he couldn't resist the odd wry comment when I refused to open letters addressed to us as Mr & Mrs, pointing out that he often – and happily – responded to the many people who addressed him as Mr Want.

That sort of gentle ridicule became part of the fabric of our lives. Nick's desire for the perfect cup of tea (stewed for three minutes, semi-skimmed milk and one-and-a-bit spoons of sugar) gave me daily ammunition, as did his love of both fine wine and fine water. His insistence on drinking only Evian unleashed my scorn. I set him a test one day, slipping him a glass of water from the tap – and whooped for joy when he failed to spot it. 'You've conned me,' he said, but he still refused to switch. At times his fastidious ways drove me crazy and I let him know it. His response was always an indulgent smile and a mild rebuke: 'Have you ever thought that *you* might irritate *me* sometimes . . .?'

Besides, he could give as good as he got. He mocked my inability to cook, questioning whether it was just unwillingness. 'You managed perfectly well until you met me,' he'd say, 'and then your skills mysteriously vanished into thin air.' I don't think he minded. He rose to the challenge of feeding us both and fell in love with cooking.

He ribbed me for other things too, like my refusal to use

first-class stamps on letters, my general irritability with life, the way I tended to harbour a grudge – and for my dreadful driving skills around town. I was good at hurtling down *auto-bahns* at 120 mph, but in residential streets, at 25 mph, I always lost interest. We laughed together – at each other, with each other, in spite of each other – more than I've ever laughed with anyone. Laughter was our lifeblood. It broke down my defences, allowing him to chip away at me gently and soften some of my jagged edges. He was brilliant at unpicking my tightly meshed but often irrational arguments, but when we fell out it was always he who brought any hostilities to an end. And there were plenty, all through our married life. But however ferocious and heartfelt our rows, he never had a bad word to say to me. He would criticize (kindly), complain (wearily), or try to reason with me, but he was never rude. He was tender and without side in his love, and I couldn't fault it. Indeed it humbled me to see how easily he could give and how much I had to learn. He showed me that nothing in life is as beautiful and as rewarding, as trying and as testing, as rich and as nourishing as love. I had thought I could live without it. When I fell in love with him, I realized I couldn't.

In 1991 we moved into a house in North Kensington, at the time an unfashionable and affordable area, and set about making it ours. Nick's pride and joy was the colour he chose for the sitting room: a deep, almost unpalatably strong terracotta, which either shocked or seduced anyone who saw it. He loved the home we made together and when, over the years, I suggested changes, he resisted. 'It's too much trouble,' he would say. I had to drag him kicking and screaming into projects to build a new kitchen and add a loft conversion, to re-decorate or re-arrange. He loved the changes afterwards, but left to his own devices he was a man content with the status quo, who preferred to put his energy into his other passions: his children, his love of cricket, and his work.

I grew to love his terracotta sitting room – so much so that I have never re-decorated it – and everything else that we created together. In this house and with this man I experienced a happiness I had only ever dreamed of. Yet sometimes my contentment was unsettled by the creeping reminder of the finite amount of sand that was, even now, running through the hour-glass measuring our time together. I wasn't alone in this. It was around this time that Nick's mother Ruth died from cancer, strengthening his fatalistic conviction that history would one day repeat itself. 'Why else do insurance companies want to know how your parents die?' he said on the rare occasions that he shared his fears.

Things never stay the same for long in broadcasting. In due course my time on *Newsnight* drew to a close. Now an experienced producer, I moved into weekly current affairs as a producer on *The Money Programme*. Once I had earned my stripes and convinced everyone that I understood something about the world of finance and business, I started to travel again. It wasn't as hectic as I'd feared: I was no longer working in a news environment so the prospect of being sent away at short notice didn't hang over me; but with more time in which to film, our reports – and our absences – tended to be longer. There were lengthy trips to the States, and in the aftermath of the fall of the Berlin Wall in 1989, assignments across Eastern Europe and the former Soviet Union. It was a dream job, even if the travelling was as exhausting as it was exciting.

From *The Money Programme* I moved to *Panorama*, which

took me away from home much more, or had me sitting late into the night in edit suites. It was high-profile and tough. *Panorama* demanded total dedication, stamina and a very thick skin: my colleagues were among the best journalists in television as well as the most ruthless. One of them made no secret of working on Gore Vidal's principle that, 'It is not enough to succeed. Others must fail.' There was little time now for wide-eyed wonderment at where I found myself: like a great many people before me, I learned that a lot of my attention had to be directed at self-preservation.

Nick, meanwhile, became *Newsnight*'s first political editor. Thatcherism was by this time on the wane and the Conservatives were tearing themselves apart over Europe. Nick presented his reports regularly from the studio, igniting his passion for presenting as a full-time role. Things went well until – as so often happens in television – a new editor arrived and wanted changes. Nick protested and, in one of the very few rows he ever had in his BBC career, threatened to leave his job. The editor, John Morrison, responded angrily, 'Well, go on then, why don't you just fuck off,' to which Nick retorted, 'OK, I will.' And he did. It was to be the making of him.

He migrated to the infinitely more civilized climes of *The World This Weekend*, a weekly current affairs programme on Radio 4, where people tend not to tell each other to fuck off. Working in radio in the late 1980s was looked down upon by most 'telly people', but Nick didn't care. He joked that the writing was on the wall for him as a television presenter when he looked at a monitor one day in the *Newsnight* studio and saw a bright shining dome in the distance. 'It was like a glowing beacon,' he said. 'When I realized it was my bald head, I knew my time was up.' Radio, he said, was his 'true home'.

After his first solo presentation in 1989 the station controller Jenny Abramsky wrote Nick a congratulatory note. 'We have a star on our hands,' she said. And so Nick started down a new path, one which would bring him job satisfaction and the sort of low-level critical acclaim that comes with the intimate anonymity of radio. He might, however, never have reached those heights without a meeting of great minds – his, and that of an exceptionally talented young editor named Kevin Marsh, a shrewd and mischievous man who didn't tolerate fools, but had, according to Nick, a brain 'the size of an aircraft hangar'.

Nick was soon presenting *The World This Weekend* on a regular basis and making his mark. It was on *The World This Weekend* in 1993 that the then Shadow Home Secretary, Tony Blair, first used the phrase 'tough on crime and tough on the causes of crime'. When James Naughtie became the presenter of its weekday sister programme *The World at One* from Mondays to Thursdays, Nick added the vacant Friday shift to his working weekend. In 1994, when Jim left, Nick took over from him, refusing to work just four days but insisting on doing all five. Colleagues were struck by Nick's commitment to the job and his commitment to the programme. Unlike many presenters, he never viewed it as a stepping-stone to greater heights like the *Today* programme or, of course, television. He was through with that.

Nick lived and breathed the news. A radio hummed in almost every room of our house at most waking hours. If I've painted a picture of Nick as a mild-mannered man it would be wrong to overlook the infuriation he expressed at people in the industry who failed to meet the high standards he set for himself. We watched the television news most nights and he would shout abuse at anything he thought of as slipshod, always ending with a reminder to himself or anyone who was listening that radio was the better medium.

'Can you believe they think that's the lead story?' he'd fume. 'It's all because of pictures. Pictures, that's the trouble with television news.' At other times a badly written script would incur his wrath: 'That is *not* English. What is *wrong* with these people?' He was particularly scathing about anyone who brought a hint of celebrity to BBC news. Fiona Bruce, whom he didn't know personally, wound him up the most and he would mimic, irritated, her eyebrow-raising sincerity and intonation. He reserved a special rage for some of Fergal Keane's reports: emotion over fact, as he referred to them. He didn't think it was the role of journalists to opine and to play with the audience's feelings, and would raise his hands in horror, imitating the soft Irish burr, then switching off in annoyance. He had nothing whatever against Fergal, but he felt passionately that a BBC reporter should not allow sentiment to over-shadow substance. In fact, he was sometimes so exercised about things that he would ring in to the BBC complaints department, the Duty Office. 'It's Mr Campbell here from Acton,' he would announce, using his middle name to disguise his identity.

Lying in bed while Nick got ready for his early starts – he had to be up at six to be in the office by quarter past seven – I would hear explosions of derision as he listened to the *Today* programme in the bathroom. 'You have *completely* missed the point of this story!' or 'We don't need to know what *you* think about it, thank you very much. You're just the presenter!' On one occasion I genuinely thought he was having a seizure and I raced to the bathroom, only to find he was shouting at Jim

Naughtie: 'Keep your questions shorter – for goodness' sake, Jim!'

His criticism was never *ever* personal. He had no gripes against any individual. In fact, his inability to actually dislike colleagues – there were plenty whom I would have loathed, I am sure – frustrated me madly. While I railed against BBC colleagues and managers who put my nose out of joint, he was never critical of character.

The World at One was a long-established daily news and current affairs radio programme with a history of big names – Robin Day, Brian Widlake, William Hardcastle – but it had traditionally been a reflective programme tackling a broad range of subjects and with little interest in breaking new ground. Now it had arguably its best ever editor in Kevin Marsh, whom Nick described as 'my great mentor and inspiration'. Under Kevin, the programme set about tackling fewer stories and in a more probing and analytical way. Nick compared his role to that of a barrister, building up a case, drawing on expert witnesses when necessary, and then subjecting a politician or similarly responsible person to forensic questioning. By the mid-1990s the political and international landscape had changed: the Cold War was a distant memory, the European Union was expanding, the Tories were in the dying stages of their reign and 'New Labour' was girding its loins for power. Political reporting was exciting and edgy.

Kevin's approach to stories was to pick them apart in order to discover whether assumptions being made about a story were correct. 'What if the opposite of what they're saying is actually the truth?' became the programme's guiding principle. Asking awkward questions, a clinical dissection of policy and political spin, was an approach that Nick loved and it began to give *The World at One* a reputation for penetrating journalism and the ruffling of feathers, particularly in political circles, whether Government or Opposition.

That ruffling of feathers soon turned to open animosity between *The World at One* and Labour spin doctors as the programme chose to run with what it regarded as the most important stories of the day – which didn't always accord with Labour's view of what was newsworthy. In 1995 when Tony Blair rejected a request to be interviewed on the programme at the party conference in Brighton, Kevin threatened to pull his staff back to Broadcasting House and run an extended interview with Michael Heseltine instead. Tony Blair's office found time in his diary to do the interview after all.

But the programme's biggest row was over the privatization of air traffic control during the 1997 General Election. The previous year the party's Transport spokesman, Andrew Smith, had declared, 'Our air is not for sale.' But on the day Labour launched its election manifesto, Nick interviewed Gordon Brown and discovered the policy had been reversed and the National Air Traffic Service was to be sold off to meet Labour's spending plans. The programme led on the story, with the glee of any journalist who gets a scoop.

The following day Nick met Charlie Whelan, Brown's spin doctor. 'He screamed at me,' Nick told me when he got home later that day. 'He pointed his finger in my face and said, "You're all fucking wankers and you can all fuck off." All because he didn't like what we'd done.' The team were thrilled when they heard this and for weeks afterwards sported T-shirts with *Wankers at One* emblazoned across the chest. They measured their success in digging up stories no one else had, and of exposing artifice.

Kevin loved nothing more than a bullying spin doctor, from whichever party, as it gave him a chance to flex his journalistic muscle, which he did without caring about the consequences. The programme's relationship with Number 10, once Tony Blair was in power, was frosty: Kevin had hung up on Alastair Campbell, Tony Blair's spin doctor, one day when Campbell had rung in, as he often did, to suggest a 'better' approach to an item the programme was planning. Kevin was having none of it.

But Campbell fought back, going public with allegations that *World at One* was biased against Labour and even claiming in *The Times* in 1998 that 'very few people – in politics or the media – take *The World at One* seriously ... so regular appearances [by ministers] are less likely'. In fact, hardly a day went by without a minister – or two – on the programme and its output became required listening in the political world. Campbell never gave up his view that it was 'inherently malign' and although Nick interviewed Tony Blair often before the election, he only did so once when he was Prime Minister.

It was the relationship between Kevin and Nick that under-pinned the programme's success. With Kevin's intellect and Nick's incisive interviewing, they gave the programme a place among the very finest of its kind – even if their working methods were unconventional. Every morning Kevin would place a sheet of paper on Nick's desk with his thoughts on what Nick should say in the programme. They were often extreme, and probably designed to provoke a debate rather than being orders as such. Nick would amend the document and give it back, after which Kevin would do the same, and it would bounce back and forth until the approach to the story became either a fusion of their thinking or the only words that had survived their arguments. Kevin never gave up. Minutes before going on air, as Nick was writing his final script, Kevin would sometimes access it on his own computer and change it surreptitiously. It was a pointless exercise, Kevin knew, because Nick always had the last say. But it was also an intellectual exercise in testing an argument to its very limit.

As with most creative working partnerships, there was, of course, friction. Kevin infuriated Nick, who would come home and complain about the things Kevin had tried to make him do or say, and then sit fulminating through his lunch until he had calmed down. Nick infuriated Kevin, too. On one occasion, after John Prescott had withdrawn from a debate, Kevin decided the programme should be devoted entirely to Prescott's cowardice. Nick disagreed. In fact he was intransigent. Kevin was so furious he stormed out of the building and had to walk round Portland Place for twenty minutes before he could bring himself to go back and speak to him.

But their mutual respect was deep, their pride in what they were doing was shared, and their mischievous pleasure at outdoing their colleagues never far away. Fearing that the *Newsnight* journalists across the corridor were trying to hijack their ideas, they once wrote the programme's entire running order in Latin. And their rivalry with, and occasional contempt for, the *Today* programme was expressed in early-morning mutterings loud enough to reach the other side of the shared office. 'What we do,' the *World at One* team would announce proudly, 'is to pick apart the half-truths on the *Today* programme. We read the papers and question what's in them; *Today* just read them and follow them.'

For all the ranting off-air, Nick was calmness personified when going out live. He finessed an interviewing technique that became one of the most respected in the industry, his words chosen with precision and accuracy and his questions shot through with disarming courtesy. I cheered at home once when I heard him ask an MP, 'For the sake of completeness, would you very much mind answering my question, please?' His velvet-lined voice, too, earned him a devoted following.

The new approach of the programme bore fruit. Under Kevin's and Nick's stewardship audience figures rose steadily and *The World at One* became required listening for opinion formers – although it was now accused of being too focused on the minutiae of politics, hence its nickname 'Westminster at One'. But that's what they were there for, they decided, so that was what they would continue to do.

Although Nick loved this job, he was never seduced by the glamour it offered. Not for him the corridors of Westminster, the late-night drinks, the gossip and intrigue. He had no desire to socialize with the people he interviewed, preferring to maintain a professional detachment that would never cloud his ability to ask difficult questions. When it came to politicians, he needed to keep a distance in order to remain unbiased and scrupulously fair. He found it helpful that nearly everyone he interviewed was in a remote studio, not sitting across the table from him. Virginia Bottomley was the one politician who insisted on being interviewed face to face. 'She thinks she can soften me by looking at me and smiling,' Nick would complain. 'So I keep my eyes on the desk and never look up.'

Jenny Abramsky, then Controller of Radio 4, had said from the outset that Nick was destined for radio stardom, so it was no great surprise when, in 1993, he started standing in for Jonathan Dimbleby on *Any Questions?*, gathering on the way a collection of engraved ice buckets and wine glasses from grateful universities, schools and church halls which hosted the programme around the country. Here he was in a face-to-face situation, but with a different format. The audience asked the questions, the panellists answered, and he took the chair as a sort of non-combatant. I often travelled with him to sit, watch and admire. As soon as he took his place on the podium with the guests, his eyes would dart round the room until they met mine, whereupon a gentle smile would crease his face. We only had to catch each other's eyes across a crowd to feel the intensity of our private world.

In 1997 Nick took the helm at *Round Britain Quiz*, radio's longest running quiz series – which, coincidentally, had been chaired by his godfather Lionel Hale in the post-war years. Nick sounded erudite and learned – an effect achieved by hours spent working over the background notes provided by his diligent producer Paul Bajoria. I listened once and couldn't follow any of the cryptic clues, so I gave up. I suspected that part of the programme's charm for Nick was that each series was recorded over the course of a weekend spent in a luxury hotel with the contestants, where the wine and conversation flowed readily in between takes.

He started to win awards: from the Voice of the Listener and Viewer in 1999, and the Broadcasting Press Guild in 2000: he was named Broadcaster of the Year. Perhaps the best plaudit he received was when the *Guardian* got in on the act – and prompted his colleagues to print him another T-shirt, this time quoting the newspaper's description of him as a 'National Treasure'.

A combination of Nick's talent and his finely honed broadcasting technique moved him from relative obscurity to relative recognition and, as it did so, I watched with overwhelming pride. I positively glowed with it and never, ever felt envious.

Though I couldn't help being irritated that, in a climate obsessed with television celebrity, Nick's talents were too often overlooked. I praised, flattered, and bolstered him, and his face would light up at each compliment with surprise and pleasure. Ever generous and ever modest, he would thank me, saying that everything that had happened to him he owed entirely to having met me. Yet the self-doubt that hounded him saddened me – and other people close to him. His great friend Will Hutton, with whom he'd worked on *The Money Programme* and *Newsnight*, once said to him, 'Nick, it's both endearing and infuriating that, however much I reason with you, flatter you or show you evidence of your success, you are still hounded by self-doubt.'

By the turning of the Millennium, Nick was regarded as one of the most skilled broadcasters and interviewers of his generation. He was also recognized as one of the nicest people in the business. Success changed him not one jot. Nor did it distract him from his great love, his home life, and a new passion that we now shared.

After Nick's mother died in December 1990, he and his sister Suzie had come into a small inheritance from the proceeds of the sale of her cottage. Nick had never had much interest in money – acquiring it, saving it, or even thinking about it. He enjoyed spending it, but not extravagantly. It just wasn't in his psyche. I, on the other hand, worried about it incessantly, a result perhaps of a childhood in which frugality was imposed on us like a curse by a father who was always fretting about our finances, and a mother haunted by the spectre of being penniless after fleeing from Eastern Europe as a child.

The inheritance, I suggested, should go towards a small place in the country. It took us two years to find Rose Cottage;

it was the height of the property slump of the early nineties and little was coming on the market. The instant I set eyes on the cottage in an estate agent's window I knew it was the one. 'What do you think?' I asked Nick breathlessly after we had wandered round it. 'If you think we can manage the work it needs, let's go for it,' he replied.

Stone-built, in a rural hamlet in south-east Somerset, it dated back to the early nineteenth century. It was painted white with black window frames and front door, and was surrounded by a thick beech hedge. The garden was a glorious managed wilderness littered with wild rose bushes, and on days when the sun shone and the sky was blue, the scene was like a picture on a chocolate box.

The cottage had been neglected for years, and still boasted a turquoise bathroom suite and brown-and-orange vinyl floor tiles throughout. However, it was structurally sound and we found some local builders to do it up – at their own Somerset pace. They took a year over a job which could probably have been done in a few months, and left us to add the finishing touches. We filled it with an eclectic mix of bric-a-brac, antiques and mementoes we had acquired together on our holidays round the world.

Rose Cottage was our labour of love and it became a love-nest, a place to retreat to at weekends, a place we dreamed about when we weren't there, and a place to hold in our hearts and minds as somewhere to retire to – one day. We spent every other weekend there, arriving late on Friday night after work, dropping into the Bull Inn at the end of the road for dinner, then slumping in front of the television with a log fire and a bottle of wine. We walked in the woods and across fields, pottered through the local antiques centre, gossiped at the pub and made friends. On summer afternoons Nick sat on the bench in the garden, reading the papers and drinking tea, listening to the cricket on the radio and glorying in doing nothing. A man who counted worrying as one of his preoccupations, he found peace whenever he was at Rose Cottage.

Some time after we'd completed the work on Rose Cottage an unmissable opportunity came Nick's way. Many writers had approached the legendary broadcaster Alistair Cooke about writing his biography, and all had been turned down. Nick's name had now been put forward as the latest to try to persuade him to relent, and he met the challenge with relish.

One summer afternoon in 1994 he paced the corridor outside a radio studio at Broadcasting House, waiting to catch the Grand Old Man – now eighty-six years old – after he had recorded his weekly *Letter from America*, normally taped in the States but whenever he travelled, on location. No one was allowed to eavesdrop or watch these recordings, apart from the producer and any sound engineer who might be present. Nick was apprehensive: Cooke had a reputation for prickliness, but on this occasion he was 'courteous to a fault' in Nick's words. The idea of a biography, however, was turned down flat. He should choose someone more interesting, or dead, or both, said Cooke. He did however invite Nick to meet him at his rented apartment in Mayfair where anecdotes of his childhood whetted Nick's appetite, and from where he emerged some hours later with nothing more than a very sore head. All Cooke had to offer him, apart from whisky – which Nick loathed – was gin, without the tonic. Cooke served it with water and Nick, not wanting to seem ungracious, drank it. He arrived home swaying, almost incoherent and convinced that he had blown his chances. It seemed he was right when a letter arrived a few days later saying, 'No bio! Positively not.'

Undaunted, Nick went away and began to delve into Cooke's past. He unearthed fragments of his early life before, during, and after World War I and kept Cooke informed of his progress. Six months later Cooke 'cracked' and agreed that, if the book was going to happen anyway, he might as well ensure that as far as possible the facts were correct. He told Nick many times later that this was a decision he instantly regretted.

Watching Nick at work and listening to him talking about his subject it became clear to me that the connection between the two men was of enormous importance to both. Nick saw Alistair as a kind of surrogate for the father he had lost as a teenager, and I suspected that Nick became the surrogate son Alistair had never quite had: a man of intellect and interests with the ability to take him on, on his own terms. (Alistair did have a son, but the relationship was different.)

It took Nick six years to complete the biography. He typed every one of the five hundred plus pages with just one finger, as he always had done, while I watched alarmed that his hand would seize up with the effort. 'I'll learn to type properly when I've finished the book,' he insisted, but never did.

The work naturally brought Nick into contact with the wider Cooke family, which was like a small dynasty with its myriad stories, long history and inevitable tensions. Nick interviewed Alistair's two children and two step-children as well as some of his grandchildren, and on more than one occasion heard about family disagreements and rifts. Yet rather than fan the flames he unwittingly brought the family together. He got to know them, warts and all, but managed to keep the warts out of the public domain while remaining objective and gently critical where he needed to be.

By the time Nick's book was approaching publication I had become deputy editor of *The Money Programme*, which meant I was no longer travelling away from home. I can't say I missed it. My time was now mine to control, and it was relatively easy to plan excursions to New York together – usually short weeks or long weekends, where Nick could work with Alistair and I could while away hours wandering through museums and shops. The city thrilled him. He loved the restaurants where he could indulge his taste for good food and wine, and although I didn't attend his meetings I did transcribe the interviews afterwards and so I knew what he was hearing and was able to share it with him.

It was a privilege to have been involved in this project. But it seemed perfectly normal. So much of what Nick and I did, we did together. We were each other's eyes and ears. We talked endlessly about his work, and about mine. Our time alone on holidays never wore thin, was never empty of conversation, but was filled with endless chat, wry observations on each other's character, and shared fun.

Yet for all the entwining of our lives we had our own separate passions. Nick loved sport and spent hours in winter watching football on television. In summer he would take off on Sundays with the cricket team he ran called 'The Money Programme', and which he had started back in the days when he'd worked on the programme. Time and again he reminded me that there would come a day when he would be too old to continue, but year after year he continued to play. In protest at the time he spent away from me, I refused ever to turn up and watch. He retaliated by refusing to accompany me on my annual visit to an Elton John concert. He loathed all forms of pop music and hated it when I played any of mine. We couldn't even agree on what to watch on television. He loved thrillers, nothing more than *Inspector Morse* or *Spooks*. I liked romantic films and documentaries. We bickered. We made each other furious. But above all we made each other laugh.

Throughout those years, Nick was always there for me. He would move mountains to help me, whether rescuing me after my car had been towed away, or comforting me after a row at work. I could call him at any time and he would be unflappable and supportive, even if it was minutes before he was due to go on air. At times it infuriated his colleagues; they never forgot the day they had the Defence Minister of Pakistan waiting agitatedly on the line for Nick, who could be heard on the phone to me promising to buy blueberries on his way home.

'No one will ever love you as much as I do . . . ' he'd remind me, whenever he sensed complacency taking a hold. I often wondered – fleetingly – how I would manage without him, should the worst happen. The haunting image of life's hourglass was never far from my mind, but mostly I chose to ignore it, refusing to believe in the notion that bad luck could befall him, or me.

Have I portrayed this as a 'perfect marriage', seen through the rose-tinted spectacles which colour our view of lives that have been blighted by aching loss? I don't mean to, because our life was also filled with the ups, downs and near-collisions that are woven into any marriage. Nick wasn't easy to live with, and neither was I. He was stubbornly set in his ways, but I could be truly horrible. We had explosive rows and at times I would lash out and even hit him in uncontrollable fury. I was unreasonably intolerant of what he called his 'little foibles', whether it was the toothpaste traces he left on his towels, or his whistling to his favourite music (Shostakovich or Mahler, which I loathed) and of course my intolerance now shames me.

For his part, Nick hated me going abroad filming. What he found hard was being left alone. It got to the point where I dreaded breaking the news of any impending trip; it was always a tense moment and he would want to know, 'Why do you need *that* much time to film?' It became worse when I joined *Panorama*. Those trips tended to be longer. I would point out that he had been away filming over the years, but he hadn't ever worked on a programme quite like *Panorama* and didn't realize how all-consuming it was. The filming alone would last around two weeks, but before that there was location preparation and the research: it could easily add up to a five- or six-week absence. On one of these he really pressed for me to end the trip sooner: 'You're the producer, you can make that decision,' he argued, and eventually I boiled over, fed up with explaining, excusing and defending myself. I stomped round the house until bedtime, when I took my rage to bed to find him lying there contrite and eager to make up. 'Never sleep on an argument,' he said, as he always did. I tried to resist, but his persistence always got the better of me in the end. He would lean over and kiss me until I grudgingly kissed him back, and then we slept. Any attempts I made the next morning to continue to be hurt or wounded were ridiculed and ignored. So the argument went the way it deserved. Out.

But our ups and downs were as nothing compared to our greatest trial, which threatened the very foundations of our relationship, as we tried, but failed, to have children. I may have come across as a career woman who loved her work and cared little for having a family, but this was far from the case. I had thrown myself into my work in my twenties and early thirties because it was fun and exciting and there was no other way to get by in a television career. It demands total dedication, commitment, long hours – and it helps if you have incredible reserves of stamina. I could never envisage a child being part of that life; indeed, I could only see a child destroying what I was working so hard to achieve. I put off thoughts about babies and hid them away in some remote, unimagined future. But that future eventually arrived and by my early thirties I was thinking about children. And it was when they failed to arrive that I realized how important my home life was. I also saw that Nick was far more important to me than anything I might achieve at work.

It wasn't for want of trying. Or for the lack of medical quests to fathom why I was unable to fall pregnant without intervention or why I couldn't keep any pregnancy I did manage to achieve for more than a few weeks. And as the months turned to years and still there was no sign of the family I longed for, the pain of the longing coupled with the fear of the void that beckoned drove me apart from Nick. Although he never ceased to have faith that we would achieve our goal, and never ceased to support me as we struggled to reach it, our approaches were different. He was a man of facts, rarely emotional, determinedly optimistic. 'We *will* get there,' he would say at night as I lay listless and sad beside him. I, however, dwelled on fear and pessimism and withdrew into myself, shutting him out from my pain, angry that he couldn't share it – or so I thought – because he already had what

I yearned for: children. I fretted endlessly that our quest couldn't mean as much to him as it did to me. I'm so glad that I eventually found out that I was wrong.

In late 2001 I went for an early pregnancy scan, expecting to be told the worst. What I saw sent me into stunned shock. I rang Nick at work. 'I've got good news,' I said, 'but you need to sit down.' The good news was that I wasn't having another miscarriage; the rider was that I was carrying twins. Nick just laughed. He had been through that before. His children – now grown up and having been through university – were less unfazed. 'I can't quite believe it,' Ali wrote from Australia, where she was travelling. 'I woke up and remembered what you said when you called yesterday and wondered if it was a dream.'

The news brought a measure of relief for me in one sense. I had never wanted to give birth naturally – it terrified me – and a twin birth meant I could have a planned caesarean. I was booked in for 5 July 2002. The operation was scheduled to allow time for Nick's annual House of Commons v. Fleet Street cricket match on the fourth, but he wasn't taking any chances. He insisted that someone sit by his mobile phone whenever he was on the pitch in case I should call.

That same day saw me tearful and scared – because when it came to it I was frightened of becoming a parent. The years of longing had now been exchanged for a dread of losing our picture-perfect life, and I was worried, deep down, that Nick and I weren't entering parenthood with the same feelings. For me, this was a first; for him, it was an action replay. My heightened emotions spilled into a letter I wrote to him that night, reminding him of how I had once told him that I felt as if I had waited all my life to meet him.

The waiting of course is now in the distant past. But the intensity of what I felt when I said what I said, and of what you mean to me, of what you've brought me by coming into my life, by finding me, by joining me and by sticking by me through all the tough times as well as all the fun ones, hasn't changed at all.

And now we're about to embark on the latest chapter of the shared adventure of our conjoined lives ... Without you I'd have no chapters and no adventures. And I want to say something momentous again, something I'll remember years hence, and yet I can't find the words because everything is so intense and so scary and so exciting.

So I'll stick to saying, I love you, because I know you'll know what I mean.

I remember leaving home for the hospital the next morning and feeling panic set in. As we shut the front door behind us I suddenly had an urge to rush back into each and every room in the house, to take one last look, to freeze the image for ever in my mind. I wanted to say goodbye properly to my old life. I didn't like life without children but, right at that moment, staring back at it through the closed door with the future so uncertain, it didn't seem so bad.

Two hours later I lay in a hospital operating theatre and panic had turned to blind terror at the thought of bringing two small human beings into the world. As doctors and nurses buzzed around me, I battled to stay calm and then noticed, with surprise, that someone in the room was crying. A second later I realized it was the sound of my own joy at hearing my two babies' first cries.

Benedict and Joel were born just after ten o'clock that morning, each weighing a little over four and a half pounds.

They were born before full term, as many twins are, and were tiny. That picture-perfect life of ours descended into chaos. Two bawling, tiny scraps of skin and bone blew us off our feet. I had no idea what to do with one baby, let alone two, and Nick claimed he couldn't remember anything from the first time around. We paid for as much help as we could and pretended to ourselves, and to each other, that we were in control. We weren't.

Nick's reaction to our mid-life collision was to immerse himself in cooking meals to sustain me through marathon rounds of breast (and bottle) feeding. When he wasn't at work, he was in the kitchen for hours on end, while I sat alone weeping. I was overwhelmed but didn't dare confess to anyone. Tears would well up for the most trivial reasons, but I assumed this was normal. I knew rationally that I was really happy so these tears could only be a natural reaction to feeling a little hormonal and maybe, I reasoned, they were also tears of sheer joy.

The truth was that the enormity of having two small, pre-term, underweight babies to care for was more than I could deal with, even with the help of a maternity nurse in the early days. I pushed the waves of panic aside though, for fear of being thought incompetent, accused of whingeing, or of just not being a proper mother. But the pregnancy, the caesarean and its aftermath, the new mother's curse of lack of sleep, all placed a huge physical strain on me. My head pounded constantly, my heart raced and I couldn't think straight.

Looking back, it should have been obvious. The fact is that new mothers who have struggled to get pregnant are more likely than others to suffer from post-natal depression. So are mothers of twins. Fitting neatly into both of those categories,

I was, statistically, a dead cert. And when the boys reached three months and I went back to my obstetrician for a routine check-up, she immediately diagnosed PND. It was a huge relief. Along with the diagnosis came the first lifting of the strain of pretending I could cope, when I couldn't.

My GP prescribed anti-depressants and the symptoms receded. I slowly awoke from my gloom to find myself in a bright and colourful place – parenthood. There I watched, thrilled, as Nick fell head over heels in love both with his babies and with fatherhood itself – all over again. I realized how blind I had been to doubt that he would relish the experience as much as I. He sat watching the boys for hours, transfixed and with tears of love and pride in his eyes, as they screamed, strutted and charmed their way along a path of total destruction to our ordered lives.

As for our relationship, it was closer now. Nick was working regular hours, arriving home just after lunch, and we were together for the rest of the day. Every day. It was a wonderful, wonderful new life.

By the time their first birthday came around we had adapted to the disorder and accepted that other things needed to change too. I realized that I couldn't return to the BBC and the long and unpredictable hours my job entailed, so when, by pure good fortune, I landed a deal to write a book, I decided it was time to sever all ties and take redundancy. Nick, as ever, was totally supportive.

During the marathon feeding rounds when the babies were tiny, my maternity nurse and I talked idly about writing a book on her methods – which were simply about coping with a newborn rather than issues specific to looking after twins. It's the sort of idle thought that I imagine other journalists have as they lie in bed wondering what to do now that they have become mothers. To that extent, it all seemed rather pie-in-the-sky. But we struck lucky and Penguin commissioned it. It was to be called *Baby Secrets* and it took the best part of two years to complete. When people asked me whether I missed my job at the BBC, the answer was an unequivocal 'no'. No, no, no and more no!

Working from home meant I could spend time with the boys during the day. As they grew older, they started to listen out for Nick on the radio. They recognized his voice, well before they could interpret what he was saying, and when he came home they greeted him like any small children, screaming 'Daddy, DAAADDY,' unable to contain their excitement when he walked through the door.

I asked him one day whether he minded having small children again, whether it bothered him that what he had done for me had brought the chaos we now lived in. 'What do *you* think?' he said, and I knew the answer. We had simply exchanged one picture-perfect life for another, and we loved it. Nick kept a diary of the boys' early years and in page after page of tight, neat handwriting he documented the minutiae of their lives.

'A measure of confusion exists over "please" and "thank you",' he wrote fondly in February 2004. 'Joel thinks that if you say please, you automatically get what you ask for. Bendy [Benedict's nickname that sticks to this day] brings you something and says thank you himself . . .'

I never once saw Nick lose patience with the boys, though the demands of having two small children often pushed us both to the edge of reason. When, at the age of about eighteen months, one of them bit the other in anger, my instinct was to slap him. Nick's reaction was, 'No, please don't do that. I never want us to hit our children.' And when they sulked and grouched and whined, and I felt my patience dissipating at their steadfast grumpiness, Nick charmed them out of their mood. 'Come *on*, boys, just make a happy face,' he would tease. 'For Daddy!' And in the end they always did.

Nick was kind and tender, and in the short time he spent with his small sons he imparted his love of sport, his love of language and his love of life. He was quite simply the best dad I have ever known.

In July 2004 we celebrated the boys' second birthday with a strawberry cake on our first real family holiday. We were in Corsica, staying in a small cottage perched on a rock over-looking the sea. It was idyllic. 'The beach is about fifty metres down a woodland track,' Nick wrote in his diary one evening,

> and our main problem so far has been persuading Bendy to make the journey on foot. He is going through a perverse stage, to put it kindly, when he needs loads of attention – especially attention which Joel isn't getting. We devised a strategy of sticks (leaving him crying on the path) and carrots (a biscuit for whoever walks to the gate) which seems to be working ... The beach itself is brilliant: sheltered, virtually waveless, clean, sandy ...
>
> ... Sitting here on this beautiful terrace with everyone asleep, boys replete with chips from an Ajaccio café and full of sea air, I feel very lucky ...

Nick always felt lucky for what he had.

I suppose we all run out of luck in the end. But for some it happens too soon.

Too soon.

*

While the boys had been changing our lives at home, changes had been taking place for Nick at work. A new Radio 4 Controller had cut *The World at One* from forty minutes to thirty in a scheduling upheaval and Nick took the news badly, never giving up his battle to get the time reinstated. He felt, as he so often had, that the BBC didn't hold the programme in the esteem it deserved, and it got him down. When, in 2002 Kevin Marsh moved from *The World at One* to edit *Today*, the team became demoralized and rudderless, and Nick took it on himself to keep things as near as they could be to the way they had been. But the strain of so doing took its toll and he never again felt the same enthusiasm about the job.

I began to notice a weariness about his work, an almost perpetual irritation at the way the programme was being run and the pressure it placed on him. His spirits lifted only after the arrival of a talented young producer called Nick Sutton, for whom Nick had the highest regard. Nick Sutton filled Kevin's shoes on an intellectual level and was also sociable and fun to be with. He understood Nick better than almost anyone, cutting through his demanding exterior (double espresso coffee with warm milk on the side from the coffee stand in the Television Centre foyer and *nothing else would do*) with the same fond ridicule that had become characteristic in those Nick respected, and who respected – and loved – him. He also gave Nick the space and support he needed to maintain the journalistic approach that had stood him in such good stead so far.

The news agenda of this period was dominated by the aftermath of the Iraq War, the search for the weapons of mass destruction, the row over the legality of the war and the Hutton Inquiry, which criticized the BBC for its reporting on a dossier outlining Saddam Hussein's capability with weapons of mass destruction. The story became a passion for the two Nicks, who questioned and probed week after week and month after month. Trying to get at the truth became a crusade.

In his spare time, Nick had completed a second book just before the boys were born. *Shadow of a Nation* was a personal commentary on the way television and celebrity had affected people's lives, and what had been lost from the Britain that Nick remembered as a child in the 1950s. And in June 2005 I published my book and we held a small party. Nick, glowing with pride, made a speech to gathered friends in which he presented me with a desk sign that he had had custom-engraved. On it was the single word which, he knew, meant so much to me: AUTHOR.

Nick often said he could never have done any of the things he did if he hadn't met me. But I would never have understood the value of love, found the happiness it brought me, given birth to my children or even achieved my ambition of writing a book – without him. We were a double act, a duet whose singers were greater than the sum of their parts and who strove always to harmonize and never to out-sing the other.

And so now my story is back where it began, in the hot summer of 2005, which most people remember for the bombs in London and for the day that England won the Ashes at the Oval. For us though, it was the last time the sun shone on our lives. We spent much of it at Rose Cottage. The boys, now three years old, revelled in being at our country hideaway. They gawped at the tractors on the smallholding next door, collected eggs from the henhouse with Elly the farmer's wife, and cooed over a calf they named 'Baby Cow'. Each had been given a set of bat, ball and stumps for his third birthday, and Nick watched them discover the delights of the game he loved. 'We've got an unusual game here,' he shouted across the garden to me. 'We've got two batsmen, and each *simultaneously* strikes his ball with a sort of scything motion. I'm the "bowler" and my job is to keep them far enough apart to avoid accidents – and to retrieve balls from the nettles!' He loved it. It was the hottest and most glorious summer we ever spent there. So beautiful that it blinded us to the tell-tale signs that something was not right.

Nick had hardly played cricket himself all season, his performance hampered by the discomfort in his hip. He was weary. He was thin. He stopped carrying the boys upstairs. And he could be uncharacteristically tetchy.

'In retrospect,' he wrote later, 'in that happy land where everything seems so simple and obvious, my inability to face up to my condition was breathtakingly stupid.'

But how could anyone have imagined the horror that was lurking ahead? Or known that we were counting down to that fateful day when we went to the GP – the day – as Nick said – that the luck ran out.

FOUR

I knew the game was up. It had to be cancer. Everybody knew that. When it started to grow it terrified the living daylights out of me. I could see the GP blanching. He told me to go to hospital the very next morning. I only dimly realized at that moment that I had crossed into a new place: and the patient's place is to do as he is told by those who understand the mysteries of ill health. I accepted meekly.

NICK'S AUDIO DIARY, MARCH 2006

17 November 2005. The day after that visit to the GP. Clutching the piece of paper he had given us, we took a taxi to St Mary's Hospital, Paddington, where the twins had been delivered just over three years before and where our nightmare was to begin unfolding.

We had had little sleep and little to eat. Wearing a thin grey hospital dressing gown, Nick was ushered from one scanning room to the next in what felt like a high-tension drama in which no one spoke but everyone knew what the story was. Except us. Doctors came and went, examined and prodded, and stared at screens across which drifted black and grey shapes – meaningless to our untrained eyes. 'They reminded me of the scans you had when the boys were inside you,' Nick said afterwards. I hovered and trembled outside the rooms, so sick with fear I couldn't speak without breaking down in tears. No one would tell us anything. Only the consultant could do that, and he couldn't see us for a week. We drove home shaken into silence.

The cancer waiting game is torture. No news should be better than bad news, but hope can be a false friend. We were frozen in the longest and most frightening wait of our lives, unable to do anything, to think anything, to plan anything, unable to eat properly as fear flapped round our stomachs. We couldn't even discuss our worries with each other: they were too great. Gazing out of the sitting-room window at the autumn gloom, I raged at the sight of the rest of the world going on as normal. *Can't they see what's happening?* I screamed quietly. *Don't they care? How can they be so bloody smug?*

There's no one to talk to in this waiting game because there is nothing to talk about. The unknown is terrifying. Questions and thoughts remain cooped up madly inside your head. I racked my brains to think of someone to speak to but could only think of the GP.

'*Please* tell me what you think this is,' I begged when I finally got through on the phone.

'You have to wait for the results of the tests,' he said.

'But what do you actually *think*?' I pleaded.

'I *think* you have to wait,' he muttered, almost irritably. He did however pass on the news that the scans had shown that, whatever 'it' was, it was in the soft tissue and not the bone. It sounded hopeful, though I had no idea why.

One of Nick's first calls to the BBC was to Mark Damazer, the Controller of Radio 4, and after telling him in confidence what was happening, he agreed to a vague 'holding position' as far as everyone else was concerned. They would be told that Nick was undergoing some tests, and a benign-sounding public statement would be issued to explain his absence.

'I'm sorry to say,' Nick's editor announced in the weekly email newsletter to *World at One* listeners, 'that Nick isn't very well at the moment. His doctor wants him to rest for another few weeks, which has the merit of enabling our Presenter to keep up with the cricket without the distraction of conducting interviews.'

Which is what he did. He spent those long, tense days resting on the settee in the sitting room watching sport on the television or listening to Radio 4. At night he listened on his small portable radio, an earphone plugged into each ear, whenever anxiety kept him from sleeping. I never once saw him break down: he never fell apart, though I was sure that in his position I would have done. But at times he slipped deep into thought, to places where I knew I would never be able to join him.

I subsided into the sofa to contemplate my fate. For the first time, I felt not just uncomfortable, but properly ill – weak and listless. These feelings were probably no more serious than they had been a few hours earlier, but then I had been trying to deny their existence, and now there was no need to pretend any longer. Dimly I realized that no further excuses would be needed for inactivity, for giving up work, for not helping with the children. It was probably just as well: I had expended considerable effort trying to conceal the pain I felt walking, sitting or climbing the stairs. Barbara, at least, would now understand what was going on.

It was scary, though, and bewildering. Was I really going to die? I had had a good life, but how would Barbara and the boys manage without me? Deep down, did I feel more sorry for myself, or for them? These disconcerting thoughts did not amount to despair. Some small part of me, viewing the scene from a safe distance, couldn't quite believe that this was the beginning of the end. I had

no way of imagining what was going to happen to me, but whatever
it was had been taken out of my hands.

NICK'S DIARY

I, on the other hand, could not stop myself crying, and hated myself for such weakness in the face of Nick's calm and courage. I knew how much it upset him, so I took myself out of the house when the tears started to flow and returned when I had found the strength to pretend that I was feeling positive and brave.

I found solace at my local church, St Helen's C of E, just around the corner. I'd started attending soon after the boys were born. It's an inner-city church with a congregation to match – African women in their finest and brightest garb, elderly people who have attended the church for decades, local families with young kids – and I loved it, though Nick, a long-time atheist, had only ever come with me once, on the day I was confirmed, a few months before. Knowing how much this meant to me, he had given me a silver cross set with light blue crystals as a confirmation gift. Now my church offered me a place to cry, and a place where I could share my fears. Preparations were under way for the Christmas Fair and the church was buzzing with people who comforted and encouraged me. One large and kindly woman called Marion clutched me to her ample bosom and gave me the benefit of years of worldly wisdom. 'My neighbour got cancer when she was only thirty,' she said, 'and she died a couple of years ago. Ninety, she was. Remember that. Then there's Stan down the road – sick as anything, he was. We were sure he was a goner. And now look at him after treatment: picture of health, you wouldn't guess what he'd been through ...' And I prayed. I pleaded.

'Give us a year, God, please don't take him yet. Please don't let him suffer and please make me strong – for him, God. Please, oh *please* . . .'

One other person I turned to was Nick's colleague at Radio 4, Eddie Mair. I hardly knew him but rang, without telling Nick, not even knowing what I wanted to say. He listened patiently to whatever sobbing ramblings came out over the phone and said, 'You do know, don't you, that what you're going through is shit.' Relief flooded through me when I heard those words. I realized I was trying to hide behind a brave face when what I wanted to do was share the awfulness of what was going on. Eddie emailed me a few days later. 'I am here if you want to talk about anything, anytime. This is not a kindness. It's a genuine offer of help which you're welcome to never use or use all the time.' We started to meet for coffee, but I never told Nick: I didn't want him to know how badly I needed support.

Whatever worries Nick and I had, we kept them from the boys. 'Daddy's a bit tired at the moment, so he's going to stay at home for a few days and rest,' he told them. But children can only take on so much, and within days they began to sense that all was not right. They started waking in the night, agitated and unsettled, and would scream to be allowed into our bed, something they had never done before. There they would fight to be by me and would reject Nick's advances and offers of comfort. It was the only time I saw him close to despair. Through tear-filled eyes he said, 'They've already given up on me.' And I could see what he meant.

It seemed important to confide in the boys' nursery head, Joyce. 'He's not well,' I said, unable to utter the word. 'Is it cancer?' she asked, and she wiped away the tears I couldn't hold back as I shared my anxiety about how the boys would be affected by the changes at home. 'Young children are very adaptable and can absorb change easily,' she said, and I began to understand how events that might be overwhelming to adults could more readily be made to fit into a child's ever-growing and ever-changing kaleidoscopic image of the world. Joyce promised that the school would provide the boys with stability, certainty and a routine to their lives which would be unaffected by anything that happened outside its walls.

Our meeting with the consultant was scheduled for Monday, 23 November. On the Saturday before I took Joel and Benedict to the church Christmas Fair. I helped out at the 'new goods' stall and in the frantic bustle of buying and selling, of a brightly lit hall packed with people, music and the sight and sound of excited children queuing to see Santa, I was able briefly to step out of the anxiety that had enveloped me and enjoy the fun. The boys ran around with their friends collecting soft toys, cakes, and cheap plastic toys, and had their faces painted as Dalmatian puppies. It mattered little to them that Nick wasn't with us, but it broke my heart.

Talking to a consultant is unlike any other hospital experience. His or her knowledge and power spill into every corner of the room. The effect, if you're lucky, can be reassuring. Nick's meeting was with an oncological surgeon called Mr Rosin, for whom, I assumed, life and death in almost equal measures were a routine aspect of his job – along with the sight of either relief or dread in his patients' eyes. 'You seem to be expecting bad news,' he said, and for a moment I dared to think that he was implying we were wrong. Over the next few weeks I learned that doctors often ask leading questions in order to measure how much the patient knows, so that no assumptions underlie any subsequent conversation. He examined Nick and looked at the scans. 'I have to be honest and say it is highly likely that this is cancer,' he said, 'so don't get your hopes up. But I'll need a biopsy and a detailed scan to confirm it.'

'Do I have to give up hope completely?' Nick asked.

'Oh no,' he replied. 'I would expect to treat this with chemo- therapy to shrink it before we try to remove it.'

Nick's face visibly lit up. 'You can treat it?' he asked.

'Oh yes, for sure.'

Treatment is not the same as cure. But for the moment it sounded promising.

Nick had always had a phobia of enclosed spaces, but I had never known how bad it was until he faced the prospect of an MRI scan. His reaction was to refuse outright, so great was his angst. He was adamant: he would not go inside the machine. Mr Rosin muttered vaguely about having his head 'outside', and we were ushered out of the consulting room. I knew it would be down to me to get Nick there. And I had had to stop myself from shrieking at the consultant that the scan could have been carried out already, during the long, long week we had spent at home. Had we not waited enough? We still had nothing conclusive, no confirmed diagnosis, no plan of action, and the lack of news, whether good or bad, was unbearable.

There were no appointments on an MRI scanner for at least seven days, either on the NHS or privately, anywhere in London. I wanted answers and decisions to strip me of the impotence I felt in the face of knowing so little, but without them I channelled my frustration into scheming to get Nick to co-operate. At the MRI reception area, where I was despatched to make the booking, I found an understanding young radiologist who made it clear that there was no possibility of Nick having his head outside the scanner. He did promise, however, to keep his head as close to the opening as possible and suggested I get some diazepam to still Nick's nerves on the day. He also agreed, when I begged him, not to tell Nick the truth until the last moment. He was as good as his word, even when Nick rang him the day before the scan to seek reassurance. I too peddled the lie.

Nick's biopsy was quicker to arrange, expedited by the surprise discovery that the health insurance I had made him take out ten years previously would cover him for all his treatment. I had always known that if Nick ever got sick his fear of hospitals and his dread of losing his privacy in an open ward would make a difficult experience even worse. It was a piece of foresight for which he thanked me, and I thank Norwich Union because they paid for everything from that moment on, right to the very end. I don't think the quality of Nick's treatment would have been *any* different on the NHS, but the private rooms, the direct access to consultants and the immediacy of appointments did ease our tortured journey.

Mr Rosin did the biopsy himself, two days after our meeting, across the road from St Mary's in the hospital's private wing. I waited outside the operating theatre – relieved that I was not allowed in, but guilty at feeling that relief – while Mr Rosin chatted to Nick about the England cricket team's progress in Pakistan. 'It's reassuring to have something else to talk about when someone is driving a needle into your buttock in order to ascertain whether your illness is life-threatening,' Nick said when he emerged, relatively relaxed.

But any calm evaporated when we found ourselves, a few days later, sitting in the waiting room at the MRI scanning department. He knew from my edginess that I had something to hide, and he wouldn't take the diazepam. 'If my head isn't going to be inside the machine, why do I need it?' he asked suspiciously. I looked pleadingly at the radiographer and he broke the news. Nick was furious. He agreed to take a diazepam tablet, but I had to cajole, encourage and beg to get him into the scanning room. 'You're going in feet first, darling, and your head will be so close to the entrance you'll be able to look out and see me. It will be FINE. I promise.' But I was terrified he would walk out as soon as he saw the machine.

He didn't. I sat next to the scanner, holding his outstretched hand in mine and talking to him soothingly throughout. It took forty minutes. He never mentioned the deception afterwards. But the experience had stressed me hugely and I took the spare diazepam tablet myself. It was lovely.

We went home to wait, again, and filled the time with mundane tasks. Nick asked me to buy him a 2006 Filofax diary insert, but I couldn't find one anywhere. I knew that if I returned home empty-handed he would see it as a bad omen, so I settled for an academic one that ran from September to August. The significance wasn't lost on him.

Whatever it was that was being scanned and investigated Nick now nicknamed 'The Beast' – and The Beast was starting to take its toll. Nick was becoming drawn and his skin was pallid, leaving no room for any illusions about what The Beast might be. His voice became weak and reedy as his energy dwindled. As I watched Nick acquiesce to illness, a terrifying thought punched its way into my fulminating brain: 'He's not going to make it to Christmas. I am losing him. Oh God, *please help me* ...' I ran over and over the events of the past few weeks, thinking of the moments of joy such a short while ago, moments we might never share again, wondering how I could have spent time in New York, wandering around the shops in such blissful ignorance . . .

It was taking its toll on me too. Leaving the house one morning to go to church, I looked in the mirror and saw a face I didn't recognize. It was etched with tension. Our plight was written into its gaunt features, worry chiselled into its eyes. The strain of taking on the domestic chores that we had always shared, of looking after the boys single-handedly, of keeping my inner turmoil at bay, and of trying to be brave in front of Nick, was getting to me. I was barely able to eat, but would pretend to do so in front of him rather than worry him, and the weight fell off me. I had just won a contract as a media consultant to a multinational pharmaceutical company, the type of work I had dreamed of finding after leaving the BBC and finishing my book, and now I struggled to perform at my best. I felt I was letting them, and myself, down, and it hurt.

At around this time I began to be visited by an unwelcome emotion which I find hard to admit to. Anger came over me in waves, and I couldn't fight it. I was angry at what was happening to us, to me, to the boys. Angry about what lay ahead, whatever it might be. Angry that I couldn't do anything to make things better. And angry with myself about the anger I felt towards Nick for taking us all to this terrible place. For the truth was that from the moment it became clear that Nick was seriously ill, I hadn't felt drawn into a struggle which united us, but rather into one that divided us by the very different nature of the separate battles we faced. Nick was a patient facing his own mortality. I was a carer, fighting not just for his survival, but also for mine and the boys', and for what we held most dear – our happy and secure life with a man we loved to bits. And I was very, very scared.

I still find it hard to think about my feelings at that time. They leave me with a bad taste in my mouth. They were, and are, unpalatable. Nick seemed to understand how I felt, though we never discussed it, and his lack of self-pity, combined with the stoicism and strength he showed, made me yet more disappointed – at myself. But however I raged, my love for Nick and the pain of seeing what he was enduring never left me. It almost exploded out of my heart. And I have no doubt that his own battle was driven by his extraordinary capacity for love – for all of us.

On the afternoon of Friday, 28 November, my mobile rang. It was Mr Rosin the consultant. He was brief and to the point. 'I'm afraid it's not good news,' he said. The biopsy had confirmed that Nick had cancer. What was alarming was that it was what he called 'high-grade and aggressive'. At that moment I was standing outside the house in the falling dusk, shaking so much I could hardly hold the phone. The thought of going indoors to tell Nick the news was too much. Mr Rosin sensed it. 'Do you want me to phone Mr Clarke and tell him?' he asked. To my shame, I said yes. I then walked round the corner to a friend's house and burst into tears.

'Nick is going to die,' I sobbed.

She started to cry too.

FIVE

People said, what sort of cancer is it, is it oesophagus cancer, or lung cancer, or bowel cancer and I had to say to them I don't really know, it's bottom cancer. It didn't sound very good.

It's actually a sarcoma. My particular type has a habit of lying low for long periods biding its time, often undetected by the patient. One website put it succinctly: 'innocuous presentation can lead to delay in diagnosis until growth prompts intervention'. Which made me feel a tiny bit better about my tardiness in seeing the doctor.

But I was under no illusions now: failure to act quickly would have only one outcome – I would die.

NICK WRITING IN THE *DAILY MAIL*, JANUARY 2006

Jeremy Whelan is tall, dark-haired and slightly dishevelled. He wears thin wiry spectacles, a shabby green coat and has the air of a thoughtful professor. He travels to work on a purple scooter.

Steve Cannon is suave and urbane with swept-back silver hair. He dresses in sharp suits and drives an Audi sports car with personalized number plates.

Jeremy and Steve. An oncologist and an orthopaedic surgeon. One diagnoses. The other operates. Cuts it out or cuts it off. A team of two halves. In the hands of these two men lay Nick's fate.

I paced the shiny blue lino in Dr Whelan's soulless waiting

room on the fifteenth floor of University College Hospital, while Nick sat awkwardly on a chair. The Beast was becoming uncomfortable. Tall, wide windows looked down on to streets enfolded in the gloom of winter. Across the rooftops I spied the grey antennae of the BT Tower, its lights beginning to punctuate the twilight. High up above the rush-hour traffic we were cocooned from that everyday and carefree world to which once we had belonged. Other patients too sat in anxious silence. I pictured us all waiting to be handed a sentence: would it be kind or would it be harsh, a stay of execution, or death?

As the clock ticked past our allotted slot of five o'clock and Dr Whelan still hadn't arrived, a secretary informed us that he was stuck in a lift. Then she confessed he wasn't always on time. Anxiety turned to irritation. My stomach was knotted, the tension spreading throughout my body; I visited the loo six times. Pace, pace, pace. I couldn't bear to look at the anxiety on Nick's face as he distracted himself by listening to the radio through his ear-pieces. Just as the six o'clock news came on, Dr Whelan strode through the double doors and swept into his consulting room followed by several pairs of vexed eyes.

Jeremy Whelan specializes in bone and soft-tissue sarcomas. The word that had seemed, in my ignorance, relatively benign when written on a piece of paper by the GP just two weeks before, indicated a very rare type of cancer. Only 1 per cent of all cancers are sarcomas. And within this group are many sub-types. I don't know how many. I asked Jeremy once and he just said 'many'. When I looked on the Internet I found that only two thousand or so people in the UK are diagnosed with sarcomas every year.

A sarcoma is a cancer of the connective tissues, like nerves, fat, muscles, joints, bone or blood vessels. Sarcomas are either soft tissue or non-soft tissue, such as osteosarcoma, which occurs in the bone. They can grow anywhere in the body, in any organ, can be hidden deep in the limbs, or grow on an extremity like a finger. They affect young and old alike. Nick's was a soft-tissue sarcoma, at the very top of his leg, between his hip and his left buttock. Some sarcomas grow slowly and some grow very aggressively with a tendency to spread, usually to the lungs and sometimes to the lymph nodes. Which means that getting one can be very bad news indeed.

The biopsy had shown that the GP's suspicion was right. Mr Rosin had referred Nick immediately to someone with expertise in this field, a sarcoma oncologist, at one of the few hospitals specializing in this particular form of the disease. Jeremy Whelan had fitted him in twenty-four hours after getting the referral – at the end of a long working day, during which Nick had been sent for a chest X-ray. It had sounded routine to the two of us: we were about to find out how enormously significant it was.

In his consulting room Jeremy talked us slowly and carefully through the information he had. Although the biopsy had confirmed that this was a sarcoma, it would need further examination to determine what sub-type it was. He didn't need that information at this stage though, he said. What he did need to know was whether the cancer had spread. 'That's why we checked your lungs,' he went on, and as the penny suddenly dropped and our faces fell he quickly added, 'It hasn't. They're clear.'

Jeremy then went through the options *we* had. Not that there were many. And as Nick often said afterwards, it was clear that one of the options was death. Which meant that when he came to the other option it seemed quite a good idea.

He never used the word 'amputation' and I remember wondering why, and wondering whether I was misinterpreting what clearly sounded like a description of losing an entire leg. In a soft-spoken voice he imparted this news with the tact and diplomacy you might expect from a Foreign Office official. Chemotherapy, he said, would have little impact on a tumour of this size. Surgery was the only option, but given the location of the cancer it was unlikely it could be removed without the loss of the entire leg. That job would have to be performed by an orthopaedic surgeon. When I realized the magnitude of what he was saying, I darted out of my seat towards Nick and cradled his head in my hands. 'It's OK, darling,' I said. 'It's OK, we'll manage.' I was scared that he would refuse this – our only hope.

'I'll do anything, of course I will, I just want to live and see my children grow up,' was all Nick could say, and Jeremy Whelan replied, 'Yes, yes, of course.'

But I noticed that he didn't look Nick in the eye.

Steve Cannon is always on time, even if it's eight o'clock in the morning – which was the only available slot in his busy schedule, just thirty-six hours after Jeremy asked him to see Nick to discuss the operation. We met him at the Royal National Orthopaedic Hospital in Stanmore. The RNOH is one of the best places to go to if you need surgery on a limb and, as at University College Hospital, it has a team specializing in sarcomas, including orthopaedic surgeons. Working together, the two hospitals make up one of Britain's key centres of excellence in sarcoma treatment, and Nick could not have been in a better place.

'Nick', 'Jeremy', 'Steve'. Professional men in their middle

years, who instinctively and politely dropped formalities within minutes of meeting – although Nick did admit that at times he found it hard to be over-familiar with a man who was about to cut off his leg.

Steve combined empathy with matter-of-factness and a certain professional enthusiasm for the task that lay ahead. A nurse told me later that orthopaedic surgeons love amputations. He stood in front of a light-box for several minutes studying the MRI plates we had brought along and then asked what we had been told by Jeremy. Nick explained he had concluded that amputation was the only course of action to remove the tumour, but wanted Steve Cannon's confirmation. 'I'm afraid I agree,' he said. 'It's what we call a hindquarter amputation,' he explained. 'We do about twelve of these a year. A quarter of a century ago just about all sarcomas were treated by amputation, but engineering techniques mean we can save many patients' limbs these days. In your case, I'm afraid, that's no longer an option.'

He then outlined what it would involve, from the risks of the operation to the eventual supply of a prosthetic limb: 'You may find an artificial leg rather unwieldy,' he warned. 'Some people only use them for Sunday best.' His eyes twinkled and I guessed he'd used this 'joke' before. We smiled meekly.

Finally he sat down and faced us. 'There are other unwelcome side effects to an operation so close to the nerves that function down there,' he said, and went on to promise 'ways' of overcoming these side effects. We giggled (afterwards) at the idea that our sex life – or rather an end to it without the intervention presumably of Viagra – might be high on our list of worries at that moment. 'I bet that's what's been keeping you awake, isn't it!' Nick teased. But we laughed more at the levity that entered Steve's mini-lecture a little while later when he contemplated Nick's chances of resuming his career. 'How many legs do you need to be a radio presenter anyway?' he asked, and as Nick said afterwards, you couldn't argue with his logic.

It was the first time we had laughed for days. Our waiting game was over. Nick's operation was scheduled for two weeks' time: we were in another 'game' now, but it was different.

While I waited for a slot in Mr Cannon's operating schedule I sat at home trying not to feel sorry for myself. To be strictly accurate, I didn't so much sit as lie on a sofa, curled up in the only way I could find to be comfortable. Sitting for any length of time was agonising. Lying in bed was no fun either: I tossed and turned through the night, with a series of pillows under my body which I hoped might provide relief from what was now serious pain. Each day, walking became more difficult, until I could barely stand up for more than a few minutes at a time. The painkillers I was using brought on crippling constipation. And all the time the weight was dropping off my body, until I could see the shock in the eyes of my visitors at my skeletal appearance.

I was dying.

It was hard for others to grasp what Barbara and I both knew: that the operation, and the amputation, would come as a blessed relief.

NICK, WRITING IN THE *DAILY MAIL*, JANUARY 2006

Nick had now been away from *The World at One* for more than two weeks without a substantial explanation. Pressure was mounting at the BBC for a statement: the programme was being bombarded with calls and emails complaining that no reason had been given for Nick's absence. 'Are you going to mention the amputation?' I asked Nick, rather stupidly, while he was mulling over the words that might be used. He managed a smile as he said, 'It'll be a little hard to hide the fact for long, won't it? I want this to be brief, simple and optimistic too. And I don't want anyone to think I won't be coming back to work. See what you think . . .' and we went over his draft together until we were both happy with the wording. He then emailed it to the BBC, where, I suspected, it had to be approved by several people in the upper echelons of management. The final copy said:

> We have learned that Nick Clarke, presenter of *The World at One* on Radio 4, has been diagnosed with cancer. We're very sorry indeed to hear this news and send him and his family our very best wishes for a swift and successful recovery. Nick will be undergoing surgery which will involve the loss of a leg, but the prognosis is good and Nick plans to be back on *The World at One* in the summer. In the meantime the programme will be presented by Shaun Ley. We would ask everyone now to respect Nick's privacy – and that of his family – and to direct any further inquiries to the BBC.

The next morning we were sitting in the kitchen when by chance we caught the ten o'clock radio news bulletin. Nick's diagnosis – and impending operation – was the last story, and it took him completely by surprise. He simply hadn't made the mental leap from his illness to its becoming news. The item was followed immediately by a stunned Jenni Murray introducing *Woman's Hour*. Clearly wrong-footed by what she had just heard about a long-time colleague, she hesitated, stumbled over a couple of words, apologized for being taken aback, and then continued.

'Poor Jenni, they should have warned her,' Nick said. But he was unsettled, and remained so for several days, especially after reading the newspapers. 'At least it gets the word out to everyone,' he said, resigned, 'and friends will understand why I won't be sending them a Christmas card this year.'

That afternoon Colin Hancock, *The World at One*'s editor, rang Nick to tell him about the arrangements for his absence and about Shaun Ley, a young political correspondent. 'He's going to step into your shoes only for as long as you want to be away,' he told Nick.

'That'll be my *shoe* soon, won't it?' Nick said ruefully.

People outside our private circle now had an explanation for what must have seemed like our strange behaviour in the previous two weeks: the to-ing and fro-ing in the middle of the day and the worried looks on our faces. Neighbours had something to talk about, even if some of their responses took us aback. As Nick broke the news to one, he commented, unhelpfully: 'Well, it gets to us all in the end, you know,' before informing us that his sister was about to die of cancer. Another passed by to report excitedly that she'd just heard the news on the radio. 'And they said the prognosis was good!' she added. I wanted to yell at her, 'But *we* wrote those words, you idiot! What do you think we're going to say? That it looks bad?'

One friend, though, made the wisest comment I heard during that period: 'This is a primary cancer, Barbara, not a secondary. It *can* be treated, so you must stay hopeful.' I had never understood the difference before, but now I learned how much the difference mattered. It's the secondary cancer that usually kills people, once the cancer has spread from its original site to other organs where it is harder to treat.

In truth though, the nature of Nick's cancer – high-grade and aggressive – meant that treatment didn't offer unbounded hope. Steve Cannon had said Nick's chances were less than fifty-fifty. Nick saw the figures as good news. I saw them differently. But we were buoyed by the knowledge that something concrete was about to happen, and distracted by its enormity. And although it was indeed daunting, a calm had replaced the edginess which had infected us. With cancer, I now understand, it's uncertainty that brings the greatest fear. A diagnosis, however grim, can be easier to cope with than the awfulness of not knowing. And now we knew. The guessing was over. The fantasizing, the pessimism, the optimism and the false bravery – all were now replaced with something we could get our heads around. There was something to fight for now, something to do.

It was hard for others to understand our relief at the prospect that Nick was to lose a leg, or to find the right words. An old friend of Nick's turned up one morning with nervousness etched into his face. His wife later told me that he had rung her on the way and pleaded, 'What *am* I going to say to them?' He said little at first, but after drinking his way through most of a bottle of wine he asked us incredulously why we seemed so relaxed.

The boys appeared to have no problem with the idea of having a one-legged father. We introduced the idea gradually. 'Daddy has a bit of a poorly leg, boys,' Nick explained, 'so he's going into hospital soon to have it sorted out.' A few days later we upped the ante a bit, moving from 'sorting out' the leg to an admission that the leg needed to be cut off. This news was greeted by a question so blindingly obvious, I kicked myself for not having thought of it myself. 'Will he get a new one?' Joel asked. 'Yes, darling, but not straight away,' I replied. 'Well, why not?' Nick said later. 'If you break a toy, their instinct is to get another toy!' Yet the simplicity of Joel's assumption and of our promise to him that that was what would happen, was to come back at me many months later.

I didn't ask Nick how he felt about losing a leg, but I noticed he had no interest in investigating, or talking about, a prosthesis. He cared little about the disfigurement, but looked at me one day as we sat alone and said, 'I'm so sorry.' He knew what an enormous impact this was going to have on us. I brushed his apology aside. 'This will just be the next adventure of our lives,' I remember saying to him. But I could see that he was struggling with what he was facing.

In the days that followed the BBC announcement, cards and letters began to arrive. They came from *World at One* listeners, from colleagues – including Mark Thompson, with whom we had worked on *Newsnight*, and who told Nick he was one of the best broadcasters the BBC had; from people who had met or known him over the past forty years and more – even an old school friend who recalled 'doing battle in athletics'; as well as from politicians who had done battle with him in the studio. There was a note from Jack Straw, a handwritten letter from the Prime Minister, Tony Blair, offering encouraging words about the advances made in cancer treatment, and another from David Blunkett. 'If there's anything I can do to cheer you up ...' the former Home Secretary wrote, and then added, 'Fancy me cheering someone up!'

Alongside those from the great and good were cards and letters from ordinary listeners, many of whom confessed to never having written in to the BBC before. More than anything we were struck by the way in which Nick was perceived by his Radio 4 audience. 'You are one of the rare broadcasters whom listeners trust and admire as a friend. We miss you,' one stated simply, while another said, 'You have kept me company for quite a while now as I wend my weary way up the A21 to my lowly sub-editing job at Canary Wharf. I always say "Hi, Nick" and shout words of encouragement when you wrangle with some awkward politician, such as, "Go on, Nick, let him have it – both barrels."'

I noticed that almost no one used the word 'amputation', referring only to Nick's 'operation', and that the only people who mentioned the word cancer were those who had suffered it, directly or indirectly. They varied from the 'keep your pecker up' type to the less helpful: 'My husband died of cancer and I know just what it's like for you.' But they all meant well – even the kind-hearted soul who sent a booklet, 'Storms of Life … Finding God' and the lady who compared Nick's absence with the end of the Routemaster – the open-backed London bus that had recently been taken out of service. 'I don't think this lady has thought her analogy through,' Nick said, slightly bemused.

As the day of the operation approached, any calm we had managed to find began to dissipate. It was scheduled for 19 December. The Beast was starting to swell alarmingly, making it harder and harder for Nick either to sit or to lie comfortably. The sudden change in size was due, apparently, to the tumour having haemorrhaged into itself and filled with blood. Nick tossed and turned at night, and spent the days lying awkwardly on the sofa. The weight was still falling off him and he looked like a man staring death in the face. That he complained so little was extraordinary. If ever anyone might have been expected to utter the words 'Why me?' it was then he might have done so. But he didn't. And I genuinely don't think he even thought them.

The operation and his terror of the anaesthetic now loomed larger in his mind than the cancer itself. 'Surely an amputation isn't as invasive or as major an operation as heart surgery?' Nick had asked Steve Cannon hopefully. 'Oh, it's not far off,' was the reply. When I realized that Nick genuinely believed he might not wake up after the surgery, I sat down and begged him to share his worries and consider the logic of the situation. 'People hardly *ever* die on the operating table, Nick,' I said, clasping his hand. 'No one has ever died on Steve Cannon's operating table, and you're not going to be the first. You're more likely to be killed in the car on the way to the hospital. It won't happen, I absolutely promise you.'

He thanked me for that. But he still went on to write farewell notes in case he didn't make it – one to me, one apiece to his three older children, Ali, Tom and Pete, one to Joel and one to Benedict. He put each into a sealed envelope and then all of them into one large envelope and wrote on it 'For Barbara, in the event that . . .' He placed it in a drawer in the Wellington chest in the sitting room and never spoke of it again.

He began, at around this time, to record his thoughts on a tape-recorder with a vague notion that they might – at some later stage – make a radio programme. The tape-recordings soon expanded to include myself and the boys as he put on tape, along with his thoughts, some of what we experienced in the days leading up to the operation, and the aftermath. It was very hard at times, but it was also cathartic – and when the boys were involved it was even fun. It would later be broadcast as a Radio 4 documentary. Nick spoke frankly of the events leading up to the diagnosis. He spoke of The Beast inside him, gnawing away, trying to devour him; he recalled my persuading him to go to the doctor, how we went along one day after a *World at One* broadcast, and how he now felt about the prospect of losing his leg.

> I can't say I've come to terms with it at all. I think of it fleetingly and as soon as the more graphic images associated with amputation come into my head I eradicate them. I've thought a lot about trying to cope with life afterwards but the actual business and the process I can't bring myself to think about at the moment. That's probably unhealthy. People say I should have counselling but I've always been a little bit sniffy about counselling.
>
> NICK'S AUDIO DIARY, DECEMBER 2005

Somewhere there was a comment about his impending disability from me: 'I feel too young to be pushing my husband around the supermarket in a wheelchair.' That was the image I had of our future and which I was finding hard to accept.

I went to church that same Sunday that Nick began his recordings and I continued to pray, clutching the silver cross Nick had given me and which I now wore all the time. Stroking it like a rosary, I felt that something was stirring for us 'above'. Someone, somewhere, somehow . . . Christmas was approaching and we had been given the reprieve I had pleaded for. It seemed I was being guided to summon the strength I needed to get both Nick and myself through what lay ahead.

On Friday, 16 December, I took Nick to the RNOH for his pre-op tests and consent forms. The RNOH is a large sprawling complex of buildings which housed injured servicemen in the First World War and in the Second took in civilian casualties from across the country. To cope with this huge influx of people, Nissen huts were put up as a temporary measure. Sixty years on, they were still there, serving as hospital wards and linked by a series of draughty corridors. This was where Nick would be staying. An empathetic young registrar joined us and went through each of the forms meticulously before warning Nick that his blood count might be low as he was so ill and that, if it were, it would need to be sorted. He took a sample and sent us on our way.

That evening, when we were back at home, the registrar called and confirmed what he had suspected: Nick needed a blood transfusion and would have to go in for a few hours the next day. His patience running thin and his stoicism running dry, Nick tried irritably but in vain to persuade the registrar to let him off the procedure. 'I can't face another journey up there and I can't bear to spend any more time away from home than I have to,' he pleaded. But there was no arguing with the registrar. 'I'm afraid you can't be operated on unless your blood count is at the right level,' he replied firmly.

So the next day we returned to the hospital. It was a Saturday afternoon. We waited for the registrar to arrive, and then we waited some more, despite promises by the staff that he was 'on his way'. When, three hours after we had arrived, he finally turned up, Nick's frustration spilled out. 'What was the point of my getting here so early and why has everyone been promising us you were on your way when you patently weren't?' he snapped, before adding, 'I could have spent the last three hours with my children at home.'

'It's a Saturday afternoon,' the registrar replied calmly. 'I'm on my own, I have a whole ward of NHS patients to see, and I've had to prioritize. I'm sorry.'

Nick looked contrite. 'OK, I'm sorry too. I shouldn't have snapped,' he said, but I could see in that moment the depth of the tension and fear he was feeling, and the difficulty he was having, trying to keep it from me.

Later that day as the last drops of blood were entering Nick's bloodstream a woman wearing dark lipstick and slightly stern glasses, but with the air of a kindly matriarch, breezed into the room where Nick was lying and plopped her well-worn handbag on his bed. 'I'm Val,' she said, beaming, 'and I'm your anaesthetist.' In the slightly super-charged macho world we had so far been exposed to, it would have been easy to under-estimate Val Taylor. But it quickly became clear that she had more than a pivotal role in keeping Nick alive during the operation – she also had a bedside manner that was second to none. Within minutes she had put Nick at ease, explaining in great detail what would happen during the operation and then what he would experience when he woke up. The sight of tubes attached to bits of his body and the sound of bleeping monitors shouldn't alarm him, she said. She expected he would be in the High Dependency Unit for a couple of days. During that time, and afterwards, she would be there to control his pain. She also said she had ordered up several bags of blood because 'huge amounts' could be lost during the operation. 'But don't worry, Nick: Steve and I have worked together for years and we make a pretty good team.'

I wandered into the corridor with her after these discussions and she looked at my drawn and worried features. 'I do know what you're going through, Barbara,' she said. 'My husband had cancer ten years ago.' And then she hugged me. In that brief encounter she gave both of us the reassurance we craved.

As we walked back out of the hospital, down one of the corridors connecting the Nissen huts, we passed a woman pushing a frail man in a wheelchair. Two small children were skipping along beside her and she was laughing and joking. I marvelled that the woman was so cheerful when her husband couldn't walk, but was soon to find out how easy and important it would become to appreciate the positive rather than dwell on the negative.

The next evening we were on our way back to the RNOH again. A friend of Nick's had offered to drive us. Nick sat uncomfortably in the back seat and we drove through the early Sunday-evening traffic in almost total silence. At one point all three of us argued furiously about which route to take, until the friend put his foot down and told us firmly he was going the way *he* wanted to, and we lapsed back into silence.

I had held back the tears in front of Nick, but by the time we arrived they were lapping at the dam I had erected. I badly wanted to stay with him at the hospital yet I also wanted desperately to go for fear that the dam wouldn't hold. My mother was staying with us, but I knew the boys would expect me home. I hugged Nick, I kissed him, I whispered to him how much I loved him, and then I left him. But as I was about to set off down the cold echoing corridor outside his ward, I remembered something, and rushed back. I reached to my neck, fiddled with the clasp of the chain and handed him my silver cross. He knew what it meant to me and at that moment I think it meant as much to him.

I wept solidly, trying to stifle the sound of my sobs, all the way back home.

*

I'm here now just hours away from the removal of the 'thing'. I'm looking at the poor old leg, which has never done anyone any real harm. Not thinking wistfully about it, because I'm in such discomfort and the thing has swelled even more with more haemorrhaging, which is what I was told was going on there rather than the cancer itself actually growing. It is unbelievably uncomfortable. I slept hardly at all last night. I'm promised extra drugs tonight in order to make all this go away and not really happening except in my wild imaginings. The plan is for the operation to take place some-time around midday Monday and it will take roughly four hours. I'll then be kept under anaesthetic and probably not allowed to wake up until Tuesday morning, because it helps apparently patients overcome the trauma. And then removed, if all is going comparatively well, after twenty-four hours and back to my little room. It's one of those occasions where you think, If only it was Wednesday now. But it isn't.

NICK'S AUDIO DIARY, DECEMBER 2005

Nick phoned me early the next morning with panic in his voice. 'Things are moving pretty fast here,' he said. I was still in my pyjamas and was dressing the boys, preparing their breakfast and struggling through the usual morning chaos, expecting to leave once I'd dropped them at nursery. Shouting instructions to my mother, I struggled into some clothes and jumped in the car, my hair still wet, and set off like a mad thing. The traffic was heavy and slow on the Edgware Road and I cursed myself for not having taken an alternative route. But I made it in fifty minutes, and abandoned the car in a RESERVED bay in the hospital car park.

When I got to Nick's room I could see he had no idea what was going on. He was sedated and was slipping in and out of sleep. His forehead sported a large gash, which had been heavily bandaged but which still seemed to be bleeding slightly. I was told that he had got up in the middle of the night to go to the loo but was so drowsy from his pre-op medication that he had walked into a wall. At one point his eyes opened slowly and he said, bizarrely, 'You really should go to Goa some day,' before drifting away and then coming round with a start. 'Shit,' he said, 'I've just remembered what's going to happen to me.'

They called him in to theatre just after lunch. I walked beside him as his trolley was wheeled along the corridor, clutching his hand and blinking back my tears. I looked down on this great man who meant so much to me, who was so clever, kind and loving, who had achieved so much in life, who was so widely respected and admired, and who had always looked so capable and strong, and I wondered . . . How could it have come to this? How fragile is our existence, how frail our human form. Though he was dopey, he knew I was there and his hand clung to mine. Through the draughty, dim corridors we went, and then into a vast operating area lit by harsh white lights which bounced off a shiny grey vinyl floor and where everybody was dressed from head to toe in blue as they darted about amongst machines that buzzed and beeped.

Nick was wheeled into a tiny anteroom where Val chatted breezily to ease the introduction of an intravenous tube into the back of his hand before administering the anaesthetic. I cupped his face in my hands, my heart breaking for him as he drifted into unconsciousness. Then they wheeled him away from me through the swing doors and into the operating theatre, at which point I collapsed weeping on the floor. A nurse was ushered in to support me back to Nick's room, where I set eyes on the tape-recorder that Nick had taken to hospital with him. I switched it on and started talking, desperate to spill the anxieties that I hadn't been able to share with anyone. What if they found that the cancer had spread? What if he lost so much blood that he died. What if? What if . . .?

I then lay on a mattress on the floor and fell asleep. A knock at the door some time later woke me with a jolt. It was Val, coming to tell me what they had discovered.

SIX

Da-da! It's gone. Nick's left hindquarter is no more. And I can't really believe it. Everything seems to have gone as well as anyone could have expected. I came round really quickly and realized my voice has changed back again. And they got rid of the Thing and my leg and I feel better.

NICK'S AUDIO DIARY, DECEMBER 2005

Nick lay in a bed in the High Dependency Unit. Small white tubes were stuck to his hands and fingers; others emerged from somewhere beneath his gown. The room was strangely hushed, with just the barely audible sound of nurses shuffling between patients, their monitors, and the boards at the end of their beds on which the medical team made notes.

Nick's head and his arms were bare. The rest of him was veiled by a thin white blanket, through which the outline of his chest was plain to see, as was his right leg. It was the expanse of flatness, the emptiness, where his other leg should have been that hit me between the eyes. It seemed enormous. It wasn't until that moment that I fully felt the impact of what had happened to him. They had taken everything – right the way up to the waist, leaving not even a stump.

'Hey, you're alive!' I said cheerily as soon as he looked up and saw me. He smiled, weakly, but couldn't speak. I think he was genuinely surprised to have survived the operation.

I picked up the board at the foot of his bed and studied it earnestly. 'Hmmmm, pregnant . . .' I said, and looked up to see him trying to roll his eyes. As I scanned the temperature charts and notes full of indecipherable medical jargon I noticed some words I did understand. 'Diagnosis: epithelioid sarcoma,' they said. So they've identified it, I thought, and then thought nothing more.

The HDU nurse looking after Nick told me that when he awoke his first words were 'Where's Barbara?' It moved me to know this – and scared me to realize how much he was depending on me, that in his very lowest moments I was the one he needed. I didn't know if I was strong enough to carry that responsibility. But I had to find the strength. I would have done anything for him.

He was out of the HDU more quickly than predicted and he got through the first stage of his recuperation rapidly. He seemed to be in minimal discomfort, complaining mainly of a sore throat where the anaesthetic tube had rested and of being thirsty. I fed him sips of cool water and stroked his head. A few short hours previously he had been a normal man. Now he was a severely disabled one who would never again be able to walk unaided. But, as Val said to me when I voiced this thought, 'You may have a husband with one leg, but you do at least have a husband who is alive.'

Once back in his room the nurses placed a pillow under the sheet and in the space of Nick's missing leg. Apparently this helps patients acclimatize slowly to the loss of a limb. It didn't stop me thinking about it though. I knew his leg had been taken to a laboratory for pathology tests. I asked Val what they would do with it afterwards and she said, 'Oh, well, it will just go in a bin somewhere – do you *really* want to know?' And I decided

I didn't. Nick didn't want to think about it either, but later, when I visited him with the children, their curiosity was less muted. Where was the leg? Had they put it in a dustbin? Where was the dustbin? What colour was it? And then they got on to how it had been cut off. They had a natural childish curiosity. They said what they thought. They decided the doctor had used scissors – *very* big and *very* sharp ones. That was how they'd done it.

The news from the operation was encouraging. From Val I learned that they hadn't seen any cancer. For a fleeting moment I construed that as meaning he hadn't had cancer after all. No, she said, it meant that the cancer hadn't spread. And that was good news – or at least as good as we could have hoped for at that moment.

A few days later the lab confirmed what Val – and Steve Cannon – had seen. They'd examined the amputated limb and at the margins it was clear. There had been no localized spread of the disease. We had reason to be hopeful. Nick was more than hopeful: he was euphoric. He came up with his own diagnosis – and who could blame him? 'Technically,' he said, 'I am cancer-free.'

He actually looked better. He had lost the awful pallor which had affected him prior to the operation. Almost overnight the colour had returned to his skin; more significant for him was the return to normal of his voice. The thin, reedy, straining with which he had been speaking before the operation had disappeared. His beautiful, mellifluous voice – the thing which defined him for so many people – was back.

Once Nick was out of the immediate danger zone we hardly saw a thing of the surgeon, Steve Cannon. He had done with Nick, and was presumably tackling his next challenge. He did come in to admire his handiwork one day, surrounded by a group of awestruck students, but to all intents and purposes he was out of our lives now.

Val, on the other hand, was a constant presence, and a real comfort. She continued to monitor Nick over the next few weeks as well as oversee his pain management. She explained that the missing leg would feel as if it were still there and would trouble him for some time, but that it would gradually seem to be shortening, until one day it should disappear. This gave us hope, until she told us the story of a man who had lost his leg in the Second World War and had never ceased to feel the strange sensation of 'phantom pain'. She prescribed a drug called Gabapentin which Nick took for some weeks until, eventually, he felt able to come off it. The worst phantom pain he felt came out of the blue when the nurses gave him a bed-bath one morning and rubbed against his wound. 'I felt as if my leg were there still and was being yanked off,' he told me later, shaken by the experience. 'I've never known pain like it. I literally howled.'

In those first few days after the operation Nick was on incredibly good form, buoyed up by the return of his voice and probably high on the cocktail of drugs he was taking. Val saw us together that week, and I remember that we were both smiling. There was relief in the air. She mentioned, almost in passing, that counselling might help us cope with what we were going through, then in the same breath said we were strong and wouldn't need it. 'You two will be all right,' she said. I felt proud that our love – and the strength it gave us – should be so apparent to an outside observer. Not that we were the least bit interested in seeing a counsellor. Nick had never seen one yet, and I knew him well enough to know that he never would, except in extremis. His public school background and the stiff upper-lip approach it had encouraged, rendered such an idea inconceivable. And with him showing such courage there was no way I was going to concede that I might need that sort of help.

How easy it is to delude oneself. Something was niggling inside me. I knew I was hiding it. And it was easy to do so, because the fear and waiting of the recent weeks had been replaced by frantic activity. I drove to the hospital every day, always in a hurry, fretting at the snarl-ups on the Edgware Road out of London, checking my watch to see whether I had time to race into Asda to buy food, already imagining the dash back home to relieve whoever was looking after the boys. Yet for all these minor stresses, my visits felt purposeful: I needed to feel that I was caring and loving, because it was now sinking in that Nick was severely incapacitated. And with the dawning of that harsh reality my mood began to sink. He was still struggling even to sit up in bed without help and nurses had to tend to his every physical need. Recovery of any kind seemed a pipe-dream. The man I loved was an invalid, crippled by what life had thrown at him and dependent on others.

It didn't help that I was sleeping so badly. The boys woke regularly in the night, often becoming near-hysterical as I tried and failed to calm both at the same time, the demands peculiar to twins weighing heavily on me. I would spend up to two hours in their room reaching from bed to bed, trying to soothe them as each one wound himself into a frenzy, trying to stop me giving attention to the other. By the time I got back to bed I was limp from stress and sobbing. Sometimes I couldn't hold it off and would break down in front of the boys, whose response was to become even more wound up, prolonging the awfulness of what was now a nightly ritual.

When the Christmas break began, the young girl who had been coming in to help with the boys and around the house left on holiday and the chaos overwhelmed me like a great wave. I placed an online food order with Tesco one evening, only to abandon it halfway through. At least, that's what I thought I'd done, until next day when there was a knock on the door. I had ordered twenty-eight bottles of bubble bath – and nothing else.

Luckily Nick was still in good spirits and visitors were filling the gaps when I couldn't be with him. 'It's awful for Barbara and the boys,' he told my friend Anita, thinking as ever of others rather than himself. 'Next year it will be better and I'm going to make it up to them with a huge Fortnum & Mason hamper.' Late on Christmas Eve he recorded his thoughts:

> Ninety minutes to go to Christmas Day and I'm not feeling sorry for myself at all. I don't know why – it's probably the drugs. This rather bare little room is not very attractive but at least I've got lots of friends and family coming to visit me tomorrow; whereas Aaron, my nurse for tonight, is going to be sitting on his own in a small hospital room, with all his relations three or four thousand miles away across the Atlantic in Trinidad; and at least I have had quite a lot of use out of my lost leg, unlike the nine-year-old girl they operated on today, who lost hers.

NICK'S AUDIO DIARY, 24 DECEMBER 2005

But by Christmas Day Nick's resilience, like mine, was crumbling. Imprinted on my mind to this day is the scene as I tried to get two recalcitrant three-year-olds, whose needs I wasn't meeting and who were running riot in protest, out of the house and into the car. The hallway was strewn with toys,

Smarties had been spilled from a tube and crushed underfoot, along with shards of glass from a tumbler thrown in anger from the top of the stairs. When we arrived at the hospital we found Nick at a very low ebb. The epidural that had been left in place after the operation in order to control his pain had just been removed. He was in severe discomfort, his pain-relieving drugs were making him nauseous and nothing could cheer him. The sight of us seemed to distress him and when he asked us to leave it was a relief, although I did so with a sense that I was failing, as a mother, a wife and a human being.

The boys and I drove north to stay with friends who had offered to share their family Christmas to give the three of us a break. On Boxing Day we tobogganed down the snow-covered slopes at the back of their house in dazzling sunshine and under a crisp blue sky, and the boys shrieked with unfettered delight.

As the old year ebbed away, Nick slowly began to regain his strength. Just before midnight he toasted in 2006 with a small glass of wine and no small degree of optimism. His drug regime was modified day by day until the pain was back under control and the anti-nausea drugs kicked in. The minute the Christmas festivities were over he was passed on to a team of physio-therapists whose job it was to get him back on his feet – or foot. It seemed an uphill task, but they assured me that when he came home he would be completely mobile and would never need to call on me for physical support. That was a relief, because I knew I simply didn't have the build to carry his weight.

At first, progress seemed to be hideously slow, but every gradual advance was greeted by encouraging fanfares from everyone around him. I arrived one day to be told that he had sat up in bed unaided and swung his leg over the edge. He was beaming with pride. I tried my hardest to share the excitement.

I've managed to sit upright on the bed now reasonably comfortably, but the idea of placing that right foot on the ground and putting all my weight on the frame and not doing what the physio says everyone always does, which is to try and put your left foot down which isn't there, it's scary ... sitting is not easy when you've lost the sitting equipment in your buttock: you're sitting on things that are much softer, and were never designed for the job. So although I can physically do all the things I've been asked to do, I do find that quite painful. I dose myself up with oral morphine beforehand to try and reduce the effect. But I'm told that over time the stump will accustom itself and it won't be so difficult and painful as it is now.

NICK'S AUDIO DIARY, JANUARY 2006

Then there was the day he made it into the wheelchair. It wasn't easy, but he persevered, and when, a few days later, he was finally wheeled out of his room and along the corridor, he was euphoric. I took the boys in that day. They dressed in doctor's outfits and ran up the corridor shouting 'Where's my Daddy, where's my Daddy?' Seeing him in a wheelchair for the first time left them completely unfazed. All they wanted to know was why it was painted blue.

'I'm a bit poorly, aren't I,' Nick said to the boys. 'I had such a naughty leg and it really hurt Daddy, but now it's gone and that's good. And when you two visit me I feel better.'

Nick was soon being wheeled to the hospital gym every day to build up his arm muscles and learn to balance on one leg with the help of a set of parallel bars, which would eventually be replaced by crutches. It was exhausting work, but he threw himself into it.

There's a certain amount of tottering but I can feel the strength coming back into those remaining limbs, which have to work 25 per cent harder than before. I was struck by the fact that at the end of the parallel bars through which you're supposed to hop or walk with crutches, there's a big floor-length mirror. It means that for the first time I see myself as others see me. With a rather bedraggled-looking trouser leg bound up towards the waist and a slightly lopsided figure above it. It's rather strange and a little bit moving, I suppose. I don't feel depressed by it. I don't feel that it's something insuperable. I think I've still got a little way to go because I still haven't looked at the wound. And the physiotherapist says I need to touch it and rub it gently and it will help to restore the circulation. But I can't do it at the moment. So there's obviously no proper acceptance of what's happened to me.

NICK'S AUDIO DIARY, JANUARY 2006

Accepting that he was truly disabled was, not surprisingly, a battle in itself.

Physical independence is very important to me. I don't want to be dependent on anybody, and I want to be able to find strategies to deal with all the little problems as quickly as possible. I'm going to have trouble feeling like a disabled person, and I was just reflecting vaguely that this wasn't really the right thing to do. I ought to accept that there are other people in wheelchairs, hopping up and down the hospital corridors and so on. We're all in the same boat.

Visitors continued to drop by, often bringing gifts that Nick didn't really want – and he wasn't afraid to say so. Carolyn Quinn, Nick's colleague at Radio 4, came with jazz CDs. 'He said he hated jazz and asked me to take them away,' she told me dejectedly. Eddie Mair brought food. He didn't want that either. Some found the visits difficult: nothing prepares you for confronting a man who has been dismembered. I was there when Will Hutton arrived, clearly not knowing where to look: he couldn't let his eyes settle on the great glaring gap in the outline under the sheets. In the end I pointed it out to him to try to ease the embarrassment. 'Look, Will. It's OK to look. Really, it's OK,' I said.

One visitor during this period was Jeremy Whelan, Nick's oncologist. He now had the pathology reports and had seen the precise nature of the growth. The good news was that, as suspected, all the localized cancer had been removed with clear margins. Nick was euphoric. Jeremy then went on to explain that this type of cancer had a high risk of coming back, which was why he was now recommending chemotherapy, as soon as Nick was out of hospital. I recorded their conversation:

'Technically speaking, I don't have cancer at the moment so I could say no to this,' said Nick.

'What you don't have is cancer that we can see,' said Jeremy. 'Why we're advising treatment is because of the possibility that there are cells still in your body that are invisible to standard detection mechanisms and that those cells gradually grow and become apparent at some point in the future. Now if that's the case then the treatment at that point is much harder to undertake with the possibility of eradicating the disease.'

There were times, looking back, when I felt that Nick and Jeremy, for all their mutual respect and ease with each other, talked at cross purposes. Nick's view was that he was now cancer-free and didn't need the chemotherapy but was having it as a precaution. I was frustrated by what I saw as a misunderstanding of Jeremy's message. In my mind the fear of how cancer can strike again was ever-present, but Nick seemed to take the view that he had been lucky. At the cost of a leg he'd been saved. He'd got out of jail. It was to take me some time – until after his death, in fact – to understand, in a conversation I had with Jeremy some months after Nick died, that this was the only way Nick could deal with the gravity of what he was facing.

'I felt he knew exactly what was happening to him and understood that his cancer could come back,' Jeremy told me then, 'but his most powerful emotion was the fervent desire to live, for you and the boys. To admit to that knowledge would have been too painful for him.'

'Doesn't everyone have a fervent desire to live?' I asked him.

'No, not at all,' he said, to my surprise. 'Some people are more phlegmatic when faced with such news. He had a fervour.'

By early in the New Year the frantic days had settled into a manageable pattern. He was still working with Val to relieve the phantom pain, which was exacerbated by pain in the stump itself. 'It feels as if someone's banging into it from the inside like a bone or a paddle,' he told her. 'I get scared to move on my side because it produces these very sharp pains and it feels as if the stump is sticking up in the air. The phantom pains I can cope with. They're not so much painful as curious. My absent left foot was very cold yesterday and I wanted to put a sock on it but decided this would be quite tricky!'

While Nick packed his days with medical matters, visitors and the physio regime, I began to feel marginalized. The visitors applauded him, cheered him, gossiped with him, and discussed world events and politics. Nick never failed to tell them how hard the situation was for me, and praised me endlessly for keeping things together, but my resistance was waning. At home I felt isolated; I was still not sleeping, still losing weight, was emotionally and physically exhausted and was beginning to feel resentful. I had no time to listen to the news or read the papers and couldn't join the conversations Nick was having. When the Liberal Democrat leader Charles Kennedy resigned out of the blue, Nick rang excitedly and told me to switch on the radio to hear his extraordinary admission of a drink problem. Distracted by two brawling boys I couldn't even get to the radio, and when, later that evening, Mark Damazer called and asked whether I had heard 'that extraordinary Kennedy speech', I wanted to scream, 'NO, I HAVEN'T! I've been feeding children, buying food, washing clothes, driving to the hospital and back, weeping, worrying, and anxiously trying to glue the pieces of my fragmented life together so I HAVE NOT HAD TIME TO LISTEN TO THE RADIO!' The fact was that I was embarrassed that I had nothing interesting to offer, no chirpy conversation, no wry observations on Charles Kennedy or anything else, because all that mattered at that moment was that I had run out of milk and was trying to work out how to get some more with two screaming toddlers in tow. I felt utterly worthless.

When illness strikes, the patient is the hero. As a carer you sit on the sidelines while bouquets are handed to the star of the show, fully aware of how lucky you are not to be ill. For me, the frustration of being the unsung hero, combined with the fury I felt at myself for daring to want a bit of acknowledgement or praise, had my mind in shreds.

Worse still, I realized that I was terrified of what lay ahead for me – of having to care for Nick and nurse him round the clock once he got home. The physical change he had gone through horrified me. I know it did him too, and it took him several days after the operation before he could bear to catch a glimpse of his wound when the staff came to take the bandages off. But I couldn't, and even when he was neatly bandaged up I found that just looking at that great empty space drained away all my strength. When I saw his gaunt, unshaven face and realized how completely helpless he was in terms of independent movement, I felt I no longer knew him. At times I found it hard even to kiss this man who seemed like a stranger – and of course I was furious with myself. My husband had cancer, had lost a leg, and was battling against so many odds, yet my reaction was to be disgusted and weak. My fury at my own reactions soon turned to self-loathing. At the same time I was weary, fed up with the effort of being brave, of holding everything together, wondering when or how I would be able to accept what had happened to Nick's body.

Finally the dam burst. It was an afternoon when I arrived early and in the middle of Nick's daily wash and bandage change. I had never sat through the whole procedure before. It was intimate and uncomfortable to watch and I wanted to leave the room. Nick, however, wanted me to stay. My struggles to accept Nick's new physical state and his limitations got the better of me. Sometimes you realize you have been battling to contain a rage and can contain it no more. It really needs to be vented, and I vented it. It spilled out in an ugly tirade. I shouted and then I screamed that he was putting me through hell. 'You've become so self-centred,' I raged. 'You have people looking after you day and night and you want me to be there for all of it. I can't do it, I won't do it. No one is helping me in all this shit. I'm there for you, but what is anyone doing for me?'

With a swiftness and a gentle tact that surprised me, a nurse ushered me into a quiet room, brought me a cup of tea and sat with me as I sobbed and ranted, abused Nick and abused myself. 'This is so normal,' the nurse told me, 'so so normal. Believe me, I've seen it many times. Don't beat yourself up about it. You're under incredible pressure and it's no surprise you feel this way. You need help, and I'm going to find some.'

Later that afternoon, when I had calmed down and begged Nick's forgiveness, the nurse took me to one side and said she had arranged for a hospital consultant psychiatrist to see either Nick or me or both of us. I agreed readily, but knowing that Nick would be resistant to the idea, I told him the consultant wanted only to see me, but that I would meet him in Nick's room. The next day I made a point of arriving late for the appointment and found Nick in relaxed conversation with a charming Greek man with a lilting accent and kindly manner. His name was George Ikkos. Seamlessly I joined the conversation, and seamlessly it turned into a counselling session. Halfway through Nick twigged what had happened. 'You've set this up, haven't you?' he said accusingly, but we carried on anyway.

In the safety and security of that environment both Nick and I opened up with undisguised relief. I told him how wretched I felt at not yet coming to terms with what he was going through, that I hated the way he looked, that I was worried about his coming back home, and that I resented what was happening to my life. 'But most of all,' I said, 'I hate these feelings because they're selfish and because I know that none of these things really matters, not really. What matters is you, and I love you.'

To my astonishment, Nick told me how guilty he felt at what he was putting me and the boys through, and he reassured me that he wouldn't come home unless he was ready to do so. 'I wouldn't do that to you, you know, I wouldn't come home if I felt I was going to be a burden to you, you have my word on that. I know how worried you must be about that and I understand it.' And then he told me how frightened he was.

I was able to reassure him that I wasn't angry at him, that I didn't resent him, but that I was angry at the situation we were both in and that I didn't for one moment blame him.

Later, as the clock struck five, I asked Dr Ikkos if he was sure he could stay the extra time that I had wasted by being late. He looked at me and said that someone who was selfish wouldn't have been thinking about him. I still felt bad that I wasn't coping, but I felt better for having shared it – and for having been able to say so in front of Nick. And to be told that I wasn't such a bad person after all. We'd moved a long way in that session.

We continued to see Dr Ikkos. He gave us a place where we could voice the feelings that even those who love each other dearly can find hard to share. When we were with him it felt safe to confront the frustrations and misunderstandings that can follow a life-changing event like Nick's illness. There was no worry about recriminations. From that very first meeting a weight lifted from my shoulders.

At home the burden lightened too – just a little. The boys were back at nursery after the Christmas break and I soon had a goal in sight. Nick had been given a discharge date: 19 January, a month to the day after the operation. I still wasn't sure he was ready to come home and was less sure that I wanted him back. I was worried that I didn't have it in me to become a carer, that I would fail the test of true love. On a practical note, I was worried about Nick's ability to climb the stairs, as I could see it would be a slow and tiring task every time. So I suggested we buy a stair lift. In his hospital room, on the laptop he used to keep in touch with the outside world, we sifted through the various websites, giggling at some of the advertising copy: 'attractive', 'beautiful', 'sleek minimalist looks', 'a refreshingly modern approach to design'. Nick sighed. 'Basically, they're all hideous, so go for the cheapest,' he said. The whole business seemed tainted with the stigma of age and infirmity and we both felt it.

People who buy stair lifts are usually vulnerable – if not for themselves then on behalf of the person for whom they are buying. At least, that is what I concluded from the way the stair-lift companies reacted to my inquiries.

First to come to the house was one of the best-known brand names in the business. Their 'trained engineer' went through an elaborate rigmarole of measuring and drawing a detailed specification of the stairs and the kind of chair we would require. It took him a full half-hour, which was strange, since our stairs are as uncomplicated as could be: sixteen steps, straight up, with no curves and no obstructions at either end. But I guess the rep had to justify his estimate, which came out at £3000.

The second rep I spoke to assured me that his company didn't do hard sell 'like the others'. He was a large man, but pointed out that his company's lifts could take the weight of people 'even larger' than himself – like the 22-stone man he had just visited. After taking the barest minimum of measurements he quoted me a price of £2500, then dropped it by £200 in view of my 'special circumstances' – which he didn't seem able to specify. As he left, he said cheerfully, 'You know, I love my job. Everyone I meet is worse off than I am.'

Though £2300 still seemed a lot of money to me, in my panic to get things organized speedily I was tempted to forget the price and go for it. Caution prevailed, however, and I found time to check a few other sites on the Internet. When the large man rang back to ask whether I was going to accept their offer, I told him that I'd found some cheaper options. How much cheaper? he asked; £1700, I replied. Five minutes later he offered me a stair lift for £1750. It was fitted the next day, a simple, low-tech piece of rattly kit which was installed in about twenty minutes. I thought I'd heard the last of these people, but they continued to call me twice a month to offer me extended guarantees, and a walk-in bath. When I reminded them that my husband couldn't actually walk, they quickly backtracked, saying, 'Oh no, we weren't thinking about it for your husband. We just thought you might have some friends who would be interested.'

While the stair lift was our responsibility, social services were offering the other items of 'homecare equipment' they thought Nick would need. Kate, a friendly social worker who spent a lot of time telling me about her attempts to get funding for a film she wanted to direct so she could stop being a social worker, brought a perching stool so that Nick could literally 'perch' at the sink, and a grubby bath lift with a seat that could be raised or lowered by means of a rechargeable battery. 'This looks like it's been used before,' I said, slightly uneasy about the grey marks on the seat. 'I wonder what happened to its last owner . . .' But she didn't get the point. 'Don't worry, it's been cleaned,' she said reassuringly.

At hospital Nick was accruing yet more aids. He now had a pair of crutches, a padded loo seat and a portable cushion made of mouldable foam. 'It's a NASA spin-off,' he told me. 'Apparently they developed the foam to give their pilots a more comfortable ride at high speed.'

The day before his return I got the boys to paint some pictures for Daddy. They set to work enthusiastically, daubing paint all over the sheets of paper I gave them. But try as I might, I could not persuade them to use any colour besides orange and purple. I stuck their efforts to the front door, and I made a large sign which covered most of the sitting-room window.

Although I was more comfortable about Nick's preparedness for his return home and my ability to cope with it, I still had one dread which I couldn't share with him, even in the presence of Dr Ikkos. I was alarmed at the idea of sharing a bed with a man who had lost a leg. I still hadn't come to terms with Nick's physical transformation, or more accurately his mutilation, and still hadn't managed to do more than glance at the dressings on his wound. Every time I thought about it, I flinched. I forced myself to talk to him about it, and recorded our conversation.

'You look so thin when you stand up on one leg, it's horrible,' I said. 'You seem to have a completely different body, and it's as if you're not the person you used to be. I try to remind myself that you are that person because your head is the same. But although the shape of your body doesn't determine who you are, it's made me realize it's a much bigger part of how one perceives someone, because sometimes I think you look like a feeble elderly man, like my father, and it's really difficult.'

'It's a shock to me at times, too, when I see myself,' Nick said. 'I can feel how thin I am, but the biggest shock is the stump. Because when you think of a stump you think of a stump and this isn't even a stump. The cut is right up against the hip, it's all gone and there's nothing left. It's just a wound. And I've found that very shocking. I've not looked at it face to face, if you see what I mean.'

'I've been wondering what it'll be like to lie in bed with someone with just one leg,' I continued.

'Well,' said Nick smiling, 'luckily it's not next to you, otherwise we'd have to swap sides,' and we both burst out laughing.

On the day I was due to bring Nick back from hospital I realized that there was still a reluctance. This was meant to be a high-point, a moment to celebrate, but the fact was we had settled into some sort of routine at home and now it was all going to be upset. Part of me resented the fact. I think I even said as much into the tape-recorder – and wondered whether people listening to it later would think me selfish and uncaring. I toyed with deleting what I'd said. Nobody would know. But there was no denying that I felt this way and I decided I wanted people to know that caring for someone can tap a seam of many emotions, some of which make uncomfortable companions.

I arrived at the RNOH to find Nick in his wheelchair struggling, as he always did, to make his tape machine work so he could record the first of his many goodbyes. I took his suitcase to the car and returned to push him on his processional tour of the ward as he sought out every single member of staff who had helped him. 'You've been so marvellous, Christine, the way you make this place run so smoothly,' he said to the ward administrator. Her eyes lit up at the sound of such praise. 'And my favourite nurse. No, NURSES!' he exclaimed as he spied first one then another of the two young women who had been with him from the start. 'Suzie, you've been so kind. Oh no, I've done it again. I STILL get your name wrong. That's my sister. I'm so sorry.'

With the goodbyes completed I wheeled Nick along the draughty corridor towards the exit, trying to remain upbeat, but utterly crushed by the sight of his emaciated and lopsided frame. As we emerged into a bleak winter day he was overcome by the moment. 'At last, the outside world. Grim and grey on this January day ... but it is fabulous to feel the wind on my face once more,' he gushed into the tape-recorder. I couldn't resist a dig at his more melodramatic broadcasting colleagues. 'You're not liberating Kabul,' I said. I thought it was terribly funny and would make great radio when the tapes were broadcast. Just in case, I got him to check that he had recorded every last word. True to form, the microphone plug had fallen out of the ageing recorder and there was nothing on the tape. We both wanted to hurl the machine out on to the street, but our professional selves were alive and well. I wheeled him back inside and we did the whole thing again. Take two.

The sense of achievement lightened the moment. 'I can't believe I'm pushing you in an NHS wheelchair which has flat tyres and is pulling to the left like a supermarket trolley,' I complained. 'What's worse is that it doesn't have a shopping basket underneath to put my handbag in.'

'Watch out,' Nick shouted as we veered dangerously close to a car, 'or you'll be the first person to claim on insurance for damage to a car caused by a wheelchair.'

As we sat next to each other in the car it felt good. We

joshed, we teased, we chatted. 'I couldn't imagine us ever sitting like this again,' I said, 'going home, having normal conversations, you telling me my driving isn't very good, telling me which route to take even though I've done the journey a hundred times. I just can't believe it. Apart from when I look down and see you've only got one leg.'

'I'm finding it hard to believe as well,' said Nick. 'Did I really think I was going to die? Did I think I'd come back? I think I thought I would come back, but I had no idea what it would be like. And sitting here like this and confronting these disabled moments is quite disconcerting.'

We remembered how much we made each other laugh. And I had a surprise for him, which was a signal that things had returned to normal. As I rounded the corner into our road I told him to look at the sign I'd pasted on the front-room window. 'Welcome home, Pegleg' he read. And he roared with laughter.

SEVEN

I've felt really cross and vexed and angry about everything and I haven't felt very much anger up to now. I spent quite a lot of today up on my crutches, and because I've been laid low by the chemo I'm not as agile as I was and not as confident as I was, so all that sense of progress after the operation has evaporated. I feel crap and I feel useless and I feel utterly helpless and I feel at everyone's whim and I don't want to ask anyone to do things for me. I feel the whole thing is lousy. I had this vision of myself today hopping around everywhere and I discovered today that the best way to do that was to be down on my bottom and to shuffle around the sitting room and try and do some work. And it's always going to be like that. So I've just said to Barbara, 'I feel angry,' and she said, 'Yes, it's shit, it's just fucking shit,' and it is. A little bit of a lapse of positive thinking. I'm tired. I'm going to have to get myself going again, get myself moving, get out of the house as soon as I'm strong enough, otherwise I'm going to sit here festering and feeling bloody miserable.

NICK'S AUDIO DIARY, FEBRUARY 2006

The man at the council was adamant. Nick's blue badge – allowing him to park in disabled bays and on yellow lines – had been issued for one year only and for a very good reason. I had rung the council in a fit of pique as soon as the badge arrived, irritated to discover that the bureaucratic rigmarole of applying and being assessed for it would have to be repeated in a matter of just months. It seemed senseless. 'His leg is not going to return,' I snapped. 'It is gone. For ever. Am-pu-tat-ed.' 'Madam,' the man replied, 'your husband will need to be reassessed because we'll want to be sure he really needs the badge. Some people with one leg are *very* mobile.'

As it happened, Nick was learning to get about quite well. His work in the gym, coupled with his determination to be as independent as he possibly could, had made him more agile on his crutches than I had expected. But I still couldn't see him making his way through a crowded supermarket car park, weaving a path between loaded trolleys with wonky wheels. He needed that badge. He had a wheelchair, of course, courtesy of the NHS, but it was unwieldy and too big to be brought indoors. We left it in the car and Nick devised other strategies for navigating around the house. In the kitchen he learned to use the worktop instead of one of his crutches and was able to hop from the fridge to the kettle to the toaster to his seat with relative ease. He even made the boys' breakfast some mornings, allowing me a welcome lie-in and sending one of them upstairs with some tea in a plastic beaker, lid firmly in place.

The stair lift was an instant hit, not just with Nick but with the boys too. They took it in turns to ride with him and then started to go up and down on their own, fighting over who got to press the buttons – 'Get OFF, OFF, OFF, it's MY turn!' – and all too often leaving the chair at the top with Nick stranded at the bottom, or vice versa. The remote-control device – if we could find it – would call the lift back, unless of course they'd managed to switch it off, which, being boys, they did.

As for our first night in bed together ... well, I survived. I never told Nick the full truth about how much I dreaded lying next to a man who was not just disabled but also disfigured. For all my outwardly brisk and matter-of-fact approach to the issue of the missing limb, inside I was having trouble with the 'in sickness and in health' bit of our marriage vows as the moment loomed. On that first evening I hovered nervously around Nick in the bathroom as he perched on his new stool to brush his teeth and wash, then helped him to undress as he sat on the edge of the bed. That was when I saw the real him for the first time: his gaunt body, his scrawny neck where once he had sported the beginnings of a double chin, the protruding collarbone and shoulder blades, the wasted muscles and shrunken waist. And then there was the huge, gaping emptiness where his leg used to be, covered by a swathe of bandages. But when I finally lay down next to him I leant over and hugged him and it really was OK. In fact, it was just fabulous to have him back, next to me, in our bed, at home with the boys, and to hear his soft rhythmic breathing in the still of the night. I lay there wondering that I could have imagined it would be otherwise – even as I realized that there was still one hurdle to clear: the bandages. Neither of us was yet ready to confront fully what lay beneath.

A district nurse visited regularly in the first few days to change Nick's dressings, and eventually to take out the stitches in his wound. I heard Nick admonish her before she'd even got started. 'You're going to *hurt* me, aren't you!' She didn't reply, just made a written note of his comment in her file and carried on. In the end it wasn't as painful as Nick had feared, and the wound was re-bandaged immediately afterwards, meaning we were both able to put off the dreaded moment yet another day.

Kate the social worker had told me that Nick qualified for six weeks of 'personal care' from social services and they were

on the case within days of his return home. The job was contracted to an outside agency. But first there had to be a long
and laborious assessment of his needs. A young Polish woman
arrived with a form that ran to twenty or so pages. It seemed
that the whole thing was more about the risks to her carers than
about Nick. There were endless questions about the state of
the furniture and the electrical appliances round the house.
Nick soon wearied of it all. 'Look,' he said, with barely concealed irritation, 'I know it's your job, but I have no idea *on
earth* how old my toaster is. Or how safe it is.' When the Polish
woman left she gave us a copy of the half-completed form.
Halfway through it, where the answers stopped, she had
written: 'Mr Clarke don't [sic] want to answer any more.'
Nick's irritation now was not born of fear and tension, as
before, but of a healthy contempt for bureaucracy – and
I thrilled to watch it.

Despite the forms being incomplete, the carers started to
arrive. There was one every morning at half past seven to help
Nick get washed, dressed and out of bed. Three of them shared
the job, all young African men, IT specialists struggling to
find work and make ends meet. They had no formal training
in the task at hand, but carried it out with great charm and
courtesy. One, named Baba, travelled all the way across
London from Catford, a three-hour round-trip for sixty
minutes of paid work. He arrived one morning, half frozen
after a particularly arduous journey. I handed him Nick's cup
of tea to take upstairs while I tended to the boys and found him
ten minutes later, hunched over it in the living room, sipping
its contents.

I made a lot of cups of tea during that time, both for Nick
and for the visitors who passed through. Among the first were

the BBC's then Director of Radio, Jenny Abramsky, and Nick's Radio 4 boss, Mark Damazer, who came together one Friday morning. Within minutes of the tea being handed round the conversation had turned from an update on Nick's convalescence to the role of the Enlightenment in the development of Western democracies. I found it hard to credit what I was hearing – and even harder to contribute. As soon as I could, I edged out of the room and left them to it. 'That was a struggle,' Nick admitted afterwards. 'I don't think I'm ready to hold my own on that sort of thing yet – *what* hard work!'

As well as visitors, there were phone calls, emails, letters and gifts. A courier arrived one morning with a case of wine and a note attached: 'Nick – some medicinal drops to speed your return to W A T O [*World at One*]. With warmest regards, Huw (Edwards).' It was one of the most generous gifts and from someone Nick knew as no more than a colleague. Eddie Mair kept up a stream of eccentric communications – mostly about radio cock-ups – which would have us hooting with laughter. He had started to stand in for Nick on *Any Questions?*, but would always ring before the programme as a matter of courtesy.

And listeners continued to send letters, some of which Nick stored in a special file he labelled 'funnies'.

'This may seem a strange thing to say, but my feelings about your illness are a bit like my reaction to the trauma suffered by the whale in the Thames,' wrote one woman (referring to a story which had recently hit the headlines about a whale that made it up the Thames and was spotted outside the Houses of Parliament). 'I don't know you and will never meet you,' she went on by way of explanation, 'but you mean something to me and I want you to be well . . .'

Another listener wrote, 'I hope you don't mind clarifying one point: are you really legless, or do you still have one leg remaining?' Another was even blunter: did Nick still need his golf shoes, he asked, because if he didn't, would he mind passing them on?

Just before the chemotherapy started, we went away. We hadn't seen Rose Cottage since before the operation, and we'd been pining for it. As Nick gained in strength and confidence we packed the car and set off for Somerset on a Friday evening. It was a hard journey for Nick. Even with the aid of the NASA cushion he found that sitting still for two hours was awkward, uncomfortable and at times painful. But as we approached, his spirits lifted and he eagerly pointed out the sights to the boys. 'This is the hill I used to push you two up and down,' he said, before adding sadly, 'We had a wonderful walk up here once when it was raining, and now I'll never walk up here again.'

I felt the burden of packing for us all, loading everyone and everything into the car, then unloading at the other end. But being back there was a sign that things were manageable despite Nick's disability. He had by this time decided that using the wheelchair was not only awkward but would represent a failure on his part to be mobile and independent. It meant that our forays to the local pub or to town the next day were curtailed by how far he could 'hop', but I respected his decision. I also realized how easy it was to be with someone who was disabled, to be cheerful at the same time, like the woman and her disabled husband I had seen at the hospital just weeks before, and on the odd occasions when I did push Nick in his wheelchair I didn't mind one bit. In fact, I relished the attention.

On the Saturday evening I brought an armful of logs in from the shed and Nick, perched on a low seat, scrunched up paper and laid the kindling. When the boys were in bed we sat in front of a crackling fire, drank wine and watched television. The weekend was a fleeting and precious reminder of our last beautiful summer there.

> I'm finding the cottage a very peaceful place to be. I don't know why, because there's no stair lift. But I find the place raises the spirits. I've been playing crutch football with the boys – it's coming on well. And I've found ways of lighting the fire and I'm trying to find some other jobs I can do to try and relieve the work that's going on all around me.
>
> It's a nice time of evening. The family noises are about, the children are having a bath, they'll come down soon and watch a bit of television and have a glass of milk and some biscuits, and then I shall read them books and I'd like to go to bed as I'm jolly tired.
>
> NICK'S AUDIO DIARY, FEBRUARY 2006

Perhaps the strangest thing that happened in those early days was that Nick started to come to church with me and the boys. It was a brave decision, as I am sure he felt uncomfortable doing so, having spent most of his adult life raging against organized religion, insisting that it was responsible for too much misery throughout history for him to have any truck with it. But somehow, I think, he was stirred to believe that the prayers I told him had been said for him at the church had in some unfathomable way helped to get him through his operation. Or maybe he had made a pact with himself. Either way, when he did show up the regulars welcomed him unconditionally, offering to bring communion to him in his pew to save him hopping to the rail. He always declined, and he wouldn't come more than once a fortnight, but it moved me just to see him there.

Around this time, during one of the district nurse's visits, the last bandages on Nick's wound were taken off for good. He was ready now to face the sight of what lay beneath, and I felt I ought to be with him when he did so.

It would be wrong to suggest it was an easy thing to do. I had to stifle a gasp of shock: an enormous scar, around eighteen inches long, ran from the front of his hip down and round to the back. The skin was loose and seemed no longer to have reason to be there, except to plug a gap. But worse was the sight of Nick's once-strong torso, now misshapen and mutilated. And yet, within moments of facing this sight I came to accept it. As did he. 'It's not so bad really, is it?' I said, truthfully. Because in the grand scheme of things that he and I had been through, it wasn't bad at all. He was alive and he was still Nick. And nothing about his body shape could change that important fact.

As for the blue badge, we milked it for all it was worth. Every time we dropped the boys off at the nursery, pulling up within inches of the gates, we cheered. 'This really was worth losing a leg for, don't you think?' Nick would say before leading the boys to their classrooms. Crossing the playground he was like a one-legged Pied Piper, pursued by a gaggle of curious children who would try to peer up his dangling trouser leg to see if they could make out what was inside. Always at the front were Joel and Benedict, immensely proud of their dad's star status. Benedict would cling to one of Nick's crutches protectively and defiantly as if to send out a warning that this was *his* dad – and no one should forget it.

*

I've been sitting here like someone in the lull of a storm, knowing that any day the chemotherapy might begin. The way I feel at the moment I could go back to work and now I'm going to have to put this off for three or four months to have this wretched treatment that, technically speaking, I don't need because, technically speaking, I don't have cancer at the moment.

NICK'S AUDIO DIARY, FEBRUARY 2006

These minor triumphs, these brief moments of optimism, gave us hope, but they were all muted by a constant awareness of what lay ahead. Like all cancer patients, Nick dreaded the start of the chemotherapy. Six sessions, at three-weekly intervals, were scheduled for the beginning of February. In preparation, he had to undergo more tests, including checks on his blood count, tests to see whether his heart was strong enough to cope with the drugs and, after a lot of to-ing and fro-ing to Harley Street, a further scan of his lungs – which, mercifully, were still clear. Everywhere he turned he encountered stories of painful mouth ulcers, sickness, nausea, hair loss, extreme fatigue. Of all the side effects, the one that scared Nick most was the nausea. 'I can't face another day like Christmas Day,' he said to me. 'I can cope with pain, but I can't cope with feeling sick.' When we went back to Jeremy's soulless consulting room up on the fifteenth floor of University College Hospital to discuss the treatment plan, Nick begged him to prescribe the absolute maximum of anti-sickness medication.

Jeremy agreed to do so, but he didn't mince his words. 'I'm afraid it'll be really awful,' he said. 'These chemotherapy drugs are particularly unpleasant ones, and they will make you feel terrible. I have a patient who had one session and simply refused any further treatment.'

Jeremy's warning weighed heavily on Nick. The day before it was due to start, he was dejected.

Sunday afternoon – the evening before the chemo, it's a wretched damp grey miserable day outside and one of my older twins – nearly thirty, I grieve to report – Tom, is making me a cup of tea the way I really like it. Which is a very difficult thing to do because I'm really fussy about the way I like my tea. The small twins are going out for a bike ride. We're going to try to use up a bit of testosterone and maybe that will ensure a good night's sleep.

Packing to go to hospital is like packing for school, where you knew you were going to be separated from home, you were likely to be miserable and people would be unkind to you, and it's just like that all over again. I feel sick inside. I can't think of anything to say because I feel so gloomy.

NICK'S AUDIO DIARY, FEBRUARY 2006

By the morning of the first chemotherapy session Nick was nearly in tears. I held his hand in the taxi and tried to find comforting words. There weren't any. It was a crisp, bright day and as we struggled out of the car at the Harley Street Cancer Centre, I heard a shout from across the road. 'Hey, Barbara, hello, over here.' It was Jeremy Paxman. He bounded up to me, but I literally had to point out to him that Nick was standing beside me; Jeremy hadn't recognized him. He turned to him and chatted for a few minutes, but the shock was written all over his face. Nick was mortified at his reaction.

In the reception area we waited, surrounded by women in black burkas and Middle Eastern men with large briefcases. It was tempting to wonder whether they were full of cash. 'I don't like yours much,' I whispered to Nick, as three veiled women sat opposite. 'What *are* you saying?' Nick always objected to any remark he regarded as politically incorrect – which made me all the more eager to goad him. 'Well, we *are* the only white people here,' I retorted. I didn't see why I should pretend that I didn't feel as if I were the foreigner – especially when we got in the lift and found that all the signs were in Greek. On the upper floors, where Nick's room was located, the staff were largely from Eastern Europe, which made me, at least, feel more at home.

I've never stayed at a Premier Inn. You know the ones, hidden away behind the trees at the back of a motorway service station or sitting uncomfortably close to a roundabout on a dual carriageway: concrete boxes with small windows looking in on soulless rooms. I say I haven't stayed at one, and I hope I never will, but the instant I set eyes on Nick's room I knew it looked like the sort of room you'd find there. Sterile, characterless, a sea of laminate surfaces and windows draped with nylon nets designed to keep out the view, a place you want to leave as soon as you arrive. And Nick was in no mood that day to tolerate bland functionalism. He found fault with everything. 'This room is just so horrible. It's like a Belgian hotel room – it's very efficient but it's got no soul,' he muttered. 'And that television screen is *far* too small and the windows won't open – which I *hate*. Why do they do that? And look at this!' He'd picked up a menu off the bedside table. 'There's no way I'm eating anything from *this*.'

I went downstairs to ask for a bigger television, to inquire whether the windows could be opened – the answer was 'no' – and to find the nearest Pret a Manger for salmon sandwiches and fruit salad.

When I got back I found Nick lying on the bed, in tears. 'I feel really low, I don't know why. Sod it. Part of the problem is, apart from the weeks before the operations, I've thought of this as a leg problem, but now I realize it's a cancer problem,' he said. I fought a huge lump in my throat. I had no idea what to do or say. A short time later a nurse came in with a drip, to which she rigged a bag full of pink liquid. He was to remain attached for more than two days, while the chemotherapy drug Doxorubicin slowly entered his bloodstream, only to be replaced by another bag, this one full of a drug called Ifosfamide.

There are, we discovered, different chemotherapy drugs for different cancers. What Nick had was rare, and researchers had yet to come up with much more than the two drugs he was being treated with. And Jeremy had explained that they offered only a marginal chance of preventing the sarcoma from returning. I don't think we realized at the time the full implications of this slim hope.

I left Nick later that afternoon; he wanted me to go. He needed to be alone and wanted to spare me the pain of watching his encroaching sorrow. He had already told me that he had entered hospital feeling gloomier than at any time yet.

I cried when I saw the chart with the schedule of drugs. I don't cry very often but something just got to me about that ...

... I hate it here. I don't feel very brave. I've never been so completely laid low. I feel crap. I just feel utterly without spirit and energy and my heart is going too fast and making me feel more depressed, but I'm told this is a by-product of the treatment. I don't want to talk to anybody. I couldn't cope with having anybody here ...

... I feel a desperation to rip my arm away from that bloody drip. Sixty hours on a drip – it just drives you mad in the end and you combine that with the uncomfortable bed. And I wee all the time – liquid is being pushed through you – into papier-mâché bottles ...

NICK'S AUDIO DIARY, FEBRUARY 2006

Two days later, when I went to bring him home, I found him looking contrite. He told me he had just been speaking to a Macedonian nurse who had had to leave a young daughter behind so that she could come to London to earn money. When Nick started grumbling about being stuck in hospital, she gently pointed out that he was lucky. He was going to go home while many of the people in that clinic would not – ever. Nick felt humbled and tried not to complain again.

I also found him looking pink. The liquid that had been drip-fed into Nick's arm had given his skin a light flush. It also made his face swell up slightly, and the combined effect made him look as if he had spent a relaxing afternoon in the sun. He admitted to feeling a terrible lethargy but was surprised at how quickly he shook it off. As for the other side effects, he was lucky. The cocktail of anti-emetics dispensed with any sickness and within a couple of days of the session ending he was bouncing back. It wasn't until the second session of treatment that he started to shed hair. 'It gets left on pillows, on cushions, on clothes,' he said. 'It comes off all over your body – I scratched under my arms yesterday. It was rather disconcerting. I can see some under the table where I had my breakfast. It's quite disgusting.' With no qualms and the minimum of fuss, he got a hairdresser in to shave off the lot in a single pre-emptive strike. He'd been getting progressively balder since his early twenties, he said, so it was no big deal. Maybe not for him, but the sight shocked me. It seemed to shrink his head, rendering him slightly haggard and ageing him, and as his eyebrows fell out his face changed shape. But several of my friends cooed at how handsome he looked. Just like Patrick Stewart, said one. No, more like Bruce Willis said another. Nick, of course, was thrilled.

As for his appetite, it hardly suffered and the mouth ulcers he was waiting for didn't arrive until many weeks later. Jeremy had warned us at the outset that he would lose weight. 'Inevitable,' he said. 'In all the research I've read, I've only come across one report of men actually putting on weight during chemo. They were Italians. Must have been all that pasta.' It is a matter of pride to me that Nick joined their ranks during his chemo months as I threw myself into cooking for him. But I can't take all the credit. I discovered a wonder food called oven chips. And I'm not ashamed to admit it.

The question that screamed out at most people who visited us now was, when would Nick get a prosthetic leg? Nick himself still showed no interest in the idea – perhaps he was remembering Steve Cannon's comment before the operation about how unwieldy they were for an amputee of his type. The amputation had been total. With no stump, he would need a full false leg, attached by straps, which would effectively be hanging from his waist. He'd have to shuffle forward a step at a time and swing from the hip, which sounded like hard work. Crutches would be far easier, he thought. If he was in any doubt, a return visit to the RNOH gym made up his mind once and for all. A fellow amputee was struggling to walk with a newly fitted prosthesis, clutching the parallel bars as he did so, making painfully slow progress. Nick instantly lost interest in trying to be 'normal'. When friends queried his decision, he just nodded at his empty trouser leg. 'This is the new normal,' he said, 'for me.'

With that decision made, I set about transforming Nick's wardrobe, a job I had always enjoyed. In fact, from the day he met me, he had never bought a single item of clothing on his own but had happily deferred to me in all matters sartorial. He had almost no interest in what he wore and even less interest in shopping, which meant that I was able to ensure he never returned to the checked trousers and beige jackets I'd first seen him in. His waist had shrunk after the operation, from thirty-six inches to thirty-two. I trawled M&S for new trousers and pyjamas, then took them to Mandy, a Greek Cypriot seamstress living at the top of our road. As we stuck pins into the fabric to indicate which trouser leg had to be cut off, she threw her hands in the air and shook her head at the thought of what had happened to Nick. 'Terrible, terrible. It [sic] so terrible,' she wailed, until I put my arms round her shoulders and comforted her. The irony of the situation didn't escape me.

It also made me realize that, for all that we were learning to live with our 'new normal', we were duping ourselves if we thought it would be easy – as I was about to find out one night in February. We had a visitor at the time: Jarka, a Slovakian au pair who had looked after the boys when they were small and who had become a cherished friend, had flown in from France, where she now lived with her fiancé, to spend the half-term helping me with the boys. She cooked for us all, woke up with the boys – who absolutely adored her – to allow us a lie-in, and restored some order to a house where order had long since been abandoned. She supported us more in that week than almost anyone in all the time that Nick was ill.

One evening, as Nick manoeuvred his way across the hall towards his stair lift, his crutches slipped from beneath him. He crashed on the stone tiles, landed hard on his wound and let out a stomach-churning howl of pain. Jarka and I raced to help him, but picking him up was a struggle even for the two of us. He may have been a shadow of the man he used to be, but he was still tall – and more or less incapable of helping himself. By the time we got him upright, I was reeling from the sheer awfulness of the process of manhandling my husband the way I imagined they might do in a hospital ward or an old people's home. This man, the love of my life, had just months before been a great physical presence by my side. I felt wretched for me and more wretched for him and what he was enduring.

In typical fashion he didn't complain at all, just continued his cumbersome progress to bed. Jarka, though, was in tears. 'I'm so so sorry,' she sobbed as we held and comforted each other. 'It's so dreadful what has happened to him . . .'

She was right. It was dreadful. No amount of pretending could make Nick's 'new normal' anywhere near normal. But we weren't going to give up fighting. And we now had a project to complete, with that very sentiment at its heart.

EIGHT

Many moons ago, when cameras used film, music was played on cassettes, and people sent real letters on paper, a close friend wrote to me asking for help. She had fallen pregnant unexpectedly and wanted a termination. Would I take her to hospital, be with her when she came round from the operation, and take her back home? She lived on the other side of London and helping her out would have meant my taking a day off work. It was a big favour to ask and she knew it. Unfortunately, so did I.

Friendship can be a funny thing. It comes with no obligations and no guarantees. Sometimes it turns up trumps, at others it bitterly disappoints. It's possible to have best friends you only see once a year, or friends you barely know who give of themselves above and beyond your greatest expectations. But when your life falls apart, you've no way of predicting how friends will respond.

I reflected on this after Jarka left. Some of our friends had been amazing. One neighbour, Liz, regularly cooked us meals. Another took the boys out every other Saturday afternoon to give us a break. Another came round with a takeaway, three bottles of fine wine and an offer to do any odd jobs that were outstanding. Mark Damazer at Radio 4, whom we had both known for twenty years, visited or rang every week. Nick was moved beyond words by the way his boss spoke calmly and encouragingly about an eventual return to work, which was always at the forefront of Nick's mind.

Other friends resorted to that old-fashioned and 'thoughtful' device: the handwritten letter. 'Your strength and fortitude will carry you through,' wrote one. Strength and fortitude were not something either of us felt familiar with and no amount of it could stop me from thinking that here was a way of excusing this particular person from doing anything more than putting pen to paper. 'We really admire you,' wrote another, although for what I was never sure.

What surprised me was how many people neither wrote nor visited. Perhaps our circle was too wide to allow for real intimacy, perhaps the close friendships were too narrow in scope. Or perhaps we were expecting too much. Whatever the reason, I was taken aback by how few friends put themselves out for us during those difficult months, though I wasn't sure exactly what I might have expected them to do.

As for my pregnant friend all those years ago, I must come clean. When I told her I couldn't help, I did it by letter. I said I didn't have the time. And I reflected, every time I thought about what I'd done, on how fickle friendship can be.

Despite all this, we weren't entirely on our own. When it comes to family you can't get away with the excuses you use with friends. I hardly knew Nick's younger sister Suzie: we'd not met much over the years. She and Nick weren't particularly close, but each was enormously respectful of the other. Though she lived in Derbyshire, she and her husband Alastair and their three grown-up daughters – all of them wrapped up in busy lives – took time out to spend some weekends with us, getting up early with the boys, taking them out, and providing company for us in the evenings. Nick's older children, Ali,

Tom and Pete, were there for him too, and my mother saw more of her grandsons than she might otherwise have done. She was also ready with a sympathetic ear.

Of course we had each other, and our shared sense of fun once more. As he dressed himself one morning, Nick turned to me and said, 'Did you know that, if you only have one leg, your knickers revolve? I don't know how to keep them in place!'

'All I can say is I'm delighted I don't have to pair your socks now,' I replied.

But nothing made us laugh as much as the newspaper cutting I found and stuck to the front door. 'Family pet loses leg,' it said. 'I hope you don't mind me asking, but what type of pet was it?' asked a courier one morning. 'My husband,' I replied, straight-faced. He left without a word. Nick just rolled his eyes at my silliness.

Throughout those days of hospital visits, home rest, visitors and endless cups of tea, Nick threw himself more and more into recording on tape some of the things that were happening to him. His openness, for a man who had always been so private, amazed me. As the chemotherapy sessions got harder to bear, he spilled out some of his frustrations.

I've reached the eve of my second chemo session and I wanted to chart my spirits. They went up sharply after I got out of hospital the first time and quite quickly felt pretty good, tired sometimes and with a pretty strange taste in the mouth, but that's about the worst of it. Then towards the end of it a little bit more tired again and not looking forward again to what's going to happen.

With a week to go before chemo number three, this week is proving a great deal more agreeable than the last when, quite frankly, I wouldn't have had the strength to pick up the microphone for two or three days. It was truly, truly awful, and a powerful reminder not to be over-confident about what's happening during this process, because I was zapped at the same time by a terrible combination of constipation and the relief of constipation and the consequences thereof which was just awful, and a cold, a cough and complete debilitation. The whole of Thursday I lost. I just lay in one position in the bed without moving. Friday was not much better, and I didn't really recover for the weekend. It was terrible for me and much worse in so many ways for Barbara, who I think almost lost it in some of that period. I don't want to go through that again. I don't know how to do it. I'll have to check that some of the drugs that I'm getting are not particularly prone to constipation, because that for me was the root of the problem. Of course, it was the period during the cycle when the white corpuscle resistance, or whatever it is, is at its lowest, and I had no strength. I ate nothing, drank practically nothing. I just lay there like a vegetable. No longer will I say I'm floating through chemotherapy because I've just come down to earth with a very large bump. I feel much better now. Almost back to normal again, and I feel greatly relieved for that.

On Sunday I felt just about well enough to get out and go to John Lewis – this was my first big outing in the wheelchair. I was wearing my little black ski cap. Frankly I look like a death mask after the previous week. I didn't feel too bad about being in a wheelchair. I found myself apologizing to people for being in their way a lot, and I guess that's normal and everyone apologizes to you if they get in your way and everyone's going 'sorry, sorry' all the time and I'll have to get over that and just assume, as I've heard many disabled people on the radio say before, you just have to be who

you are, where you are, what you are and then treat life as normal –
but that will take a while. My wheelchair use has been so minimal
I'm not used to it at all at the moment. I'd feel much better on the
crutches, but I guess that would be too tiring at the moment.

The other great adventure I've had is the first ever bath. Last
Saturday. To clean me up. And it's incredibly easy. God knows
why I haven't done it before. March twenty-fifth, first bath since
December eighteenth. That's a very very long time to go without a
bath, and although most bits of me have been regularly washed it
was absolutely glorious to feel the water lapping round me for the
first time. I think it's quite pathetic of me not to have got it going
before. I felt reluctant, but it's damned easy. You have a chair that
rises to the top of a couple of pillars with four suckers on the
bottom of the bath and you slide on to the seat via a little flap, sit
down, press a button and down, splop, into the water – it's
incredibly easy. The electronic gadgetry is all protected against
water – otherwise it would be a quick way to finish me off if
Barbara can't stand it any longer.

NICK'S AUDIO DIARY, MARCH 2006

The recordings seemed such a natural thing to do for a
broadcaster that I never asked Nick why he had decided to
do them – although many others asked me the same question.
I think it was a way for him to avoid looking too deeply at
the awfulness of what was happening to him. There's only
so far you can go when you articulate your innermost
thoughts, knowing that they might one day have an audience
of strangers – hundreds of thousands of them. You have to
marshal them and keep them from straying into painful areas.
As a story-teller you're your own editor. And this was a
story for which Nick badly wanted to compose a happy

ending. There was no self-pity on Nick's tapes. Quite the opposite. I am humbled now by how much concern he had for me:

> Barbara's felt like cracking a bit, I think, in the last few days. It is difficult. We both come a bit close to the edge sometimes. I can't do anything to help really – and that's the problem. I do everything I can to help. But for her it must just be absolutely hellish, the prospect of cooking for the rest of our lives and never getting much relief from it, the prospect of fetching and carrying ... I think sometimes it just strikes her as being really shitty. I don't blame her.
>
> I've had a huge amount of attention and it's a big issue that people don't recognize that next to me is somebody who is scurrying around doing everything. In my case, all the things I used to do are being done by Barbara. Some people recognize it, some people get it, and some people just don't get it. They say, 'Poor Nick, poor Nick,' and I say, 'Look, I'm fine.' I'm lying here in stately grandeur watching the sport and having a nice meal brought to me, then I'll wander off and take a bit of fresh air and then I sit down again. And all the time the shopping's got to be done, the cooking's got to be done, the children have got to be picked up from school – all these things have to go on and some people don't recognize it.
>
> NICK'S AUDIO DIARY, APRIL 2006

Nick didn't tell anyone at the BBC about the recordings until he felt comfortable with what he was doing, about three months after his operation. At that point Mark Damazer assigned a producer to put the rambling thoughts and observations into some sort of order, and Nick handed over the raw record of his painful, private journey to a man he didn't know – but whom he had to trust. He asked for no control over the way it was to be edited. In the following weeks, however, he did talk to the producer about the themes that were emerging in the way we had described the huge changes in our lives. Somewhere in amongst it all we had spoken about our growing sense that we were fighting to be normal, and the phrase struck a chord. *Fighting to Be Normal* became the title of the programme.

One of the changes I spoke about was my worry that we would never again be able to take a 'normal' family holiday, and I wistfully remembered the last one we'd had in Corsica just two years before. But in May there came the chance to take a break with the boys – in Slovakia, where Jarka was getting married to her French fiancé. It was only to be a weekend trip, and Nick was sad to miss out on it. He was undergoing his penultimate chemotherapy session just before the boys and I were due to fly out with my mother, and it never entered our heads that he would be fit to join us. But he had other plans. He rang me from his hospital room. 'I don't want you to go without me,' he said. 'I don't want to spend a weekend alone and I want to be with you. I'm feeling fine. I'm coming.' Then he added that he had managed to find one remaining seat on our flight. My first reaction was to think how hard it would be to get him to, and through, the airport, on to a plane and off at the other end. My second was shock at how much it would cost – almost £600 for his plane ticket. My third, however, was to jump at this opportunity to do something together as a family, to overcome the hurdles, forget about the obstacles and live for the day. 'Go for it,' I said.

We arrived in Bratislava late on a Friday night. Our airport transfers had been easy, all five of us crammed on to a transit buggy, the boys whooping with delight as we zoomed along the corridors and navigated a path through knots of shuffling passengers.

We were swept from the departure lounge to the gate in one of those buggies and because there was no sky-way – there were no steps up to the plane – we had a special lorry with a hoist to lift us on to the plane. When we got off I was carried like a traveller from the nineteenth century in a sedan chair into our own wheel-chair coach, swept to passport control, right to the front of the queue and out, and the whole thing went like a dose of salts. If ever I do get a bit gloomy I can always think about the wonders of travel like this. I feel fantastic for being here, if a little knackered.

NICK'S AUDIO DIARY, MAY 2006

A taxi took us from the airport to Jarka's home town of Stupava and deposited us at the best hotel in town. We found the lights dimmed, the restaurant long since closed for the evening, but we couldn't complain: our two-room family suite cost £20.

We awoke to the sight of a sun-drenched park outside our windows and the sound of a rowdy gaggle of French guests eating breakfast. After lunch in the best restaurant in town, a pizza parlour, we were driven in a brand-new Touareg four-wheel drive to the Catholic church in central Stupava. Jarka's father had worked all his life for Skoda, now VW Skoda, and had been loaned one of their finest models for this special day. When the boys saw Jarka on the steps of the church they fell into a stunned silence. They'd never seen her like this before – utterly mesmerizing, her raven hair tied back with white flowers. As they followed her into the church, she asked them to lift her train and carry it down the aisle – which they did, awkward and self-conscious. The music seemed particularly poignant in the circumstances and the 'Ave Maria' brought a lump to my throat. As the boys looked around the church their eyes were out on stalks at the sight of the tortured figures nailed to crosses – not the sort of thing we had back home at St Helen's C of E. 'Daddy, is that *really* Jesus up there?' Benedict asked in a stage whisper. 'And what is all that blood on his hands?'

Afterwards we adjourned to the romantic setting of the dining-hall at the town's cement factory. I'd like to say the wine flowed – and it did for the other guests – but Slovakian red was a bit of a challenge for our palates. Conversation with our non-English-speaking hosts was a struggle, but the party enfolded us in its warmth. Late in the afternoon a photographer was ushered in. He called first for a gathering of 'All the Slovaks', and then for one of 'All the French', after which Nick hopped into the middle of the room and shouted for a photo of 'Tous les sans-jambes' (all the legless people). For a split second there was stunned silence. Then whoops of laughter and applause.

By the middle of the evening, as the dancing got under way, Nick and the boys were exhausted. We headed for the exit, worming our way through a cross-cultural swirl of gyrating bodies and swinging limbs, the raucous laughter drowning out the sound of the band. It was more than good to have been there. It felt significant, an achievement perhaps, and much more than a simple weekend away with the kids. Our Slovakian adventure turned out to be the last event we put on tape for the radio programme. And the first really to give us hope that all was not lost in our new life.

Nick's next chemotherapy session finished on 9 June, a day which gave us two reasons to celebrate. It was to be his final session, and it was his fifty-eighth birthday. He came out of hospital feeling remarkably upbeat. 'I would skip if I had the appropriate number of limbs,' he said to me when I collected him.

My birthday present to him was a stylish new jacket which I bought at the Fenwick sale. It was made by Strellson in a fine cream-coloured linen-cotton mix. I knew he would need a smart outfit for his imminent return to work and one that would fit his new slimline shape. My shape meanwhile had reverted to more than normal. 'You need a tummy controller under that clingy dress,' my mother said as I prepared for the small party we had planned. 'I've already got one on!' I laughed, looking down at my waistline, expanded by a return to normal eating as some of the stresses and worry had faded.

A few friends, colleagues and neighbours turned up that evening, and we ate pizzas and a birthday cake from one of the best bakeries in London, the Hummingbird in Notting Hill. We lit candles on the cake and the boys helped Nick to blow them out. They sat close by his side through an evening of warmth, of caring, of laughter, of hope. My eyes filled with tears as I watched Nick, relaxed and happy and doted on by his little boys. He'd been to hell and back, but had survived both in mind and spirit, and seemed ready to move on to the next chapter of his life, wherever that might take him.

Later, when I looked at the photos from that day, I saw a different man, one with worry etched across his face and sorrow seeping from his eyes. Or maybe it was just exhaustion. It had pervaded every part of him. He was worn out by the havoc of the cancer, by the aftermath of his operation, by the daily struggle to find reserves of energy that weren't always there, by four months of invasive, debilitating chemotherapy; and he was tired of the worry, tired of being brave. Tired, in fact, of fighting to be normal.

I wonder whether Nick knew at that time, deep down, that the next chapter of his life might take him somewhere he didn't want to go. If he did, or if he even suspected it, he never shared the thought with me. His one overriding concern was how soon he could get back to work. 'It makes me twitchy not being there,' he said many times. It was as if the return would signal above all else that something in his life really had returned to normal.

A week after the birthday party we packed and drove to France, confident now that we could travel abroad. For a number of years Nick had taken his cricket team, 'The Money Programme', on a summer tour to the small town of Saumur on the Loire, where they played against a loosely assembled team of expats and sat through mammoth drinking sessions in local bars. This was the first time I had joined Nick and was able to witness what really went on during these weekends. It turned out largely to be what I had imagined: a bunch of slightly over-excited blokes flew en masse with Ryanair, arriving drunk and believing, contrary to the evidence, that they were in warm, sunny climes. They sat in open-neck shirts outside a bar in the middle of the town square all afternoon and well into the evening, drinking beer and chatting about things blokes chat about before going to bed in the early hours and waking late to play a game of cricket with huge hangovers.

We planned to take a week's holiday around this year's tour so we had travelled over early. A lovely young Hungarian woman called Zsuzsanna, who had been helping us out on Saturdays at home, came with us as an extra pair of hands and she sat in the back of our people-carrier trying to entertain the boys, whose rivalry and incessant warring had reached epic proportions. It was asking a lot of two three-year-olds to sit still for hours on end. As I drove, Nick finally began to succumb to the effects of the chemo, becoming more and more listless. Jeremy had warned us that chemotherapy robs the body of its immune defences and that any serious infection, if not caught and dealt with in time, could be fatal. People die, he told us, not because of the drug regime, but because they get sick and don't react quickly enough.

Seeing Nick slumped in the passenger seat next to me I was filled with fear. He had clearly picked up a bug and his temperature was rising. He had also developed sores in his mouth and was finding eating extremely painful. He was pale, thin and looked terrible. I had no idea whether I should be taking him to hospital and neither did he. We were in silent distress for most of that journey, both of us desperately wanting the holiday to be a success. We decided to break our trip halfway, and stopped in a market town where Nick was ushered to our room up and down narrow stairs and along winding corridors – only to discover that the hotelier could have taken him to the room in thirty seconds through a back door in the car park. While he collapsed in bed, the boys, oblivious to what was happening, could barely contain their excitement at the sight of a double bed all to themselves, along with their own bottles of mineral water on the table. Then, the icing on the cake: an unprepossessing little balcony with two rickety chairs on which they sat and sipped and babbled the private nothings that only small children understand. It was a bittersweet feeling, not to be able to share such a moment with the man who loved those boys as deeply as I did.

Nick had gone straight to bed without eating, but when

I awoke beside him next morning he announced that he was beginning to feel better. Maybe that's what the prospect of playing cricket can do for a man, I told him.

I didn't watch the matches, preferring to catch up on some sleep, and I'm sad about that as it turned out to be the last time Nick would ever play the game he loved – even though he was relegated to the role of umpire. But the moment lives on in the boys' memory, so thrilling did they find it. 'When the batsman hit the ball over the fence Daddy put both arms in the air and stood on one leg and everyone cheered.' They have recounted that moment time and again, and still do.

Fighting to Be Normal was scheduled to be transmitted on Radio 4 while we were still away. Mark Damazer had told us he was going to 'go big' on it, and although we didn't hear the trails we received text messages from friends back home telling us they'd been running through the week that preceded it. Nick wasn't happy about this. He was worried that Mark, along with the whole Radio 4 audience, would be disappointed when they finally listened to what he had to say. A CD of the nearly complete programme was couriered to us for our comments and input, but it didn't arrive until the day before the programme was due to go out, and only after some highly charged phone calls between Nick and the producer about the delay.

We listened to it in the car, in a supermarket car park, while the boys slept in the back. We shed tears when we heard the recording of them praying in the church in Slovakia: 'My Daddy is poorly. Please look after him, dear God.' We spotted two factual errors which had cropped up in the editing – and Nick, ever the professional, cringed. But what upset him far more was the last line in the programme – spoken by me: 'There's cancer in the air,' I heard myself say, 'and it's scary.'

Nick thought it was horribly downbeat and was on the phone to the BBC as soon as we finished listening, but the producer didn't seem to share his concerns about the inaccuracies and claimed that they couldn't be changed anyway at this late stage. As for the last line in the programme, he said he would think about it.

His response came a few hours later, by text. 'I think a happy ending would be pat,' he said. Nick was furious at what he saw as a glib response in the face of the enormity of the subject matter. 'Actually, it's my life and a happy ending is what I'm hoping for,' he texted back. 'I don't find it pat at all.' Ever the conciliator, however, he declined to fight his corner any further. But he was saddened and hurt, and felt that his trust had been abused. And I felt desperately guilty for having uttered those words. It may have been the truth, but it seemed cruel that someone else was trying to force Nick to face it against his will.

On Saturday night, long after the boys had fallen asleep, we lay on a rickety French bed sharing the headphones on Nick's pocket radio, which was by now his constant companion, straining to hear the weak and crackly signal of Radio 4 on long wave. As I listened, I worried that my honesty in describing how I had found our experience would be misconstrued as whingeing. But I knew the risk had been worth taking for the many thousands of carers who felt the same way but had no outlet for expressing how hard their role can be. In any case, the main thing to come through in the programme, the thing that transcended all else, was Nick's extraordinary courage, openness and humanity in the face of enormous personal adversity. Yet as we listened that night, neither of us had any inkling of the impact his story would have on those listening back in the UK.

When we returned home we read the first of many articles in the papers. In the *Daily Telegraph*, Gillian Reynolds wrote, 'my notes were covered in tears and my hand was shaking so hard I could barely hold the pen'. Word got back to us that the BBC's Chairman, Michael Grade, had also cried in his office. 'The man who once described me as a middle-class, middle-aged, public school old fart,' Nick smiled as he remembered an affectionate spat he'd had with Grade a couple of years before.

But more touching than anything we read in the papers were the many hundreds of letters we got from Radio 4 listeners. We worked our way through them together in the evenings, though Nick could only manage a handful at a time, finding the task slightly overwhelming as the strangers to whom he had broadcast over the years came alive on the pages before him, became real people with names, voices, stories to tell and feelings they wanted to share. The letters ranged from the tearful to the sympathetic to the comical. A peer of the realm, writing on House of Lords notepaper, said,

> I listened to your programme as I drove down to Ascot. I found it very moving and it made me realize that 'I am so lucky'. A horse of that name was running, and being a complete novice I placed a small bet on it – and guess what, it won!!

Many listeners wrote to tell him how highly he was regarded:

> You say in your audio tapes 'The World at One has got on very well without me.' Not true. I for one have drifted away from the programme. Don't forget, you really *are* the best political interviewer/commentator – better than Paxman or Marr.

Others could not contain their affection:

> I did wish I could give you a big hug (permissible, I think, at my
> ripe old age of nearly seventy-six!) and say, 'Oh, Nick – remember
> us your listeners. There are thousands of us out here rooting for
> you, holding you in our thoughts and prayers, and WILLING you
> to pull through.'

> I am almost blind, eighty-eight, and this is my first fan letter.
> Hang on in there, I'm hanging in with you – you dear man.

Most moving were the letters expressing simple gratitude:
that at last someone had gone public and told the audience what
it was like to live with this modern curse.

> To hear you and your wife face the unthinkable with such honest,
> undiluted courage and humility was profoundly moving and
> uplifting.

A fellow cancer sufferer wrote,

> Your audio tapes showed me that it is OK to admit to psy-
> chological and emotional lassitude.

Another said,

> I spent most of the listening time weeping, both for you and for
> my very close friends who have fought in varying ways.

'Please remember you are not alone with this illness,' said one
lady, while every one of those who wrote with direct experience
of amputation – their own or that of a close relative – was
upbeat and sometimes funny:

> My father was Head of Russian service at the BBC. He had a leg

off, and while recuperating was asked by a friend to interview a Russian called ... Oleg Bitov.

A man from India, a World Service listener, even tried to sell Nick a 'Jaipur leg', a rubber prosthesis invented and made in India for victims of landmine explosions.

Amongst the earnest good wishes and heart-felt, empathetic letters, were, as ever, a few odd ones – from a reverend gentleman, for example, who had suffered from cancer of the larynx and sent a collection of limericks he had made up, along with an audio cassette of himself singing hymns. A copy of *The Tibetan Book of Living and Dying* sent by one listener was put straight in the bin.

We read each and every letter and I could see the frustration Nick felt at not being able to reply individually as he had been used to doing with the day-to-day correspondence that arrived in the *World at One* post-bag. If he was ever in any doubt, these letters made him realize that he was admired and loved by a wide spectrum of the BBC's listenership. Had he died earlier in his illness he would never have known the extent of the respect and affection in which he was held. That programme opened up a new vista for him, one in which he was a star. It was something he had always wanted, deep down, but when he realized it had happened he was baffled.

Sharing private pain is not to everyone's taste. But it seemed to me that Nick had, more by accident than design, tapped into something that unites us all: an awareness of the human condition, and the dark and difficult places to which it can take each and any one of us at any time. It was rewarding to know that the courage Nick had shown in describing the brutal and traumatic effects of his illness had had such an impact. We were moved by the reaction of our listeners, but the comment which touched me most deeply came from an old friend and colleague from my *Panorama* days, Jane Corbin. 'When I listened to your programme,' she said, 'I realized that I was listening to a love story.'

NINE

On Friday, 30 June we opened the *Guardian* to find that Nick was the subject of a leading article, headed 'In Praise of . . . Nick Clarke'.

> In the absence of Jonathan Dimbleby, BBC Radio 4's *Any Questions?* tonight will be chaired by Nick Clarke. This is less of a routine announcement than it might seem, since it brings to an end the eight month absence of a familiar and trusted voice. Though he crops up in many guises, his most regular slot over the years has been the lunchtime news review, *The World at One . . .*
>
> He's been absent all these weeks because of a serious illness – a cancer which required the amputation of a leg. He and his wife, Barbara Want, with interventions from their three-year-old twins, kept a radio diary which was broadcast on Radio 4 last week: wry, rueful, largely devoid of self-pity, but vivid and poignant and sometimes painful to listen to – in its way, another Nick Clarke model for how things ought to be done. But it isn't just for his courage in this adversity – an adversity which, as he'd no doubt insist, thousands of less famous people share every day – that we salute him today, but because he's the kind of radio presence we can't do without, and one which, for the good reputation of broadcasting, those who aspire to practise his trade should set out to emulate.

Finding himself the subject of a leader column in a national newspaper bewildered Nick. He wanted his return to work to be unremarkable and routine. He had been ill, and he was on the mend. That was all. But of course it was never going to be that simple, and his colleagues at *The World at One*, still awaiting his return a few weeks further down the line, called to tease him. There were jokes reminding him about having been described as a 'national treasure' in the same newspaper all those years ago, and quips about his being a suitable successor to Terry Wogan, a subject for *This Is Your Life* – and when would he get the call from *Desert Island Discs*?

Any Questions? is a kind of road-show, broadcast live from a different location every week. It might be the guest of a school, a church, a community centre – anywhere that an audience of local Radio 4 listeners can gather for the chance to grill a panel of four politicians and commentators about events in the news. This particular week it was to be at Tring School in Hertfordshire, where Nick had spent many a weekend watching his older sons playing football when they were young. Not that the actual location was usually of any great interest to him, other than that he always preferred to be able to get home quickly after the programme had been transmitted live. What exercised his mind and excited him whenever he presented *Any Questions?* was the make-up of the week's panel. Would they be big political hitters, lacklustre has-beens or something in between? And how hopeful could he be of a programme that would romp its way argumentatively through fifty minutes of airtime rather than drag its way awkwardly to the end? The fact is, he never really knew until it got under way. Sometimes a weak-looking panel could deliver a sparky and entertaining programme; at other times he might have a senior Cabinet Minister and a feisty spokesperson for the Opposition producing a programme that was unremarkable and tame. Provocative and clever questions from the audience were an essential part of the mix. The fun was in the unpredictability.

The panel on Nick's first week back included the writer Frederick Forsyth, disgraced former MP Jonathan Aitken, and former minister Barbara Roche. It wasn't the most promising line-up, but that wouldn't detract from what was, for Nick, a momentous occasion, his return to the microphone after several months' absence, his re-acquaintance with normality. Going back to work was the closest he could get to saying, 'I've put a whole terrible episode of my life behind me – for now at least – and it hasn't taken away what I had before.'

I wish I could have gone with him that day but I had no one to baby-sit the boys, so after he'd got dressed in his new Strellson jacket, a white shirt and an orange silk tie, I was left to help him into the BBC car and see him off. Mark Damazer made a point of going, however. To him, Nick's return was a moment to note – and to honour.

I listened to the show alone, at home, with a lump in my throat, thrilled at how easily Nick seemed to slip back into doing what he so loved. The programme was good, if not remarkable, and an hour after it had finished he arrived home. 'You were *fabulous*,' I gushed, and as always happened when I said such things, his eyes lit up. 'Thank you. It was OK, wasn't it . . .?' And he said no more, before taking himself to bed.

Typically, he made no mention of what I later learned from Mark. As Nick arrived in the school hall that evening and hopped up the steps on to the makeshift platform, which was one of the *Any Questions?* props and went along to every venue, the audience of around three hundred started to clap, cheer and stamp their feet in appreciation. Some stood up. They carried on applauding for several minutes. Mark, who had spent years talking to, thinking about, and trying to understand the Radio 4 audience, could only watch in wonder as the walls reverberated to a sound more in keeping with a rock concert or a religious revival. Looking surprised and ever so slightly awkward, Nick tried to subdue the tumult by waving his hands. When he eventually succeeded he quietly picked up at the microphone from where he had left off eight months before, with no mention of his absence, nor of the extraordinary, emotional response that had greeted his return.

As well as telling me what had happened, Mark later confessed his regret that it was only there in Tring that he fully realized Nick's unique connection to loyal Radio 4 listeners. The BBC, he admitted, had been too slow, too lazy or too caught up in other things to recognize it. It had simply failed to acknowledge something that was staring it in the face.

But Radio 4 listeners knew and they had come to view Nick with affection and respect, recognizing his skills as an interviewer, the strength of his journalism, the quiet, methodical and courteous way in which he questioned people on air, his seductive and mellifluous voice – the whole package of qualities which set him apart. These were things he had brought unobtrusively into the privacy of listeners' homes or cars, installing himself in their collective consciousness quietly, unwittingly, permanently. That was what they were applauding that night, along with his courage in sharing the story of his battle with cancer in the radio diary. Now, upon his return, the strength of their admiration had come out in an extraordinary, public, and unscripted display.

For Nick, the reaction in the hall that evening, the words

printed about him in the papers that summer, and above all the hundreds of letters sent to the BBC in response to the radio diary, made him realize for the first time that he had achieved what he so longed for, which had been accorded to many others in the same line of business but had too often passed him by. Recognition. And I think it mattered to him hugely.

In July we celebrated our fifteenth wedding anniversary. Shortly before the day I had a flash of fear about how many more anniversaries might lie ahead of us. Without saying why, I asked Nick if he would give me a memorable present, telling him, 'Fifteen is an important number, you know.' For years he'd been buying me jewellery from Wright & Teague – long before they became fashionable and expensive. This time he did so again in style. Unable to get there himself, he arranged for a taxi to bring the gift over from the exclusive Mayfair shop, wrapped in swathes of orange tissue paper inside a black box tied with a large satin ribbon. It was a set of seven silver bangles. I loved them, and told him so. In the evening we went for dinner at Cibo, an Italian restaurant in Notting Hill where good seats were at a premium. When the waitress tried to show us down to the basement Nick took one look at the steep steps and said, 'That's going to be really tricky for me.' Without another word she found us a table upstairs. Free parking; the best seats in the house: there were clearly quite a few advantages to having only one leg.

We began to go out more often, Nick often the centre of attention while I maintained a vigilant presence at his side. I took him to the Radio 4 summer party, where he drank wine and gossiped with the likes of Jenni Murray and Sue Lawley, glowing with delight at being there, at being normal again. He became a star attraction. Everywhere we went people had heard *Fighting to Be Normal* and wanted to tell him how much it had touched them. I felt so proud of him – overwhelmingly, stomach-flippingly proud.

He made an important concession to me that summer – one that told me how much he thought of me. In the radio diary I'd talked about my attendance at my local church. Someone at BBC TV's *Heaven and Earth* programme had picked up on it, and called to ask whether we would talk to the presenter, Gloria Hunniford, about how our faith had helped us during Nick's illness. Nick was horrified. 'I don't mind coming to church with you every couple of weeks, but being quizzed on national television about it is going a bit too far,' he said. I persisted: 'I can talk about faith and you can do the other stuff, and anyway they'll film the boys, which will be fun.' And so one afternoon Gloria Hunniford and a camera crew arrived at our house. I waxed lyrical to her about the support I'd received from my fellow churchgoers while Nick fielded her questions deftly, turning on the charm to hide his awkwardness. 'Do you have a faith, Nick?' she asked. 'Not in the same way as Barbara,' he replied, 'but this experience has aroused my interest, not least because of the numbers of people, hundreds and hundreds of people, praying for me, for us. And not just one religion either – several religions. I mean, this is pretty powerful and you're bound to think about the power of prayer. It's possible that it's had an effect . . .'

When the recording was finished Gloria talked to us, candidly, about her own daughter Caron Keating's recent death from cancer. I was touched by the way she made it clear that she was drawing no parallels between what happened to Carol and what might be in store for Nick. She talked too to the boys about her grandchildren's rabbits and pressed them on whether they had ever thought about having one. For a moment I could see her turning up at the house with a spare bunny – but my 'no way' look put paid to that.

With Nick's chemotherapy completed, the summer of 2006 stretched ahead, blissfully free of hospital appointments – until his first review, which was due in early September. Thereafter, Jeremy Whelan told us, he would be called in every three months for a check-up and a scan. After a year, assuming he was still cancer-free, those visits would come at wider and wider intervals. We knew that each scan would fill us with trepidation, that our lives would remain clouded by the shadow that cancer casts over all its sufferers. But, for that summer at least, we felt safe. No more visits to consultants, no more hospital waiting rooms, no more procedures.

The one person we did continue to visit was our psychiatrist, Dr Ikkos, at his practice in Marylebone. I think I got more out of those sessions than Nick, being more open to the notion of spilling out my innermost feelings and having so many questions, worries and agitations bubbling away under my skin. There were a lot of things agitating me, not least my own behaviour. It is with great shame now that I remember the times I got irritated with Nick or with day-to-day trivia that summer. Caught up in my own struggle to cope with what had happened, I would snap now and then, or retreat into edgy, sulky silence for short spells. When Joel tripped up the step coming into the house and cut his lip and I had to rush to the pharmacy in search of plasters, I tutted loudly and pointedly as if somehow it wouldn't have happened had Nick not been disabled.

I don't know why I was so uptight. I like to think it was a

sign of the near-normality at which we had arrived: our marriage had always had its fair share of minor conflicts. But underlying my agitation was an utterly unjustified anger at Nick for having fallen ill. And although we talked endlessly about the practical stuff that it had thrown up, we never really discussed our fundamental, gut fears. And so it was just as well we could talk to Dr Ikkos. Without him I never could have said, 'Nick, I'm angry at what you've done to me, to you and to our family, and try as I might I can't stop that feeling.' I expected him to be furious that I wasn't more sympathetic to him, and to what he had endured. Instead he said, 'I completely understand that and I don't blame you. I feel so, so guilty at what I've done to you and the boys.' I was mortified, not to say deeply moved.

In those same sessions I raised another issue we were bickering about. With Nick's treatment completed, I wanted to go away for a long spell and for the four of us to take the type of holiday we would never have taken had we not stared death in the face. What Nick wanted was to get back to *The World at One* as soon as he was strong enough, and I found that hard to take. His BBC bosses had never pressured him, but he yearned to return to the maelstrom of daily news and I think he felt that by getting back there he would be closing the door properly on this whole episode in his life. In the end I gave way: a short holiday and then back to his desk, his colleagues, the microphone. I now thank God that things turned out that way.

Nick had spent many a summer, when his older children were small, on the North Norfolk coast, and that's where he longed to return. We booked a room at the Blakeney Hotel, a beautiful old building perched on Blakeney Quay with breathtaking views across the salt marshes and out to sea. We were joined by some old friends: Richard Tait, who had known Nick since schooldays and been our editor nearly twenty years earlier at *Newsnight*, his wife Jane and daughter Rachel, who was the same age as the twins. The hotel could not have been more accommodating of this noisy trio of (now) four-year-olds. The summer of 2006 was hot, unbearably so in the city, where the temperature hit the mid-thirties on several days, but we enjoyed a soothing and caressing coastal breeze.

On the beach along the coast at Cromer, Nick struggled determinedly with his crutches, slowly working his way to the water's edge to be near the boys or to sit in the beach chair I carried out for him. His lack of self-consciousness was as remarkable as his lack of self-pity. He struck, without a doubt, an almost comical pose; perhaps the boys' unquestioning acceptance of his physical condition helped him to feel at ease with it. Although I found it hard to watch him sitting there, I was determined never to let him see the struggle I had had in coming to terms with what had happened to his body, and the deep sorrow I felt at the mauling he had taken, both physically and psychologically.

As he sat in his chair a small boy came up to him and stared him in the face. 'You're weird,' said the boy, 'you've only got one leg.' Unfazed, Nick replied, 'It's not that weird, lots of people only have one leg.' Without missing a beat the boy responded, 'Yes, but you've only got one leg *and* you've got no hair. Really, you're weird,' before running off. Nick just smiled.

In the mornings we swam in the hotel pool, Nick mastering a lopsided swimming technique, or lazed in the garden. Later, as the tide slowly came in and filled the creek outside the hotel, we decamped to the edge of the quay with crabbing lines, nets, buckets and a packet of bacon to tempt the crabs lurking below. Nick became king of the crabbers, hauling in one after the other to the sound of shrieks from the boys. I can still hear their voices. 'Look, he's got a HUGE one! Look, Mummy, look what Daddy's got! He's the best, he's better than your dad, Rachel. Daddy, let me help you, I've got the net, pleeeease . . . !' On our very first session, distracted with the thrill of this new game, we caught so many crabs we didn't notice them dying because we hadn't put enough water in the bucket. When we tipped the contents back into the water out fell a lifeless mass of around fifty limp crustaceans. 'They're tired,' Nick told the boys hurriedly. 'They'll soon be crawling back to sea. Just leave them and we'll find some more to catch.'

In the late afternoon Nick rested while I took the boys for a swim in the silty waters of the creek. We splashed and screamed, and emerged slimy and spattered with black mud. It was fun, but something was wrong. We weren't together; that's what it was, and from that realization came the moment when a shadow passed over me, as I reflected that Nick couldn't be with us right then, and never *would* be able to be with us at times like this. I raged at the world to keep at bay a deep, visceral fear. When I brought myself up sharp, reminding myself how lucky I was that he was alive, I understood that the tendrils of terror which cancer brings in its wake were more tightly wrapped round my mind than I had realized.

As Nick's return to *The World at One* approached we spent the last few days of our break at Rose Cottage where, for the first time since we had moved in, we were able to sunbathe in the garden. Never before had it been so warm for us in that chilly, wet part of the country. Thomas the Tank Engine came to the East Somerset Railway in Cranmore, a few miles up the road, and we took the boys for their first ride on a steam train. Nick refused to be daunted by the steps up into the carriage and managed, with the help of the guard, to haul himself inside. As we made our way to our seat a woman across the gangway said, 'You're Nick Clarke, aren't you?' Nick paused for a second and then pointed to his one leg. 'I guess that's a bit of a give-away, isn't it!' 'I started to listen to your radio diary,' the woman went on. 'But I had to switch off after a few minutes. It was so gruelling . . .' It was refreshing to hear someone say the programme wasn't to everyone's taste.

There were moments during that summer when I felt we touched again on the perfection of the life we had achieved in the months and years before Nick got ill. The physical load eased as his strength returned and he was able to share some of the daily duties of life with young children. He would man-oeuvre his way round the kitchen in the mornings helping me to get the boys' breakfast, and even in the middle of the night as I struggled to settle a wakeful child, I would hear his crutches tap-tapping along the landing to join me. He would ease himself on to the side of one of the beds and tell me to go back to sleep while he dispensed daddy comfort.

We had the bathroom adapted so Nick could sit in an easy access shower and as the builders scurried round trashing the house, Nick alternately encouraged and admonished them (in typical style they left before completing the job). We bought a new car, an automatic Chrysler Grand Voyager with electric sliding doors; Nick was thrilled to be able to drive again. And he presided over the church quiz while I sat at his side, unable to contain my laughter at my first question: 'How many legs does tonight's chairman have?'

There was one moment that summer when I felt total

happiness wash over me. It's painted vividly into my mind, not for anything startling, just for its very ordinariness. I was driving home from Sainsbury's with a car-load of shopping bags, the sun was shining and at home I knew there were three people I loved. I feel so blessed, I thought. I am so happy. We've pieced together the shattered fragments of our lives and the glue is setting. We'll be able to see the break-lines, probably for ever, but it's OK. It's OK. Even an uncertain future couldn't dull that moment. In our newly adjusted timescales, any future seemed a long way away.

Nick returned to *The World at One* in the middle of August. A BBC car took him to work where a photographer from the staff newspaper *Ariel* was waiting to record the event. To Nick's great joy, a large chunk of one of his first programmes was devoted to the story of alleged ball-tampering by the Pakistani cricket team. I could hear the thrill in his voice as he explained the ins, outs and complications of this heinous sporting crime to 'his' listeners.

'The fact that a ball has one shiny side, and one rough, causes it to swing towards or away from the batsman. But after forty or fifty overs, as the shiny side itself starts to become rougher, some bowlers can make it move in the opposite direction. It's known as reverse swing,' he said, with the meticulous precision he always used with words.

At the end of his first programme, champagne was uncorked and Nick was presented with a cake in the shape of a clock – with the hands at one o'clock – made by two of the studio managers who, like so many of the people Nick worked with, adored him. He came home buzzing.

I was surprised, then, a few days after his return when he

rang me mid-morning – as he always did – and I heard him whisper, 'I don't want to be here.' 'Why?' I asked, my stomach flipping. 'It just doesn't feel right,' he replied, before moving on to more mundane stuff. He never expanded on this, and I decided to put it down to a restlessness he had had about work before he got ill – the sort of weariness that comes with any job after so many years. Either to that or to the simple fact that he missed the comfort of being at home.

A couple of weeks later he had lunch with the head of radio news, Steve Mitchell. He told him he was still very tired and that coming back to work had proved harder than he had imagined. Steve's response was instantaneous. 'Don't do so much,' he said. 'Cut your days back, now – until you feel more like it.' Which is what Nick did.

I should have seen the warning signs. I reassured both Nick and myself that the tiredness was the fallout from the chemotherapy. I was sure it was. I could think of no other reason. Nick was sure it wasn't, but offered no explanation. I didn't know what else to say. Lots of things went unsaid.

Something else should have rung alarm bells. As August drifted by, Nick's mood became tetchier, but I assumed, as with my own unforgivable irritations, that it was just part of 'returning to normal' and reacting to life's daily niggles. He began to immerse himself in sport on the television, more so than usually, and seemed reluctant to communicate with me. It was as if he was retreating into a distant and private place and it upset me, so much so that I shouted at him one evening. 'Nothing in life really makes you happy. Just your bloody sport.' He didn't say a word in reply.

Why didn't he tell me what was happening?

But there were more pressing matters distracting me. The

boys' first day at school was approaching and Joel was becoming increasingly fretful. By great good fortune the boys had been offered a place at a highly admired Church of England school in Kensington: St Mary Abbots. But whenever the name of the school was mentioned he screamed and ran off. 'I don't want to go. I'm NOT going there,' he shouted. When I asked him what was worrying him, he put his hands over his ears and sang, at the top of his voice, to drown me out. I was perplexed and as the big day approached, increasingly worried. It took Nick, patient and caring, but also getting quite desperate in the last days of the holiday, finally to fathom what the problem was. We'd taken the boys to look round the school in July, and nobody had thought to show Joel where the loos were. He had assumed the school didn't have any and was panicking at the idea he would have to get through a whole day without being able to visit. And he'd been too embarrassed to tell us.

On the first day of term Nick and I posed for a photograph with the boys in their new uniforms outside our front door. We, of course, were just as nervous as they were. When we arrived we were allowed to sit with the boys for a few minutes in their cosy classroom with its tiny seats and colourful walls and Nick joked, 'Let's count the legs. Oooops, it's not difficult to count to one, is it!' Reluctantly, we tore ourselves away, reassured by the sight of their new teacher, Miss Keck, talking quietly in the Home Corner to Bendy while Joel chattered, loudly, to the rest of the class. Our precious boys had passed another milestone. Sharing it with Nick reminded me again of the sheer wonderment of parenthood – and of parenthood shared with the one you love.

Two days later that perfect world fell apart.

TEN

Daddy got a very poorly leg, that's all that happened. He went to the doctors and they couldn't get a plastic leg so he died. If he had his plastic leg he would still be alive.

JOEL, 4½

I was in Boots. I was standing at the No. 7 cosmetics counter. It was 3.20 in the afternoon. Nick had gone to see Jeremy Whelan for his first routine check-up but I couldn't be with him as I had to be at the school gates. I had arrived early and was killing time in the shops on Kensington High Street.

I had accompanied Nick to every single appointment with Jeremy, but I didn't go to this one. And I thought no more of it. There was a 'buy two get one free' offer on the face creams and I couldn't decide on my third item. And then the phone rang. And nothing was ever the same again.

'It's not good news,' was all Nick said.

The horror of that moment was physical. A bullet of ice seemed to penetrate my body and shoot through my heart, my limbs, every nerve, every finger and every toe. And then I started to shake.

It felt more real this time, more final. I felt conned, except that I was the con artist. Had we not deceived ourselves, had we not basked in confidence, had we not been oblivious to the words being written on the wall? Had we not been bloody stupid to hope that this moment might never come?

There was a lump, Nick said. Where there shouldn't be one. He sat on the dark blue chair in the sitting room. I sat at his feet. We looked at each other across a deep, dark well of sadness. 'I'm so, so sorry,' he said. And I said, 'You never, ever have to say you're sorry.' And he said, 'I love you,' and I said, 'I love you more than anything, and you're the best friend I have ever had and could ever have had, and I'm so sorry if I've ever been undeserving of what you've given me and I'm so sorry for all the times I've been rotten to you ...' And he smiled and said, 'You know none of that matters to me.' He was right. I did know.

This time there was no barrier between us as there had been that day, nearly a year ago, when we first knew he was ill and when we embarked on our separate journeys. I felt myself start on a new journey now, alongside Nick and close to him, and I could feel it taking me towards a point of unconditional love, which is an exceptional, overwhelming thing to feel. It is like becoming the other person, where you are so joined, conjoined, that you really are one. If he had asked me to jump off a cliff, I would have jumped. If he died, I would die with him. Sitting opposite me was my lifeblood, my heart, my soul, my very breath, part of the blood that coursed through my veins. Where his flesh ended, mine might begin.

Two days later we were back at the RNOH where a softly spoken Indian doctor carried out a biopsy. I hadn't asked Nick where the new lump was – I had flinched from knowing. It turned out it was on the side of his neck, in a lymph node. He lay on a hospital couch staring up at the ceiling as the doctor guided a large needle into the growth and then scanned it with an ultrasound. I crouched on the floor beside Nick, holding his hand throughout. I couldn't look at the needle. I only looked at him. He was calm as he spoke to the doctor, though inwardly I have no doubt he was as terrified as I was. The scan showed signs of necrotic tissue, the doctor said, and Nick immediately knew what it meant. 'It's another sarcoma then,' he said. I was staggered. He clearly knew more than I had imagined he would want to.

We went to Harley Street the next day for a CT scan of Nick's lungs. We knew that it was to the lungs that sarcomas usually migrated if some of the cells got away from their primary location, and that their arrival there was a sign that the game was up. We didn't know there were other places they could choose to re-locate. Particularly with Nick's type of sarcoma. Or what it meant if they did.

Back home we waited for five days for the results. We tried to talk of other things, of the boys, their new school, Nick's forthcoming recording of *Round Britain Quiz*, but it felt false. Nick reverted to lying in bed again, a patient once more, listening to his portable radio through his earphones, trying to watch sport on television, but actually subsiding into deep, deep thought. I lay beside him hour after hour, watching, waiting, just being. Being together. Living, breathing and being. Together. Sick with fear. Not eating. I couldn't eat.

We jumped every time the phone rang. I always passed the handset to Nick to answer, out of respect for the fact that, if it was THE call, it was his news.

Finally it came. It was late on Friday afternoon, the end of one of the longest weeks of our lives. It was Jeremy Whelan.

I heard one side of a tense and difficult conversation. At one point Nick said, 'Nothing at all?' Which set me panicking.

Then he said, 'So there is something that can be done?'

He came off the phone. 'I was worried they'd say they couldn't do anything,' he said, 'but they can.'

You see, that's what they can nearly always do with cancer. They can do something. Rather than nothing. They can offer treatment. And that's what you want to hear. At the point at which they say there's no treatment and there's nothing they can do, then there's only one way things can go.

For us, treatment offered hope. The hope was only a shred. But it was a distraction from the facts. Because once a cancer returns, once it migrates to a new place in your body, there is nearly always no cure. Treatment only delays its progression, suppresses its symptoms, and to us it offered hope that maybe the 'final conclusion' could be headed off at the pass, for the time being at least. Hope can be very welcome when what you are feeling is despair.

Jeremy explained that chemotherapy was not an option now; Nick had had as much as he could take, and anyway, it hadn't worked. Neither was surgery. You can't cut out cancerous lymph nodes. I never found out why, but there it was. It would have to be radiotherapy, high-energy X-rays designed to slow the lump in its tracks. Or maybe, we hoped beyond hope, to kill each and every cell that was growing there. Jeremy now needed to bring in another member of the sarcoma team at University College Hospital and he arranged a meeting at the beginning of the following week.

That evening Nick was on the road for *Any Questions?* again. It is unlikely anyone had any inkling of what he was going through. I was standing by the front door, waiting for him to return when his taxi pulled up outside and I overheard his customary banter with the car driver. He sounded almost jaunty. But the minute he shut the front door I could see his spirit crumple from the weight of what he was carrying. I looked at his face, the creases I knew so well and loved so much, the fluffy coat of new hair that had grown since the chemotherapy, and I smelled the faint warm scent of his skin, as familiar as my own. I could have lived in it. He had his shirt open at the neck to relieve the pressure on the spot where the biopsy needle had been and I saw the black and grey hairs sprouting on his chest. The wound had started to weep and no amount of dabbing at it could stop it oozing. It had seeped on to, and stained, the lapel of his new Strellson jacket.

Anna Cassoni was the next consultant recruited to Nick's medical defence team. She specialized in radiotherapy and was upbeat and calming. I could see Nick relaxing as she spoke. She would need yet more CT scans of his neck, she said, to assess the size and shape of the tumour so that she could calculate very precisely where to target the radiotherapy.

'I can't promise to kill every single cell, but I will try,' she said, smiling.

'Well, I'm going to be positive and hope that we get *all* the little blighters,' Nick said, and smiled at me.

His main concern was how soon he could return to work. Anna Cassoni told him kindly but firmly that he shouldn't expect to work again before Christmas. 'You can't rush back, Nick,' she said. 'This treatment will really tire you out.'

Afterwards, as we stood waiting for the lift, Nick looked at my taut and worried face and said, 'Cheer up, it's not *that* bad.' Ever the optimist, ever the man whose love for me could brook no pain.

That day, and in the weeks that followed, I was sometimes

baffled and often frustrated that Nick seemed oblivious to the reality of what he faced. But looking back now, I think he simply couldn't bear to see my hurt, in the same way that I couldn't bear to see his. We both shied away from sharing our fears, from talking about what might lie ahead, and in so doing we took ourselves to a place where we both began to believe our own propaganda, that this was no more than a temporary hiatus on the road to recovery. Occasionally I emerged, briefly, from this Neverland and raged inwardly at Nick's denial of how bad things were. Many months later I asked Jeremy Whelan why he thought Nick had faced his horror this way and I was astonished to hear how common such a reaction was. 'Denial is something intrinsic to coping with life-threatening illness,' he said. 'It is a very black-and-white word, but the emotion is more subtle. It is an important strength.'

The strong and courageous man broke down on just one occasion. A few days after we had received our devastating news, Nick's older twins, Ali and Tom, emailed a photo of the two of them with their younger brother Pete at their thirtieth birthday party, which Nick had been too weak to attend. It brought tears streaming down his face. I held his hand and pleaded softly, 'Don't cry, darling,' because his tears scythed through my fragile defences. But he needed to cry and depriving him of the chance to do so was wrong.

I myself broke down regularly and, just as I had done barely a year before when we first found out he was ill, I did so when he wasn't around, leaning heavily on the support others offered me. One person who steadied me was the vicar at St Mary Abbots, the church attached to the boys' new school. His name was Gillean Craig. He had an inner strength that I hunted out when I was overwhelmed. One morning, after I had dropped the boys off, he and I sat together in the vast and calming silence of the cathedral-like building where so many must have prayed for help over the years. After listening to my outpourings he asked me whether Nick would like to see him. I urged Nick to accept the offer. Talking to a man of the cloth was not high on his list of priorities, but neither was talking to anyone about the turmoil that must have been in his mind. I thought that unburdening himself to an outsider might help him.

And so Father Gillean came to the house, and the first words he uttered when he saw Nick were, 'Do you want to do this with God or without?' 'Without, please,' Nick replied with open relief, and I left them to talk in private. I believe it was the only frank and honest conversation Nick had with anyone about what was happening to him. I asked Father Gillean months later whether he thought Nick knew he was dying. 'Oh yes,' he said, 'without a doubt.'

Once Anna Cassoni had established the nature of the treatment she needed to give Nick, we began three weeks of journeying daily to University College Hospital. The radiotherapy machines were in the basement, behind heavy doors along a long brightly lit corridor with a shiny vinyl floor. The treatment was uncomfortable. Nick had to place a close-fitting mask over his head and neck to hold him completely still while the X-rays were directed at the tumour with the greatest precision possible. He hated it, of course. I never saw the process first-hand and was relieved to be excluded from the radiation area. Nick urged me to get out of the hospital while I waited for his treatment to finish. 'There's no point sitting here doing nothing,' he insisted – and so I wandered round Heal's department store where I chose things for the 'next stage' of our lives together, when Nick was recovered and things returned to normal. In our Neverland. I fancied a brand-new bed.

When I returned to the hospital I usually found Nick sitting in the corridor reading a thriller to distract himself, or talking to other patients. There was a woman who brought her teenage son for treatment every day, all the way from deepest Kent. And a young man who recognized Nick and said he'd lost the lower part of his leg to cancer but had now been told the cancer had spread to his spine.

At the end of September it was my birthday. We had nothing planned so at the last minute we invited a few neighbours round for a drink and cake. From the day he had given me the lucky heather Victorian pin brooch, Nick had showered me with beautiful and tasteful gifts, many of which he bought in his favourite antique shop in Brighton where every autumn one of the political parties would hold its conference. That autumn he had been determined to make it to the conferences despite the huge obstacles his disability would present. But his deteriorating health had knocked this idea on the head. There was no birthday present either. For the first time in nineteen years. But I got a card which meant more than any gift and which turned out to be the last thing he ever wrote to me and from which shone his love, eternal optimism and selflessness. 'Thank you for being there,' it said. 'You amaze me. With a bit of a fair wind let's hope that your next 29th [sic] birthday is a lot less stressful. You have transformed my life – from drab to brightly coloured. I love you.'

Nick was cheerful and chatty that evening, though I noticed that his appetite was beginning to wane. I didn't know then how sinister this was. We put it down to the side effects of the radiotherapy, as we began to do with almost everything. The list grew. It made Nick feel tired. It burned the skin on his neck. Slowly it began to weaken his voice, the cruellest blow of all. Worst, it seemed to have little impact on the lump on his neck, which was growing at an alarming rate, clearly visible now for all to see. And when the three weeks of radiotherapy ended, Jeremy Whelan dropped a bombshell. He'd seen a shadow in another lymph node by his stomach. He would need a second course of radiotherapy.

And so Nick embarked on another three weeks of treatment. Still we persisted in thinking everything would be fine, despite all the signs that should have warned us that things were not right in our Neverland. Nick grew more frail. When he could no longer get from the car to the radiotherapy department on crutches, I had to push him in a wheelchair. He ate less and less. His stomach became more and more uncomfortable and distended. He stayed in bed for most of the day and I lay next to him rubbing his tummy gently in slow circular motions as I had done to the boys when they were babies. At one point my hand slipped upwards towards his rib cage and I felt a hard lump beneath his skin. Horrified, I pulled my hand away, shaking. 'What's the matter?' There was alarm in Nick's voice. 'Nothing, nothing . . .' was all I could say as I felt my own stomach churn. I had felt it, touched the cancer that was eating him up inside.

In early October Nick was booked to speak at the Cheltenham Literature Festival, as he had done just a year before. Nothing would sway his determination to get there and meet his commitments, though it was abundantly clear it would be a huge struggle. My mother, who was awaiting a hip transplant and could barely walk herself without excruciating pain, came with us. 'I'll manage,' she assured me. 'I'll just take extra pain-killers.'

We set out on a Saturday morning. I drove and Nick dozed. Mum sat in the back of the car and distracted the boys. I wept silently, knowing Nick wasn't noticing. When we reached the town centre, the familiarity of the locations we had grown to know together and the warmth of the hotel we had always stayed in took me back to happier times – times I was beginning to fear we would never have again. It really hurt.

The event was at the Town Hall. It was full. On the panel were some eminent names. Libby Purves, Tony Benn, the journalist Danny Finkelstein, Jeremy Paxman. Jim Naughtie was chairing the session. The subject was the relationship between politics and the media. I drove Nick to the venue and wheeled him to the Writers' Room where participants gathered before going on stage. People wanted to talk to him, as they always did, but I could see how little energy he had. When the time came, he hopped up on to the podium with the other panellists and the audience clapped and cheered. His welcome outdid that of everyone else. To listen to him, to hear the fluency of his arguments, the mastery of his subject and the still intact but weakening voice, you might not have known. But to look at him you might have questioned. So used was I by now to his gaunt and hollow look that I didn't register how sick it made him appear. He signed books afterwards and made conversation easily and readily. Several people approached him to comment on *Fighting to Be Normal*. After-wards I took him back to the hotel to bed. He was utterly exhausted. I fed the boys and settled them before going to bed myself, crying again. At midnight Nick woke up, disorientated. He waved his arms wildly and talked as if he had no idea where he was. He seemed to be hallucinating. I was petrified. I thought he was about to die. I calmed him back to sleep but I felt very alone, and very scared.

After Cheltenham Nick's voice grew hoarse and strained. Although a return to *The World at One* was out of the question, he badly wanted to record the *Round Britain Quiz* programme at the beginning of November, but there was no way he could do so until his speech returned to normal. Three or four times a day he would gargle aspirin or paracetamol, desperate to bring his precious voice back to life. Helping him one evening and seeing how hard it was becoming for him to hop the short distance from the bedroom to the bathroom, I saw his frustration spill out. 'This is ridiculous,' he cursed, 'I'm not getting better. I just want to feel better again.' In our Neverland we still told ourselves the symptoms were the side effects of the radiotherapy and that he *would* get better. Some day . . .

There was nothing more guaranteed to dent that state of disbelief than the visitor who arrived on our doorstep one afternoon. I opened the door to a young woman whose first words were, 'Are you Mrs Clarke?' Instinct told me what this was about. 'Yes,' I said.

'I'm from the *Daily Mail* and our showbiz editor got a tip-off that your husband Chris [sic] Clarke has had a relapse. Has he?' My blood went cold.

It was the only time I broke down in front of Nick. 'I'm just so scared of losing you,' I said as I told him what had happened and started to cry. 'Don't worry, I'm not going anywhere just yet,' he smiled. I had denied everything and told the journalist that if she couldn't even get someone's name right it was no surprise that her other facts were wrong too. She left, but returned ten minutes later to knock again and, when I didn't answer, leave a bunch of nasty-looking flowers on the doorstep with a note thanking me for talking to her and saying she looked forward to talking again. We called Mark Damazer at Radio 4 and he promised to intervene. I don't know what happened, but we didn't hear from the *Mail* again.

Nick's unerring conviction that he had time on his side gave me courage – most of the time. There were moments when I really did believe things would be all right, and other times when I caught myself thinking the unthinkable. I looked at photos of Nick and wondered how it would feel – as I thought I soon would – to be looking at a picture of a dead man. As I sorted his T-shirts and pyjamas in the wardrobe I imagined how empty the shelves might soon be. The light of reality was starting to penetrate the cracks that were opening up in our Neverland.

New, practical fears began to surface. If Nick died, how would I manage financially? He had been a freelance journalist for most of his career, effectively self-employed. He had no BBC pension and, like many people, only a meagre private pension. It felt vulgar to ask, but I had to. Mark Damazer arranged for me to talk to a woman from Human Resources and we met in a café at the end of my road. It wasn't a comfortable meeting. She had clearly left her empathy folder in the office. I asked first whether the BBC would continue to pay Nick's salary, as they had done up to now, even though he wasn't working. We might have deluded ourselves about how sick he really was, but we both knew a return to work was some way off. 'We'll pay him as long as he plans to return,' she said, and then asked pointedly, 'He *is* planning to return, I assume?' I nodded, dumbstruck at the tone of her voice. I realized that if I told her I feared he might die, she might take him off the payroll. We talked further about BBC benefits for 'death in service' and Nick's lack of pension, to which she said with equal censure, 'Did you not know he was freelance?' Then she added, '*Surely* you have life insurance for the mortgage?' I'm not sure why I expected any more than facts and figures from someone working in a personnel department, but I decided then and there to have nothing more to do with her.

As we slipped into the shortening days of October the visitors became fewer and fewer. I think some people were afraid. Maybe they scented the wounded animal's last journey. One weekend some old friends of Nick did visit. Despite its being autumn, vestiges of the glorious summer of 2006 still lingered. We went to the park and sat in unseasonably warm sunshine. I sensed our visitors' awkwardness at the sight of him, now weak and thin, having to be pushed in a wheelchair. The ugliness and discomfort of illness can be hard for friends who have only ever shared the good times.

That evening Nick felt sick. He struggled with his food and when his tummy bloated alarmingly he became distressed. Terrified, and realizing I was getting out of my depth, I knew I needed medical help – but where to go? We had never been given an out-of-hours number for Jeremy Whelan so I called University College Hospital and got the oncology registrar on duty. She had only the barest notes on Nick because he was a private patient. I needed to speak to Jeremy, but even she had no means of contacting him. Despite the thousands of pounds Norwich Union had shelled out on Nick's treatment, here we were, on our own on a Saturday evening. Had he been treated on the NHS, I found out later, we would have had twenty-four-hour access to every member of the oncology team and each would have been able to familiarize themselves with his case instantly.

The registrar did her best with limited information and established that Nick hadn't taken the right dose of Tramadol, a drug designed to ease the discomfort he was experiencing. Within an hour he felt better, but I felt very alone that evening, despite the presence of Nick's friends, who sat silently downstairs through the crisis, too embarrassed and too powerless to offer help.

The following Monday morning I joined a private out-of-hours GP service so that I would have someone to ring at night if we needed support. And every one of those doctors gave Nick respect, sympathy and time whenever we consulted them. Which was just as well, as we received little help from a local GP when I rang a few days later during the day to plead for advice. His response floored me. He was curt and cold, and when I asked him for a home visit he agreed with seeming reluctance before cutting the call dead without a goodbye. He came at lunchtime, looking inconvenienced at having to do something he clearly didn't want to do, barely looked me in the eye, and on seeing Nick said, without an ounce of sympathy, 'Well, I'm sorry things are so grim.' 'The only thing that's grim around here is him, the Grim Reaper,' I said to Nick afterwards. The GP wrote out a couple of hurried prescriptions and said he would send a Macmillan nurse round. I saw Nick's shock at the suggestion. In Neverland you don't need Macmillan nurses because you are *going to get better*.

I didn't consult the GP again. The visit was bruising and Nick took it badly. When you are very sick you yearn for kindness, an encouraging word. Or perhaps it was just that the truth had been revealed, that no one could do anything for him now – except set up a team of last resort, into whose network we had now been plugged. He didn't even want to hear the words. Palliative care.

And so a Macmillan nurse arrived later that week from the palliative care unit at the local hospital – formally known as a hospice – and when Nick winced at hearing where she came from she tried to reassure him that palliative care was not always 'end of life' care these days. 'It's more about symptom control,' she insisted. 'Many patients come to our unit for a few days to get their medication sorted and then go home.' It was what Nick needed to hear. But it was probably the only helpful thing she did. The reputation of Macmillan nurses may precede them, but I was bitterly disappointed by ours. Far from bringing us reassurance, knowledge and understanding, she had little to say and little to offer beyond coordinating Nick's prescriptions and medicine collections. Whether it was by design, I don't know, but when we asked her about the symptoms he was experiencing, she offered only one explanation: it was the fallout from the radiotherapy. But she would go no further than that: her visits were brief and involved lots of note-taking on her part. I don't know what she wrote down.

Between our local support services, the GP and the Macmillan nurse, we felt utterly abandoned. A social worker from the palliative care unit offered the prospect of real help when I admitted I wasn't sure I could cope any more, but it was never forthcoming. 'It is fucking humiliating to admit that I need social fucking services to help me care for my husband and family,' I emailed Eddie Mair in despair. 'You have been pushed way way beyond what any person should be asked to do,' he wrote back, sympathetically, and I replied, 'I'm so, so scared.'

At the end of October, Nick's radiotherapy course finished and in early November we saw Jeremy Whelan one more time. Nick sat gaunt, pale and listless in his wheelchair. Anxiety filled the room. I felt both desperation and anger that Jeremy – consultant oncologist, leading light in one of the largest sarcoma units in Europe – that things had become this bad: rightly or wrongly I wanted to blame him. He had little to say beyond, 'I'll see you again in a month.' 'No please, I can't take it,' Nick pleaded, 'can't we leave it to the New Year? I'm just so tired.' Jeremy looked unsure. I hesitated before asking a question I hadn't even raised with Nick. 'Are there any clinical trials Nick could go on?' Nick responded before Jeremy. 'Please, no, I can't face any more treatment,' he begged, and in a quaking voice I said, 'I know, darling, but I'm just so worried.' 'Do you think I'm not worried?' he snapped back. 'All the time I'm thinking, worrying, wondering if I'll find another lump. Don't think I'm not aware of how bad this is.' It was the only frank admission he ever made to me about the fears he harboured and hid from me. 'Yes, there are trials, but let's wait for a moment,' said Jeremy. He must have known he was looking at a dying man.

Would the awfulness of those days have been any different if we hadn't had our Neverland to distract us from the truth that was too terrible to face? One friend urged me to ask someone outright whether Nick was dying, but I couldn't. I needed hope to keep going, even the wafer-thin shreds of hope I clutched at like straws in the wind. We both had to keep cheerful for the boys, who were remarkably unfazed by Nick's increasingly haggard face and decreasing mobility. He had spent so much of the last year lying down, either on the settee or in bed, that they had come to see it as normal. He now struggled to make it downstairs but managed to do so on 5 November, when he sat with the boys at the back door watching me light fireworks in the garden. Looking at photos of them from that evening it breaks my heart to see Joel's and Benedict's trusting innocence, their ignorance of the horror that was enfolding us and their joy in a childhood world which was about to be ripped apart.

What it was like for Nick during this time I don't know. I couldn't break into his mind or into his thoughts and I didn't know that I wanted to. I felt like the world's greatest coward as terror engulfed me and I froze. We never talked about what was happening, about what was *really* happening and Nick made it very clear he didn't want to talk, even though there were ample opportunities to do so. Many months later I came to understand that Nick was facing his approaching death the way he wanted to, quietly and without fuss, and to some extent in private. You can love someone to the ends of the earth, but when they face a journey that will take them beyond those ends you cannot go there with them. That's one journey they have to take alone.

For me though it was like living in a horror movie, my stomach pitted with fear, feeling its fibres spreading through my body and tingling in my fingertips as I tried increasingly desperately to keep faith that we would eventually turn a corner and find respite. I started doing deals with myself, often as I read to the boys at bedtime: 'If I get to the end of this sentence without hesitating, he'll live.' 'If I read this page in less than a minute he'll be OK.'

The horror was now coming between us. I started to sleep in the spare room, at Nick's request: he was worried that his unease at night, his shifting and stirring, would keep me awake.

He fell asleep mid-evening, leaving me to while away a dark
and silent couple of hours on my own with only the madness
in my mind for company. I spent the time reading to distract
myself or surfing the Net for meaningless things, like looking
for sheets for that new bed I was hoping for, for when Nick
'got better'. The bed linen became an obsession, and so obses-
sive did I become that I had some shipped over from New
Zealand. I even organized a Top Shop party at home. Yes, you
read that correctly. I held a Top Shop party. A van-load of
clothes were delivered to the house with a couple of Top Shop
style advisers, and five girlfriends came round to try and buy.
One after the other we stood in front of the long mirror in the
bedroom, chatting to Nick while he lay in bed, remarkably
cheerful as he watched us, in various states of dress and undress,
filing past him.

Most of the time I chose not to see that Nick was dying in
front of my eyes. But had I faced the truth, what good would
it have done?

In mid-November I had booked two nights away at a health
spa with Tessa Jowell, the politician, whose uncle married my
mother when she was divorced some years ago, connecting us
circuitously. She and Nick would laugh at their family relationship. 'I think you're officially my step-cousin-in-law,' Nick
teased her when they met, either at a party conference or at one
of our annual get-togethers with her uncle and my mother.
Having chosen never to have politicians as friends, he was
concerned it would compromise his ability to do his job, to ask
difficult questions, and sometimes the connection with Tessa
worried him. She seemed to understand, though I am sure she
got a worse deal because of it. Whenever they sparred in *The
World at One*, Nick, anxious to prove that the rigour of

his interview was in no way compromised by the family connection, would end up being tougher on her than he had any need to be. She never complained. She always struck me as one of the most thoroughly genuine and empathetic of people. It was she who suggested going away; I think she realized how much I needed a break and she found time while being a Cabinet Minister to share it with me. Just before we left for the spa, she sat down with Nick, held his hand, talked and listened, and showed real compassion for what he was going through. I could see in his eyes the supreme effort he was making to be positive. He had pride. And he badly wanted me to have this break.

When I got back forty-eight hours later I was struck forcefully by how dreadful things were and I was racked with guilt at having been away. A friend had been helping Nick and, having once trained as a nurse, she sensed things were not right. She told me categorically that we needed nursing help and that I shouldn't even try to carry on alone. Nick hated the idea. We argued. The boys overheard us and talked for months afterwards about our 'Mummy and Daddy having a talk fight about nurses'. Eventually Nick agreed and my heart wept silently as, finally, reality began to sweep away the veil in front of my eyes and the walls of our Neverland began to crumble.

An agency nurse moved in. She would cost well over a thousand pounds for six days, but we had nowhere else to turn, having been let down by both Macmillan and our local NHS services. I felt I was letting myself down too, though. I loved Nick to the ends of the earth, but I couldn't be his nurse. It was beyond me.

Released from some of the pressure now of the constant worry about his medical needs, I sat by the bed talking to Nick on Saturday evening, 18 November, feeling buoyed that he had managed to eat a couple of chips. 'I'm feeling a little better,' he reassured me. On Sunday I took the boys to John Lewis with my friend Daniel, Benedict's godfather. We bought Christmas decorations. When we got back, Daniel went up to see Nick; later he told me that Nick had said, 'Daniel, make sure Barbara gets a lot of love.' He was dying and all he could think about was me. On the Monday Nick seemed severely dehydrated and by now had barely eaten for six weeks. I pleaded with him to go to the palliative care unit. I hoped they would feed him intravenously, which the agency nurse couldn't do. 'It will only be for a couple of days,' I said, 'I promise you.' Nick agreed, very reluctantly.

An ambulance took us there. Nick had to be carried from his bed in a chair. As the paramedics settled him, tears began to slip down his face. I sat next to him and wiped them away, feeling sick to the core of my soul.

When we arrived we were told to wait. And wait. For an assessment. Nick began to drift in and out of sleep. A young doctor examined him and went away.

That night they brought him his medicine, but his dose of sleeping tablets had been halved. I could see Nick panic that he wouldn't sleep and I think he now yearned for sleep as a haven from this horror. 'I'll get you another tablet,' I said after the nurse had left, knowing full well that the nurses would not, under any circumstances, give him an extra one unless a doctor prescribed it. It was late at night and there were no doctors around. Nick sensed this too, and knowing me as well as he did he said, 'Please don't do anything rash,

I implore you.' 'I won't. I promise you,' I lied.

I went to the pharmacy. The door was open. A man was working his way round the shelves piled high with bottles and pots. He looked at me warily. I beamed. 'Looking for something?' he asked. 'No, just lost,' I laughed. I scanned the room and saw Nick's medicine tray sitting on a table. I turned to leave and as the man turned back to his shelves I stepped back silently, heart racing, and took the box of sleeping tablets.

Nick slept fitfully. I lay on a bed beside him, desperate for the sleep I knew I would need to cope with the day ahead. During the night, nurses came to turn him and he screamed in pain as the subtleties of dealing with his stump were ignored. The staff were calm and polite but without warmth. It was not a place I would want a loved one to be. Nick woke throughout the night and each time I jumped out of bed to help, to be there, by his side. At one point he looked at me lovingly and said, as he had often done, 'You really are the best.'

The following morning the palliative consultant stood by his bed. Her name was Ann Naismith and she treated Nick with kindness and respect. 'What is your main worry at the moment, Mr Clarke?' she inquired with genuine interest and enormous compassion. 'My voice,' he replied. He was dying, but what he was thinking about was his voice. His voice was him, it was what had made him, it was his identity, his being, and as it died, so did he.

Then she took me outside and told me the truth – but not in so many words. I was standing in a brightly lit corridor. 'Do you have any legal documents you need Nick to sign?'

In other words, your husband is about to die.

I doubled over and sank to the floor, grabbing my head with my hands, curling into a foetal ball. I didn't sob, shake or cry.

I just lay there silent, in shock, in disbelief and in horror as she confirmed what I already knew.

In her office Dr Naismith spelled it out. 'He is in the terminal stages of his illness. I doubt he will still be with us at Christmas,' she said. 'I may be wrong, of course. Sometimes people surprise us, confound our expectations.' And then she asked the wisest question of all. 'Does Nick know what is happening to him?' 'No,' I insisted, and I said that at all costs I didn't want him to know.

In truth, I couldn't face having to watch him realize the game was over. Though I now think he already knew. She told me that people usually found out for themselves. Their bodies eventually told them, if they didn't already know, she said. And I asked how they reacted. 'There's shock at first, of course, and anger and despair, but it doesn't last as long as you might fear. People seem to come to terms with the news, and quite soon,' she said.

She looked at me with concern. 'You have a tough time ahead of you. You need to know that death can be brutal,' she said. 'It isn't what you see on celluloid. It isn't *Love Story*. It can be very hard indeed.'

They didn't want him to leave the palliative care unit. They tried to persuade me to let him stay. They needed to 'sort his medicine regime', they said. He couldn't go home until a special bed was provided, they said. He couldn't go home because there were no ambulances available, they said.

Then I heard Nick's voice. 'I just want to go home.' They were his last words to me.

I called a private ambulance and he was home within an hour. I will never regret doing that.

Suzie and Alastair had moved in and a new agency nurse arrived that evening to help for the next few days or weeks, however long it might be. Her name was Charlotte and she arrived with a broad Midlands accent, long blonde hair, layers of make-up, a low-cut T-shirt and slightly too much perfume. The first thing she told me was how much she loved her job. Her job was helping people to die. Trained as a nurse she found palliative care the first field in which her work made a real difference to the quality of people's lives. And deaths. She was twenty-seven.

Everyone who dies should have a Charlotte with them at the end. And everyone who has to live through the torment of watching a loved one die, should have a Charlotte beside them to guide them through the experience and beyond.

Charlotte brought empathy, understanding and experience to my disintegrating world. She made Nick comfortable. She gave him sips of tea. She knew instinctively what he needed. She took care of him medically and physically. He was drowsy now but at one point he looked at her and whispered, 'Thank you.' He knew he was with someone who really understood. And I thank her because I could not have managed that last leg of the journey alone. And again I thank Norwich Union for paying for her, because people like Charlotte do not come cheap. Though at that stage money was hardly uppermost in my mind.

I slept in our bed that night, next to Nick, covering myself loosely with a blanket, barely able to move for fear of disturbing him. He slept so, so peacefully, though I lay awake, love and horror and pain and fear and yet more love tormenting me.

I love this man to the ends of the earth. I want to grow old with him. He is being ripped from me and it hurts like I never knew pain

could hurt. I am crossing the Rubicon. I am becoming one of those
people for whom life will never be the same again. My soul mate is
dying before me and I am going mad. I am howling, and screeching
and dying inside because I just love him so so so much and I don't
know if I can live without him.

At lunchtime the next day Nick was still sleeping peacefully,
drifting occasionally into brief wakefulness. Although he was
at times uncomfortable he was never in great pain and never
needed morphine. Something happened that will seem strange
but wasn't strange at all at the time. I came down to eat and sat
in the kitchen with Charlotte and my mother and I heard a
familiar sound. It was a tap-tapping coming from upstairs. It
was the sound that Nick had always made when he walked with
his crutches along the landing. This time it sounded loud,
urgent and very clear. Charlotte and my mother looked at me
in surprise. Without thinking, I said, 'It's the ghost.' I realized
that I had heard this sound before, several times over the past
few days, but it had never been as loud, as purposeful, as clear
and yet it was only now, when confronted by others' quizzical
looks that I thought to wonder what it was.

Nick hadn't walked for some time. He was now barely con-
scious. There was no one else in the house at that moment.
I knew the neighbours were out, but went to double-check.
We heard it again, as clearly as before. Mum and Charlotte
said nothing. What can you say? I have since wondered if it
was Nick's parents coming to be with him at the end and then
to take him away. Or maybe he himself was already taking his
last journey. I have not heard the sound once since he died.

I have thought long and hard about writing down Nick's last
hours, and minutes. I have kept to myself some of the very

private moments and always will. But Nick chose to tell his story. And I feel a duty to finish his story for him – with the dignity he deserves, and with the dignity with which he died.

So this is how it happened.

None of us knew of course that it would happen so fast. Death has no timetable. That evening Mark Damazer came round. Nick, awake for a spell, didn't at first want to see him, kept shaking his head weakly, but then changed his mind. He insisted he sit up in his wheelchair. Charlotte and I lifted him out of bed and into his chair. He was still heavy and it was a struggle. He couldn't talk but made himself understood.

Mark sat with him in private. He held Nick's hand and told him how much he was loved by his audience and how much he was admired by the BBC. Nick tried to say something back, but was too weak to speak. Afterwards Mark said to me, 'If at any stage he becomes lucid, call me *instantly*, even if it's in the middle of the night. I want to hear what he wants to say.' It cannot have been easy for Mark. I admire him to this day for what he did.

Suzie spent time that evening just sitting quietly with Nick when I had to be away from his room.

Tom, Pete and Ali sat with their dad, together and alone. Tom kissed him goodnight and told him he loved him.

Joel and Benedict raced into his room before bedtime to say goodnight. Benedict kissed his face and Joel kissed his arm. Benedict said, 'Why does Daddy look so strange?' Both boys told him that they loved him.

At eleven o'clock Nick woke up and was restless. He was trying to say something to me but I couldn't understand. It was as if his whole body no longer responded to anything he asked of it, no longer worked. 'Darling, I *think* you want to listen to the opening of the Ashes and I'm really sorry if I've got that wrong. You know me and cricket...' I switched on his portable radio and twiddled with the tuner until I found the commentary from Down Under, then put his headphones in his ears. But I knew that wasn't what he wanted.

At around midnight he grew more restless and his breathing became heavy and laboured. Because I had Charlotte at my side I was calm. I asked her to stay in the room. Had she not been there I would have been terrified. I did not know how to be with someone who was so ill. Thirty minutes later it came to me suddenly that Nick was about to slip away. I didn't want to hold him back. I wanted to release him, allow him to step through to wherever he was going easily and gently. I was suddenly fearful that he would die slowly, agonizingly. I willed him to go now. 'It's OK, my darling,' I said. 'You can go.'

I stroked his head, put my arms around him and told him how much I loved him, thanked him for loving me, and said that when he woke up he would find himself in the garden at Rose Cottage with me by his side and the boys running in the grass.

And then he left me.

Death can be brutal. But it can also be beautiful.

ELEVEN

I remember kissing Daddy before he died. I woke up and called his name really loud but no voice came. I thought he'd gone shopping.

JOEL 4½

The angels took him to Heaven. I don't know what happens there because I've never been.

BENEDICT 4½

If it was hard to watch the man I love die, it was even harder to tell his children they had lost their father.

They bounded out of their bedroom as they did every morning, with tousled hair and crumpled blue-and-white checked pyjamas, one behind the other, together as always. Bendy clutched his favourite soft dog Patch by the hand and made me think of Christopher Robin. Both boys' faces were lit with excitement at the dawn of a new day.

I crouched down in front of them and looked them in the eyes. 'Darlings, something terribly sad has happened. Daddy died in the night. It's really, really sad and I'm so so sorry.'

They paused. They took in what I had said. They looked at Suzie, who was standing behind me. We all stood motionless. Then Bendy asked, 'Can we go and watch telly now?' It was not that they hadn't understood. It was the way any four-year-old would take in news so momentous, so impossible to comprehend, and process it, putting it away until the time felt right to take it out again.

I hadn't stopped to think how the boys would react to Nick's dying, so engrossed was I in caring for him and fearing for myself. But at that moment my instinct told me that what they needed was for as many things as possible to continue as normal. Or as near as dammit. They needed to know that the foundation stones of their small lives were still standing, even if the walls had been hit by a wrecking-ball.

I rang the boys' head teacher, Mrs Doyle, and told her the news. Then I drove them to school. Over the past few days, as I made that journey, I'd been looking at the winter sunlight angling across the tops of the bare trees, grieving to think that Nick would never leave his bed and see the sun shine again. And now he was dead.

The boys were muted, thoughtful. For all that I was relieved to be handing them over for the day to somebody else, I felt wretched about doing so.

Miss Keck, their class teacher, promised they would be cared for with compassion and understanding. I trusted her. Totally. Mrs Doyle gave me an envelope filled with sheaves of paper. It was material she had printed off the Internet. How to help bereaved children. It came to me then, in a flash, that I carried a double burden. I had my own grief to bear, and I could already feel it beginning to crush me. And I had my children's to bear too. The realization nearly brought me to my knees as I struggled back up the road to the car. It was months before I could look inside that envelope.

*

The first person I had called in the night was Mark. He never did find out what Nick had wanted to say to him, though some time later he told me he had worked it out for himself. He asked me when I would like the announcement to be made. 'On *The World at One*, of course,' I said. The timing of Nick's parting was perfect for news management. By dawn, Mark and the programme editor were in the office preparing an extended hour-long programme of dedication.

I rang Eddie first thing in the morning. He was there when I got back from school. He sat on the sofa where Nick had sat for so much of that last year, and cried. I spoke to Nick Sutton, Nick's closest colleague, and he cried too. 'I really loved him,' he said. Their tears meant much to me. For some reason I didn't cry at all. I was stunned. And exhausted. And totally disbelieving.

By mid-morning the house had filled with people. There was a sea of faces in my kitchen. I saw them all looking at me, as if I were an animal on the other side of a glass screen being subjected to some cruel and awful experiment. They offered to make tea. Suzie organized them, sorted food, took calls. Tom, Pete and Ali came, but I didn't know what to say to them. I had to remind myself that they had lost a father, that Suzie had lost a brother. But my own loss seemed so absurdly huge that I couldn't, in truth, see past it.

I removed myself to the sitting room to sit. Just to sit. And to be. Alone. Jeremy rang to ask after Nick and I told him. 'I'm so sorry,' he said, and I wondered whether he was sorry he hadn't been able to keep Nick alive. An old colleague rang on the off-chance to ask after me and when I told her what had happened she screamed. Then I spoke to a good friend of Nick's who said, 'Oh no, that's another one of my friends gone.' But this isn't about you, I thought furiously. It's about Nick, about me, about his children. It was an early lesson in the bewildering way some people react to death. And in the way that bereavement opens the floodgates to suppressed anger.

At one o'clock Shaun Ley, who had been standing in for Nick on *The World at One*, came on the radio and said, 'Our main headline today is that our colleague and friend Nick Clarke died this morning.' His voice cracked audibly. Over the next hour a succession of people – friends, colleagues, politicians – spoke about Nick's greatness. The tributes were superb, fitting, funny, moving. Nick was described as a great journalist, a great interviewer, a great broadcaster, one of the very best of his generation. At one point it occurred to me how strange it was that I, who knew him better than any of these people, wasn't there to say what a great husband and father he had also been.

Later that day Suzie and Alastair went to Chelsea Town Hall to register Nick's death. The certificate came home tucked inside a purple cardboard folder with a flower on the front.

The next day they took me to the undertakers, where a small and elderly-looking woman, who said her husband had died seventeen years before, smiled a lot and was uncomfortably cheerful. She showed me pictures of coffins and I stared at them, uncomprehending. She broke my silence with, 'If you're having a cremation we can only do the plywood ones, I'm afraid. The wooden ones don't fit into the furnace.'

Plywood or wood. I was supposed to make a choice. 'He's being cremated.' But even as I said it, I winced at the thought that the last thing I would ever buy for Nick was made of something as cheap and functional as plywood. But then

I reminded myself that he wouldn't care at all, that nothing mattered any more.

The woman closed her brochure happily. 'Plywood it is, then!'

I came home with the morning papers. Every one of them ran an article. Even the *Sun*. '*World at One* star Nick dies,' it said, and there was a photo of him with a caption – 'True pro'. Below it was a piece about Britney Spears.

I dumped the whole bundle on the table and sat down. So it's true, I thought. It's in the papers. He really is dead.

Then Suzie took me to see Father Gillean. I wanted him to lead the funeral at St Mary Abbots, rather than my local church. Father Gillean had offered Nick solace, and Nick had drawn comfort from the fact that St Mary Abbots School offered the boys a safe haven in their troubled world. It seemed fitting that it should take place in a building which displayed the kind of grandeur you'd associate with a cathedral. Beyond that, I had little interest in the proceedings. But in the blur of disbelief, indecision and confusion in which I stumbled through the preparations, Father Gillean guided without pushing, was compassionate while remaining dispassionate, made suggestions when I drew a blank. He thought of fitting hymns and suggested a variety of possible readings. He handled the process with extraordinary sensitivity, and for that I am for ever grateful. As Suzie and I sat in his study at the Vicarage that day and again a few days later, he was patient and thoughtful as we tried to create a service that would ... Would what? I didn't really know what I wanted beyond something that felt right. Right for me, that is. Funerals aren't for the departed. They are for those who are left behind.

As for my faith, I could feel it ebbing away that week. But

when Father Gillean said, 'You will meet him again one day,' I didn't share my doubts with him. Had I really believed I could join Nick by one simple act, I would gladly have gone to him there and then, and left this earth behind me. But right now I couldn't be sure Nick had gone to God, nor indeed that he would have wanted to. I couldn't work out where he was, and the only logical thing I could think was that his soul had entered mine. I thought it had probably done so just after he took his last breath, and there really were times when I sensed there was something of him in my heart, in my being, should I choose to seek and feel it there.

As I mused on these possibilities, I was interrupted by a phone call from Mark Damazer telling me the BBC was offering to pay for the funeral. So I chose an expensive and up-market florist, Orlando Hamilton, described in the newspapers as 'florist to the stars', though the truth is it was a matter of convenience, his shop being around the corner from home. Orlando was charming and promised me a stunning display. He suggested flowers I had never heard of and said he would be in the church from dawn creating the designs. People would later tell me they were indeed stunning, and I had to take their word for it. I wasn't going to be taking much in on that day.

Two days after Mark's call another of Nick's colleagues popped by. He told me he had 'great news'. 'The Beeb aren't just paying for the funeral,' he said, 'they're paying for the party too!'

I had no idea there was going to be a party.

Nick Sutton came round and helped me draw up a list of people who should be invited. Somehow I managed to put out of my mind the idea that everyone else would be 'celebrating' that day as we compiled our lists. Nick's, of course, included the names of a lot of very eminent people, politicians mainly. He asked me what I thought. I just wanted the people (my) Nick would have wanted, but it was too late to ask him now. There were, however, three or four on the list whom I really loathed. I asked Nick – who was going to be an usher – if he could ensure they sat right at the back, together on the same bench, which he did, and which brought a brief smile to both our faces. Before the day, I asked him to choose one of Nick's silk ties, to take it as a gift and to wear it at the event.

Then came the business of getting myself an outfit. It should have mattered so little, yet I cared so much about how I would look. I wanted to show people something about the woman Nick had married and I wanted to feel confident in myself. If Jackie Kennedy could do death with dignity, so could I. On eBay I bought a beautiful 1940s crepe wool dress, and I got a black coat and black shoes from Jigsaw. My friend Angela Levin took me to Harrods, where I bought the most expensive hat I have ever owned. It cost £275. It was black with a pheasant feather in the trim, and she assured me it looked very stylish. Angela made me feel I had chosen it myself when clearly I had little idea what I was doing. She held my hand as I stood at the cash desk.

As the days passed I fell into a strange, trance-like state. I looked at other people and barely saw them. I certainly didn't connect with any of them. I felt numb and exhausted, wobbly, mouldable, trying limply to put on a show with no script and no props. It was a show of coping – and I coped. Perhaps there was an echo of Nick's final performance on *Any Questions?*. I couldn't give in until the final curtain fell. Grief was slowly invading every cell of my body and setting to work at crushing my soul, but I had to keep it at arm's length for now. There was so much to do and all of it seemed unreal. I was sure that before long I would break down, but right now there was no space or time for that. Nothing stood still for long enough. I was being bombarded with questions, asked to make decisions, and I marvelled that people thought I was capable of rational thought. The funeral directors wanted to know how to dress Nick's body for the coffin. Reluctantly I handed over the Strellson linen jacket I had bought him for his return to work in the summer, reluctant because I hated the thought of it being consigned to the fire. I chose a tie, too. An orange silk tie, bright and bold, the one he had worn on his first day back at work. I asked them to return his wedding ring and I hung it on a chain around my neck.

As the funeral approached I was also struggling with the sense that Nick was in effect public property, his death an excuse for public grieving, his funeral a very public display of respect. Reading the articles in the papers, watching the reports on television, or listening to the radio, and seeing the tributes that listeners wrote on the BBC website, it was as if two men had died, my Nick and theirs. The public Nick and the private. 'He was my lunchtime companion for years,' wrote one lady on the BBC website, while another said, 'I had not realized how many tears one could cry for someone not known personally,' and another, 'It's a dark day for the listening audience.' He had touched so many people, been a friend in their homes, a trusted confidant they felt they knew personally through the power of electronic communication, who had seduced them with his velvet-lined voice. And now these fans — these conquests — wrote in their thousands. 'Perhaps God needed a powerful voice up in heaven. Certainly if I ever meet God I would expect him to have a voice like Nick Clarke,' was one comment that made me smile, but the many who said, 'I hope you find comfort from the knowledge that he was loved and admired by so many,' brought little. Because nothing, but nothing could comfort me at that moment.

There were times when being reminded of what a great man I had lost made my already unbearable pain feel even greater.

Two days before the funeral my burning desire to claim back the private man did find an outlet. I was asked to write an article for *The Times* called 'The Nick I Knew', a tribute to a husband and father. And so in an outpouring of love I talked of Nick's joy of cooking, his love of good food, of good wine and good hotels, of his generosity and modesty, of the lessons he had taught me in how truly to love, of his wonderment at becoming a father second time around and of the love he had showered on his two little boys. It was a burden released. The article appeared with photos of our wedding day and of our family holiday in Corsica, just two and a half years before. And as I re-read the piece I had written through eyes blurred with tears I realized that something remarkable had happened. I had never had any confidence in my ability as a writer and would always pass my words to Nick, the master of language, watching anxiously as he went through them line by line, refining, correcting and improving my prose with his inimitable, pared-back style. Yet now the words had tumbled out, and when they landed on the page they looked good. Phrases grew from the jumble in my head and spilled out almost poetically. In my grief Nick was giving me a voice. Or maybe I had been right about where he was, and he really had entered my soul.

*

And what of the boys in that mad, disorienting week where people worried about parties, flowers and frocks, and I stumbled about, hobbled by the pain of loss? At home the stream of visitors distracted them for me, when I could no longer manage to give to them, so drained was I from surviving myself. At school they had real, solid, bedrock support. That first day, after I had entrusted them to her, Miss Keck sat the class down in a circle with Joel on one side of her and Benedict on the other. 'Joel and Benedict, I'd like you to tell your friends what has happened to you,' she said, and when they had done she invited other children to share their own stories of losing someone precious. One had lost a dog, another a grandmother. One child said his granddad was so old he was 'nearly going to Heaven' too. Above all, she tried to normalize the boys' loss so that there was no awkwardness or embarrassment. Then she took them to see Mrs Doyle, the head teacher, so that they could tell her their story too. Between the four of them they tried to figure out where Daddy had gone. They concluded that the angels must have taken him to Heaven in the night, that he was now watching his boys from Up There. They couldn't see him, of course, but he could see them, of that they were sure. 'Will he be able to see us if we go on holiday to France?' asked Bendy. Yes, said Mrs Doyle, he would. Then Joel asked if he could go and play with his red toy bus.

The next day was harder. They didn't want to leave me and ran screaming round the house. I think they were scared the angels would take me next if they weren't by my side. We arrived at school late and Miss Keck met us at the side entrance to shepherd the boys indoors, calmly and assuredly. She did the same thing for the rest of the term and it seemed to ease their anxiety about being parted from me. That same day the boys were spared having to attend assembly, where the rest of the school was told what had happened. Miss Keck was determined that everyone should hear the same story, that there should be no whispering, guessing or rumours. For her, the shared faith of the school made the task of answering the children's questions easier.

In the following days, as reality sank in, the boys clung to her more and more. She carried on talking openly about their dad so that they would know that the subject was never out of bounds, and when she did so she reminded them that he had died and wouldn't be coming back. It seemed harsh, but she knew about 'magical thinking', when children believe they can make something happen just by thinking about it. And who could blame the boys if they thought they could will their daddy back, especially in the run-up to Christmas, when Santa makes every child's wishes come true.

There was, however, one moment that week that left Bendy distraught. One of his friends claimed he'd already been to Heaven *and come back*. If it could happen to him, it could happen to Daddy. It took Miss Keck's gentle intervention to make the friend admit to Bendy that he had made the story up.

We have much to thank her for. Through her sensitivity, intuition and compassion in those early days, when I was incapable of offering the care the boys needed, she single-handedly helped them to understand that their father had died, to absorb that knowledge and to cope with it – as they still cope, to this day.

I never doubted that Benedict and Joel should go to the funeral. My only worry had to do with the coffin, and the questions they were bound to ask. If Daddy had gone to Heaven, how could his body still be in there? Children will find any chink in your intellectual armour. The solution I came up with was to tell them that Daddy would need a few things with him in Heaven and we had to choose what to send him. Someone would then put everything into a big wooden box which we would take to church and leave for the angels to take up to him when they had a spare moment. We agreed Daddy would want some clothes and some nice wine. 'I think he'll want tomato ketchup and lasagne,' said Benedict. 'And mayonnaise,' said Joel.

The funeral was on the morning of Friday, 1 December 2006. The boys wore their school uniforms: dark blue sweatshirts and grey trousers. They were wide-eyed, sombre and subdued. We each held a single rose, terracotta-coloured, like the ones I had bought Nick two weeks before he died and which I had placed opposite the bed, against the light of the window, where he could see them all day. 'That's my favourite colour,' he said. All those years and I had never known.

We waited in silence outside the austere Victorian wooden doors leading into St Mary Abbots Church. Next to us was the school, around us were the old gravestones. It was cold. Two policemen slipped out of a side door. I guessed they were doing security checks. After all, some very important people were coming to the funeral. Nick's coffin was held aloft by four men in black. On the sides were pictures the boys had made with Miss Keck. And messages. 'We love you, Daddy.'

We must have made a tragic scene as we walked up the aisle, the boys and I. I was struggling to work out how it could be that the lifeless body of the man who had made sense of life, the father of those tiny and bewildered boys at my side, was lying there in that box. I remember feeling strong, and being surprised by the fact. Maybe it was the tranquillizers I had taken; maybe it was Nick giving me strength. There were hundreds of people, but I only noticed a handful of faces. We sat down next to Suzie and Tom, Nick's oldest son. Behind us I noticed a dog, then realized it was David Blunkett's guide dog. I noticed John Humphrys had taken a front pew, which seemed strange as he wasn't really a friend. The choir sang beautifully. Mark Damazer and Tessa Jowell both spoke, and then I read a Bible passage, from Corinthians, the one with the memorable phrase, 'without love I am nothing', the one which ends with, 'And now these three remain: faith, hope and love. But the greatest of these is love.'

Then I read some words I had written.

I chose that reading because love lay at the heart of everything Nick and I shared, everything we did, everything we felt. We gave and received in abundance and in the last, difficult year of Nick's life we found new heights – a level of unconditional love that carried us through and brought us even closer together. How true I feel it is that without love I am nothing.

I wish that sharing this moment with so many people could bring me strength. In truth, the outpouring of loving tributes serves only to highlight the enormity of what I have lost and to increase my pain – for there is a gulf between your loss and mine.

We have all lost a friend. I have lost the man I loved and with him all the hopes and dreams that mapped out the landscape of our joint lives. My grief is deep beyond anything I have ever known.

But I am lucky to have shared nineteen years with a man whose kindness, goodness, generosity, humour and brilliance shone in every aspect of his life, the professional, the friendships, the loving husband, the doting dad.

I am sad though for two little boys who knew his love for just four years – too short – their loss is greater than any of ours. Joel and Benedict are here this morning to help send this wooden box to Heaven where Daddy is already waiting. They know it's full of all the things he needs: clothes, nice food, tomato ketchup, mayonnaise and most important, of course, lots of bottles of wine. The angels will be carrying it to Heaven later today, my darlings.

Towards the end, Nick showed so much courage, selflessness and even humour.

I want everyone to know that Nick died peacefully at home, in my arms, as I told him how deeply I loved him. Death can be brutal, but Nick's was not and for that I will forever be thankful. I thank God that I was by his side and that he knew to his last breath that he was truly loved.

Everyone laughed at the tomato ketchup bit. At the end when I looked up I saw that nearly everyone was crying.

The boys sat almost perfectly still through the whole service, overawed and mesmerized by the electrifying atmosphere. People sitting near reached out hands to comfort them. Miss Keck sat behind us and passed them cuddly toys when they looked distracted. Afterwards they went back to school with her while I stood outside the church, a wraith-like figure in black, on her own, lost, as people came up and spoke to me. I saw Father Gillean watching me the whole time. Watching, checking, caring. Too many people kissed me. I started to feel grubby. A couple of the politicians were humble enough to tell me who they were. Like Lord Falconer, whom I didn't recognize and who just said, 'I'm Charlie Falconer.' I did recognize Michael Howard and noticed he had an incredibly kind smile. Mark Thompson, the BBC's Director-General, towered over me. I remember thinking that he and the BBC's Director of Radio, Jenny Abramsky, standing next to him looked as if they had just come out of a meeting and were off to another. I had nothing of any consequence to say to anyone. I mumbled my thanks, over and over. Thanks for what, I wasn't sure.

I noticed that a lot of people didn't come up to me. Perhaps they were worried about getting to the party. Paid for by the BBC.

Only the family and very close friends came to the West London Crematorium, but I left the boys at school. Father Gillean had everything organized. He led the prayers, and took charge of proceedings. I didn't like it one bit. After the magnificence of the church service, the babble of talk coming through the walls from the people who had preceded us made the whole business seem mundane, routine, peremptory, an everyday event, whereas this was one of the rites of passage which either accompany our arrival on earth, or our departure, or some of the momentous occasions in between. In the end, the whole thing hinged on me. It was I who had to give the nod, to choose the moment when Nick's coffin would start its move away from me over the roller-bars towards the brown curtains, behind which, I imagined, was the wall of fire waiting to consume it all. I wondered as I stood there, leaning against the platform on which the coffin lay, my hands clinging to its sides, why I didn't scream, break down, fall to the floor, try to hold on to the coffin and refuse to let go. But I just stood. And then said goodbye.

I thought briefly of that hour-glass, the one which I always knew was measuring the span of my days with Nick from the very beginning, the one that had too little sand in it from the start. It was saying to me now, Your time is up, and you always knew it would be, so don't be surprised.

As the coffin slid away I read for the final time the note I had written on my wreath of terracotta roses. 'My Darling Nick. Thank you for the greatest gift: Love.'

At home, cakes and biscuits and cups of tea appeared for the handful of people who were with me rather than at the party. Mark told me I had spoken magnificently, and I felt proud because I wanted Nick to be proud of me and because I wanted to show everyone else what I could do for the love of him.

By the time I had sent everyone on their way it was Saturday afternoon, and the house was quiet but for the sound of the boys. I had a journey to make, a journey that felt as wide and as long and as deep and as vast as an ocean – and just as cold and daunting. I desperately wanted to start that journey, though I had no idea what lay along its route. I simply had to move somewhere, to put some distance between me and the utter wretchedness of the place where I was just then. All I knew was that at some stage along it things could only be better than the sheer horror of where I was now and I wanted to start making my way to that place.

What I didn't know was just how hard the journey would be.

TWELVE

Mummy's sad because of Daddy. She misses him, she wants him on earth ...

JOEL 4½

Yes, she misses his kisses, his hugs, his cooking and his talking.

BENEDICT 4½

When all the visitors had finally left and the house was empty, I was free – almost free – to let my grief explode. All I had to do was hold it at bay for an hour or so every morning until the boys were at school. Then I could succumb, sinking to my knees on the kitchen floor, sobbing uncontrollably, my face contorted with pain and my fists beating the floorboards in an agony of loss. I begged Nick to come back to me. I pleaded with him to tell me that he understood how much I loved him. And I wailed and wailed until my voice became hoarse.

It was unlike anything I have known. It was inhuman, bestial. Gritting my teeth, clenching the muscles of my mouth and neck and locking my hands and arms in a fierce grip, I tried to brace myself against the waves of what I knew to be the worst emotional pain that I, or any human being, ever, could have felt. It was piercing, searing, stifling. Instead of offering me some sort of release, it seemed to tighten its hold on me.

I thought it was going to destroy me, and was genuinely surprised when I survived each successive onslaught. The discovery that I could withstand it encouraged me to face the pain head-on and step as deep inside it as I could. I had no desire to shy away from any of it. Besides, I knew there was no hiding from it. It would find me anyway.

The grief came in waves, pounding against me relentlessly, with a tidal insistence. The distractions of daily life only made things worse: every time I found escape in some routine task like preparing a meal I would have to face reality all over again. There were three plates, not four. Three forks, three spoons, three baked potatoes. Not four. It seemed that each day Nick died a hundred times over as the horror of my loss hit home afresh, leaving me gasping with shock as I lost him yet again. And when the broken waves of grief eventually ebbed away I lay moaning like a sick animal, blinded behind more tears than I ever knew I had.

I soon discovered that tears bring no real relief. Yes, they stop flowing eventually, but only because, finally, you exhaust the supply. Then your body gets to work and replenishes the well, and it starts all over again.

Somehow I managed to hang on to a semblance of normality when I had to. I'd brush my hair, put on a pair of sunglasses to hide my swollen eyes, and set off on the school run or the trip to the supermarket. When the boys were at home I did my best to stem the flow of tears, but more often than not I was defeated. '*Please don't cry, Mummy, pleeeeease stop,*' became the boys' mantra. These two perplexed four-year-olds were trying to cope with the loss of their father – and my incessant crying was making it worse.

I knew that I had to try to pull myself together for their sake.

I sensed that we had to talk, however painful it was for me. So at bedtime, when the boys were in a reflective mood, I would encourage them to explore a subject that was beyond their comprehension – even though I was no further along the way to dealing with it than they were. They searched for logic in a world that made no sense:

Mummy, why did Daddy die?

Because he was poorly . . .

So why did they have to cut off his leg?

Because it was very poorly. But then the poorly things spread throughout his whole body and he became very, very poorly.

But if he had had a plastic leg he wouldn't have died. Why didn't you get him one . . .? Mummy, WHY?

I watched in amazement as they did what grieving children do, as their young minds flitted in and out of grief with astonishing ease:

Mummy, did God want Daddy to die?

Well, no, but he can't stop people from dying.

Mummy, can I look at a picture of the Eurostar on your computer tomorrow?

I had no such facility. Once the boys were asleep, the waves of pain would visit me again and I began to understand for the first time why no one ever tells you about the torment that is grief. It is greater than you can know. It takes you to a terrifying place located at the outer edges of human tolerance. And at its furthest and most frightening point it plays one last card as it reminds you – with seeming glee – that the one person who always rescued you from the brink, who was always there for you at the worst of times and whom you now need more than ever, is not there, is not anywhere, and never will be again. The breast that you would lean on, the arms that would embrace you, are not there. In their place is a howling void.

My evenings were empty and bitingly lonely. The phone had virtually stopped ringing and when it did ring I couldn't muster the energy to conduct a conversation. Neither could I find the strength to return messages left on the machine. Sometimes a caller left a follow-up message, some of them bristling slightly with irritation that I hadn't responded to the first. None made a third. What struck me most in those early days and weeks was that I heard nothing from most of Nick's closest friends or colleagues, nor from people with whom we had shared the roller-coaster ride of the past year. Nick's sister Suzie rang regularly and listened to my outpourings, as did my friend Daniel. Two ladies from my church called. My neighbour Liz brought food to coax me into eating, though the sight of food turned my stomach. From the rest there was silence or formal letters.

What I wanted, more than anything, was for people to keep calling even if I couldn't talk, to leave messages of comfort even if I could barely bring myself to utter a thank you, or to come and sit with me while I cried and share my grief – and our memories of Nick. But people heard my silence, saw my withdrawal, and misinterpreted it as a desire to be left alone. Or simply couldn't find the courage to confront my pain.

So my evenings dragged by. Watching television in the room where Nick and I had done so almost nightly was now out of the question. I retreated to my desk and sorted through paperwork that was stacking up frighteningly fast as I began to take over the bills and cancel direct debits in his bank account. I trawled through websites on sarcomas trying to establish why Nick had fallen prey to this disease, or searched for information on clinical trials – one Google search threw up: 'Sarcomas:

Feed your passion on eBay.co.uk.' – before I realized the utter futility of what I was doing. I found comfort though in reading what I hadn't had the courage to read when he was alive: 'The prognosis for patients with epithelioid sarcoma is poor.' It helped to know that Nick's death might have been inevitable, rather than a statistical anomaly.

Eventually exhaustion got the better of pain. I would go to bed as quickly as I could so as not to dwell on the fact that I was lying where once we had lain in each other's arms and where, just weeks before, Nick had lived his last. Sleep came slowly, but when it did, there was no respite there. I entered a world of dreams, in which Nick was well and unaware of the fate that awaited him, smiling happily and chatting obliviously, though I knew he was days from death. *He mustn't know what's going to happen*, I would think as I kept up a pretence of good cheer. I smelled his skin in those dreams, heard his voice, saw his smile, felt his warmth, felt the tension of fear rising in me as I shielded him from the awful truth. Waking from his presence was torture.

And so, un-refreshed, each new day was a screaming, moaning, snivelling hell of unwanted isolation. Occasionally I wondered what the neighbours thought about the animal wails they heard through the walls, but I hardly cared. I was existing in a different place from everyone else. While the world carried on as if nothing had happened, I started to feel I was no longer part of it.

People say that time is a great healer. I knew from the outset that time wouldn't heal this pain. Grief is an illness for which there is no cure. I could only hope that time would teach me how to live with, and survive, this cruel new state of being. And survive I had to, because I had two small sons to care for, and Christmas was approaching. The boys deserved the best I could offer.

A few days before the end of term, St Mary Abbots Reception Class performed its nativity play. This was the first event of many that I would attend on my own, the first of many where the boys would perform only for their mother, and I realized that each and every event like this would now serve to remind all three of us that we were a family without a husband and a father.

Benedict had been cast as Joseph. He sat in the middle of the stage beaming, delighted to be the centre of attention. Joel, as a shepherd, was due to introduce the play, but when it came to it he almost refused to go on. I watched with a proud but heavy heart and marvelled at those small boys' bravery at coping with their loss even when all eyes were on them. But throughout the performance I felt the spotlight was in fact on me, illuminating a huge sign above my head which read 'tragedy'. Whenever I looked at any of the other parents they hastily averted their eyes.

I don't know what I expected, but I hadn't expected this. Since the day Nick had died only one mother had spoken to me and offered her condolences as I made the trek to and from the car to the school. And now at this poignant moment where parents watched their children's first Christmas play, all of us squashed together on tiny seats and ostensibly sharing the joy of the moment, only the head teacher came and offered me a quiet word about how hard it must have been.

Lonely and isolated as I felt, I still had to go to the school every day, but it was becoming unbearable. As I walked down the narrow path to the school gates, edging my way past other parents, I felt so exposed I may as well have been naked. Everyone knew what had happened to us yet nobody said anything. Slowly my wretchedness turned to anger that a group of people who wore the badge of Christianity were unable to give me what I so needed – a few brief words of comfort, an embrace, a welcome into a fold of which I and the boys were an integral part. What was wrong with them? Even my postman managed to find words – and the courage to say them to my face.

But school wasn't the only place where I met this wall of silence, this apparent indifference. It was a pattern that would be repeated over the following months, and a pattern – I came to realize – that is experienced by most people who are bereaved. I learned that others seem unable to look us in the eye or speak about loss. For the most part they are probably scared, but their silence exacerbates the very pain of the isolation that the bereaved person is suffering. From my local church I heard almost nothing, save the concerned ladies who dropped by. I stopped attending. And I stopped praying, for I felt there was nothing left to pray for. Hope had been taken from me, now I cared little that only despair remained. Thank goodness for Father Gillean, who was at the school gates most days, reaching out a hand of understanding or a word of sympathy. 'Jesus sat by Lazarus's grave and wept,' he told me one day. 'He knew the pain of loss.' I nodded irritatedly, wondering how Jesus could ever have understood pain like mine. Father Gillean must have sensed that his religious offerings left me dry, as he never made a biblical reference again. I confessed to him many months later that I had stopped praying and he responded by saying gently, 'Maybe you could think about praying for the boys.' And I did.

Many a morning my destination after the school run was Sainsbury's, but there in the entrance, amongst the flowers on display and staring me in the face, was another wounding reminder, the very same roses I had bought for Nick when he was dying, the ones he said were his favourites, the ones the boys and I had carried down the aisle at the church and placed on his coffin at the crematorium. Such is the delirium of grief that I seriously thought of summoning the manager and asking him to put the display somewhere else.

Wandering round the shop, my body feeling like lead, my sunglasses hiding my eyes, trying to summon the energy to buy food when I had no interest in eating, I looked in envy at the people around me, unburdened by loss, dry of tears, some on their mobiles to husbands, wives, partners, discussing dinner, an everyday act, insignificant, instantly forgettable and one which I yearned to be able to follow.

Where I stood I seemed to be at the edge of a ravine, with the rest of the world on the other side of a deep dark chasm. On my side it was windswept and cold. On the other side, visible but utterly out of reach, were the red and green hues of Christmas preparation and celebration, families with fathers, wives with husbands, parents with confident, smiling children. The casual Christmas greetings, the whole frivolous business of people dressing up as Santa, made me want to lie on the floor and weep again.

On Christmas Eve I took the boys to the children's service at St Mary Abbots Church where, just days before at Nick's funeral, people had wept openly in an atmosphere tense with disbelief and sorrow. Now children ran riot in the aisles, and everyone wore their Yuletide cheeriness. Across the pews I saw the school head sitting with her husband, their two young boys intertwined between them, a family, whole, untouched by tragedy, close, together, loving, alive. As I watched in envy her husband stretched his hand carelessly across the back of the pew and ran it down the ponytail of blonde hair on the back of her head.

On Christmas Day the boys were up at six thirty, dragging me from my bed to open the few presents I had managed to buy. My task that morning was to prepare Christmas dinner for eight – Suzie and her husband Alastair and their three grown-up girls were travelling from Derbyshire that morning to be with us. I started on a chestnut roast from the recipe that Nick had used every Christmas we had spent together. It was so much harder than I had anticipated. How often had I complained to Nick about the time he took to prepare this very meal while I paced around in the early afternoon buzzing with hunger. I was soon way behind time and didn't serve the meal until well past three o'clock. The roast had disintegrated into a brown mush, the vegetables were cold. It seemed like a hackneyed metaphor for my state of mind.

Somehow we contrived some brighter moments. The girls had decorated a box and filled it with shredded paper in which they had hidden presents for the boys. We laughed at the sight of them delving into the box and ripping the paper, their delight at what they found lasting a few moments before they dived in to pull out the next gift. The cloud of tragedy that hung over us seemed to have retreated briefly.

That afternoon Suzie, Alastair and the girls took Joel and Benedict to the park: they realized that I wanted to be on my own. I had been putting off this moment, but now I was ready to face it. In the bottom drawer of the Wellington chest in which

Nick stored his papers was that envelope marked 'Barbara, in the event that . . .' Inside were the letters he had written the day before his operation, just over a year ago, six in all, one for each of his five children and one for me. They were all sealed.

My letter was short and although written in his tight, neat hand it betrayed the tension he had been feeling in the uncharacteristic slope of the words across the page. It was filled with love, with honesty and a few wry asides, and it ended, 'I know that in the weeks to come you will find the strength to cope.' It was designed to be read when he was dead and was worded in the present tense, as if he were speaking from beyond the grave. He told me to be brave and he said he had faith that the strength I had shown in the weeks since he first fell ill would carry me through now. The words, and that writing that I knew so well, took me to the deepest place I had been. 'You have no idea what this is like,' I screamed at him in my head and as I tried to feel sorry for him for having lost his life, for having left his boys, for having forfeited the right to see his children grow up, for not having lived until his three score years and ten, for missing out on the mellow years that he could have looked forward to in retirement, for simply not being there to see, breathe, hear and feel, I couldn't. Because I knew that it was worse for me. To be left behind. And as I cried, all I could think, selfishly, was why was it not me who had gone and been spared this horror? Why, indeed, not me . . .?

With the festivities over, I decided to take the boys to Somerset. My friend Daniel refused to allow me to go alone and came with us. I was shocked by the way our country retreat appeared to me on that winter's day. The place on which Nick and I had lavished so much love was now etched in misery. The seat where Nick had sat on warm afternoons reading the papers now stood bare and awkward on a wet lawn strewn with black twigs and dead leaves. I hated being there.

A friend brought round a present for the boys. It was an electric train set. A fight broke out immediately, the boys tussling over an electric coach and yanking the wheels off. I let rip. I screamed, I cursed and I called them names, grabbing the carriage brutally from their tiny hands and flinging it against the wall. The two terrified faces looking at me in bewilderment pulled the plug on my fury and I collapsed on the floor, sobbing hysterically. It was the first time the boys had seen the full stranglehold that grief had on me, and they didn't understand. Daniel came in from the greenhouse where he had been fetching firewood. He gently picked the carriage up, put his arm round my shoulders and soothed the boys.

I'll never know what damage I did to them. That incident wasn't the last. As the reality hit home that Daddy was never coming back, so the fear set in for them. I could not cope with the continuing burden I bore. I was exhausted. For a year I had been a carer and I was now a griever, widowed, bereaved, emotionally depleted, depressed. My sleep was interrupted night after night as Joel would wake, scared, shouting for me. Through puffy, barely seeing eyes I would stumble down the corridor, where I found him confused and agitated, with Benedict starting to wake up as well. My patience with them would last mere minutes before I lost control. Then I would resort to shouting, screaming and cursing as I let loose all my frustration, pain and growing anger on the only two people who really mattered to me. The boys would run after me as I returned sobbing to my room and plead with me to love them. Riddled with guilt, I took them into my bed and held them through the night.

In their grief and bewilderment at the loss of their dad, the boys looked to me. And I wasn't there for them. Indeed, I grew to envy them. It was all right for them, I reasoned. They had me. I had no one. It shames me to think of what I did and of what I thought. They didn't cry in grief and they didn't express their sorrow verbally, and so, too readily, I set their needs aside. Only once did Joel put into words what he felt when Nick died: 'It was like an electric shock going through me,' he said. But I know their pain was very, very deep. For months Joel would fly into rages, panic if he lost sight of me and complain of a tummy ache, a classic 'symptom' of child bereavement. Made worse, no doubt, by the stress he felt from my dreadful behaviour. Benedict reverted at times to baby behaviour, lying on the floor and asking for a bottle of milk.

Early in the New Year we were visited by the palliative care unit social worker who had been assigned to us when Nick was ill and I was struggling to manage things at home. Marion was a grey-haired softly-spoken woman who arrived with a bundle of books which, she explained, I might want to read to the boys. During the course of our conversation she offered to come and talk to them and to do some 'bereavement work'.

The very idea of having some kind of support with the boys flooded me with a sense of relief and gratitude. A few days later I kept the boys home from school and waited for her arrival.

It started well. Joel and Benedict wanted to put on a 'show' for us and we accepted 'tickets', watched and applauded. The show consisted largely of their racing round the room, banging into things, screaming and hitting each other.

We sat down at the kitchen table and Marion produced a glove puppet for each of the boys. She then handed them some coloured pencils, paper and a ruler with brightly coloured dinosaurs etched on it. The boys were overcome by the sight of these new toys and started to play up: both the ruler and the puppets soon became weapons as they started to fight. Marion tried to get them to focus on the task in hand, to pretend to be the glove puppet and to tell her what they were feeling. The chaos simply escalated. I suggested I leave the room as I thought I was distracting them and I sat on the stairs listening intently. The role-play wasn't happening and the fighting wasn't stopping. One phrase she uttered has stayed in my mind. 'Now, boys, we did agree not to be naughty, didn't we?' It was a farce, and it finished in a chaos of screams. When Marion left she smiled wearily and said, 'We didn't achieve much, did we?' I closed the door after her and burst into tears at what I saw as my own failings. The boys needed help, but I was the least equipped to provide it.

I couldn't bear to see Marion again. And luckily I didn't need to. When I spoke despairingly to Miss Keck, the boys' teacher, about what had happened she didn't hesitate. 'Why don't you let me do something with them?' she asked.

Sally Keck had never counselled a bereaved child before, but she combined her intuition and instinct with professional drive and curiosity. She also held an ace in her hand: the boys adored, respected and trusted her, a relationship already cemented by her being so readily available to them in the days after Nick died.

Her plan was to take each of the boys out of playtime once a week and sit together in a private room talking, openly, easily, safely, and building a set of memories for the boys of their father before and during his illness. At the beginning of their first session Miss Keck took them to W H Smith on Kensington High Street to choose a file, pencils and paper, which they did with relish. She then stuck a label on the front of the files: 'My Memories of Daddy, by Joel aged 4', said Joel's. By the end of the first session he'd persuaded her to amend the figure so that it read 'aged 4½'.

Working with a book called *Puddles, Muddles and Sunshine* – produced by the charity Winston's Wish, which offers help to bereaved children – she began a tour of the boys' minds and memories, and in doing so drew from them a version of their grief which they would never have shared with me. It was the kindest and most helpful thing anyone did for them.

Every word they spoke was transcribed into their files, creating a record of how they were feeling. The first time I parted the pages I could hardly see the words through my tears.

I didn't know why the angels took Daddy away. I was cross. I was shouting all around the house like a tiger roaring.

JOEL

I wasn't expecting him to die and when I woke up he had just died and gone to heaven. I felt cross at myself … I don't know why … I said half his name and I realized he wasn't there.

BENEDICT

I'm lonely and worried because it's just Bendy and Mummy now. I'm scared that when Mummy is in her room the angels will take her. There's been a pain in my tummy all day.

JOEL

I've never felt happy since Daddy died, not ever. He made me feel happy when he was alive because he always hugged me when I was sad. I miss my Daddy. I miss his hugs, his kisses, him talking … He used to say nice things like 'I love you'.

BENEDICT

I do know Daddy is hugging me but I don't know if it's a real hug or hugging my brain.

JOEL

They never cried during these sessions with Miss Keck. They were as matter-of-fact about Nick's passing as they were about the sibling frustrations that rankled day after day – and which did make me smile:

I'm cross with Bendy because he's got more furry dogs than me. I've only got three and he's got seven. I feel like stealing all his dogs and never giving them back …

Their words sketched a picture of death seen through a small child's eyes, watching without fully understanding and always trying to make sense of something that essentially made no sense at all.

I don't know how Daddy got poorly – I think his leg muscle broke. He went to the doctors but they couldn't get a plastic leg so he died. If he had had a plastic leg he would still be alive. The only people who make people alive and make people die are God and Jesus …

JOEL

Cancer is the baddest illness in the world and sometimes you die. You can only get better if loads and loads of doctors come. Daddy only had ten or eleven. I think he needed thirty to be alive.

BENEDICT

I hate cancer. I wish I could see it and hurt it.

JOEL

I began to see how different their grief was from mine. They had no sense of the magnitude of what they had lost, of the tragedy of it, or of the size of their loss projected into the future. They didn't look ahead and see a life without a father in the way that I recoiled at the sight of my life unfolding without a husband. Neither did they grapple daily with the angst, guilt and torture I felt as I remembered Nick's last days and thought of what he himself had lost, of all the years he might have lived, of all the love he still had to give and to receive and of all that he was missing from watching his two small sons grow up. The boys dipped in and out of their sorrow, puzzled that they could still feel happiness when everyone around them was so unremittingly sad.

I feel happy about Daddy when I am busy and I forget to think about him. I feel confused because I don't know how you can feel sad about Daddy and feel happy too.

BENEDICT

I feel happy about Daddy today. I heard him in the night – he called me Darling. He said, 'Don't worry, Darling' just before I went to bed. I think he's saying he's OK in Heaven and I have lovely food from you and Bendy and a lovely lasagne. Maybe he's saying thank you, the mayonnaise is delicious … I still love Daddy, even more actually, I love him all the same, because he's my Daddy, he always will be.

JOEL

What they never told Miss Keck was that I shouted at them at night, or that they often found me sobbing on the floor.

I confessed to her, but she said they never mentioned it, whether out of loyalty, disbelief or fear.

While bereaved children only get whatever help is offered to them, bereaved adults can seek help out. And I now needed some myself. It came in the form of a woman called Sarah Kershaw, a volunteer for the bereavement charity Cruse, whose local office I called just days after Nick died in the hope that someone, somewhere, would really understand what I was feeling and be able to stop me falling apart. Sarah came with many years of experience counselling people who had lost loved ones, and a listening and understanding ear that I could find nowhere else. She wasn't paid for her skills and she didn't even know me, yet she gave me more than anyone. She said she would see me once a week for as long as I needed her to. 'It might be months, it might be years,' she said, 'but one day you'll tell me you don't need to see me again.' Once her visits started I found it hard to picture a day when I would *ever* say goodbye to what she offered.

Sarah's promise to me was that I would, in time, get stronger. She couldn't make the grief less painful and she couldn't make me feel 'better', but she could, and did, help me make sense of this hideous new world in which I now lived. I cried. I talked. And I began to unburden myself, sometimes nervously. Confessing to what I was doing to the boys was hard, but I needed to find a way to stop. What I went on to admit to her was even harder. 'I don't think I love them,' I sobbed, appalled at the very words I was speaking. 'They feel like a burden to me and I can't find any love for them. How could I lose that most basic instinct, maternal love? There must be something wrong with me.'

'Grief is the most powerful emotion there is,' said Sarah. 'It wipes away all other feelings, even love, but the love *will* return, I promise you.' And she helped me work out ways to manage my rage with the boys, by dealing with it as soon as I felt it rising, rather than leaving it to take control of me. 'When you feel the anger coming, find something to hit, a wall or the floor, and do it before the anger escalates,' she said. And I did, and it worked.

It was the first of many times that Sarah helped me to piece together the splinters of my life.

Coursing through those delirious days and weeks after Nick died was a nagging practical worry. Money. Overnight, my income had dried up. The consultancy work I had been undertaking had drawn to a close some months earlier. Laying my hands on any of the money due on Nick's death would take weeks, if not months, and even then I couldn't see how it would provide enough to live on.

Nick and I had always haemorrhaged money, though we never quite understood why. Since the boys had arrived we had lived a comfortable life with few extravagances, but we never got to the end of a month without running up an overdraft. Now the sight of our regular monthly outgoings petrified me. They ran into thousands, from the mortgage on the house, the cottage, and on a rental flat we had bought as a retirement investment, to credit-card payments and a long list of monthly payments from household bills to the £200 Nick gave every month to a cancer research charity.

Looking at the figures knotted my stomach. I wondered whether those around me assumed it 'would all be taken care of' and that I would be a wealthy widow. But it's rarely like that and wasn't going to be for me. I was going to have to work out a way of using what assets we had to keep the three of us going until I was in a fit state to find work.

The worry helped me dry the tears for short spells, sort through the paperwork and start the process of claiming the money due from various investments and a couple of small life policies. I thought I could manage the process myself, but the simple act of finding and sorting the papers required more stamina than I could muster, so I decided to hand the process to a solicitor.

I made an appointment at the practice in Chiswick in West London where, a few years previously, Nick and I had drawn up our wills. Thankfully we had agreed on the simplest and most straightforward formula in order to ease the way of whoever would be the one carrying out this task. We'd both left everything to the other and had had a private agreement – trusting each other totally – as to what should happen to everything.

I took an instant dislike to the solicitor I met. She had a brusque and charmless manner, which seemed inappropriate in the circumstances, and she reminded me of the ugly mother in the film *My Big Fat Greek Wedding*. Well, she had a Greek name. Her first words were, 'Do you have any questions?' to which I replied, 'How much do you charge?' She told me it would be £185 an hour, plus VAT. OK, I said, we'd better not hang about.

She wrote a list of Nick's and my joint and individual assets and told me I had to get a valuation for 'everything' we owned. This seemed a monumental task and I felt my defences crumbling as I thought about it. She talked a lot about probate, but never explained what the word meant. I now know that it is simply the process of dealing with the affairs of a deceased person, verifying their will and distributing their estate to their beneficiaries. Obvious, really, except that she never bothered to explain it. She then told me to get the process going as quickly as I could in case there were changes to the inheritance rules in the next Budget.

People seem to assume that the bereaved know what they want and what they are supposed to do. With no clear definition of probate I had no idea what part I was expected to have in it. In my bewildered and confused state I felt I was on my own, and I felt I was easy prey, a suspicion confirmed when a letter from the legal practice arrived a few days after my visit outlining my instructions to them, and confirming their charges. The ugly mother had omitted a key piece of information in her conversation with me, namely that, in addition to her hourly rate, I would be charged a 'value element' of 1 per cent of the gross value of Nick's estate and 0.5 per cent of the value of the house. Think of the value of a four-bedroomed house in inner London and do the maths ... It's a tidy sum, and it meant that at the end of the process, *in addition* to her hourly fees, I would hand over several thousand pounds more for ... for what? It was 'one measure of the extent of responsibility falling on the firm' according to the letter. I was incensed. The will could not have been more straightforward, and I couldn't believe that calling in life policies was onerous, nor that the transfer of our house into my sole name was more of a responsibility than conveyancing during the purchase of a home. Death is a money-spinner, I thought, for those who meet the bereaved when they are most vulnerable.

I rang the head of the legal practice, furious not just at the size of their charges but also that they hadn't been mentioned when I had asked outright. I rang the Law Society and asked them to explain why solicitors were allowed to charge a 'value element' on estates, but they never came back with an answer. And then I rang five local probate solicitors until I found one who was willing to negotiate – and thereby saved myself thousands.

Money began to come in, including a lump sum death 'benefit' from the BBC which enabled me to pay off the mortgages on the house, the cottage and the 'retirement' flat, wiping off the largest outgoings at a stroke. After trawling through some government websites I discovered I was eligible for a State Widowed Parent's Allowance, which in my case would bring in £400 a month. My university friend Anna did me the kindest favour of sitting me down with pen, paper and calculator one day and helping me to work out my income and outgoings so I knew exactly where I stood – something I hadn't had the courage to do. The figures weren't great. I knew something had to give. Rose Cottage cost money to run and was clearly an expense we could live without. Selling it would break my heart – and the boys' – and besides, I had decided not to take any major financial decisions for at least a year. I put it with a local letting agent, but this was January, and people weren't rushing to rent houses in the country. We would have to wait.

There was one other solution: to work. I found it hard to imagine how people could hold down a job straight after losing a partner. Yet I know they do, usually because they have no choice. And I discovered how hard this must be when I was offered, and couldn't refuse, some work that month, producing footage and interviews for a pharmaceutical company video. It was far from demanding, but I struggled. Shaking with nerves as I left the safety of the house, I was in no fit state to engage with anyone I was working with, and yet I had to coordinate a team of people. I battled to talk to them coherently, yet I couldn't connect to what I saw as 'their world', a world without pain and without understanding, and a world in which they seemed oblivious to the enormity of my struggle. As with every encounter I was having, an embarrassed awkwardness stifled acknowledgement of what had happened to me, leaving an uncomfortable silence. In between filming takes I sat alone in a corner writing fiendishly in a memoir that I had started as a release from the churnings inside my head. On two occasions I was overcome by a sensation I had never before experienced, a howling, rushing sound pounding in my ears and head, while all sight and sound of everything including the people around me vanished. My body froze as I panicked at my incapacity to see, speak or move. The episodes lasted less than a minute but were shocking: they were like out-of-body experiences totally out of my control.

I knew then that I couldn't cope with working full-time. Besides, the boys needed me to be there for them, and single parenthood meant the weight of daily household chores now fell entirely on me, a job in itself. And I realized, with no small amount of sadness, that I would never again be able to work in the way I had before Nick was ill, would never achieve the ambitions I once had, would never be able to pursue opportunities at will. Those I had lost, along with so much else.

There are many layers to loss. With Nick's departure I had lost companionship, company and intimacy. I'd lost a co-parent, the sharer of my days. I'd lost the life we had lived, the interpreter of all that happened to me, the reason I wanted to live, the life I expected to live. My future had disappeared. Where once there had been hopes and dreams, now all I saw was a blank canvas. I was scared. Scared of this new life, scared of the loneliness, scared of the future, scared of my own emotions.

Loss changed the way I related to everything and everybody. In a house that felt like a mausoleum, haunting memories filled every corner. My bedroom was the place I hated the most. What had once been a private sanctuary from the outside world, shared with the man I loved, was now a place I dreaded to enter. I'd go to bed, switch off the light so I couldn't see the emptiness around me and lie in the foetal position, clutching the sweatshirt Nick had been wearing when he died, shredded by the scissors Charlotte had used to cut it off him before surrendering his body to the undertakers, burying my nose in the scent that he had left behind. I changed sides in the bed so that I wouldn't have to sleep next to the space that once Nick had slept in. As I lay where he had done in those last weeks of his life I started to wonder – and then fled from the thought because it was too painful – what he had felt and thought as he lay there, as his body prepared itself to leave us.

All the while I lay there praying for sleep, the memories of his final days seeped into my mind. I found myself remembering over and over those words he spoke when the cancer came back and started to spread. 'Come on, it's not too bad . . .' I re-lived the daily trek to University College Hospital, pushing him in his wheelchair, staring down at his emaciated shoulders, the protruding tendons on his neck, his skull whose ridges and contours I could outline for the first time because his skin was so thin, his newly re-grown hair, fluffy, almost childlike, black streaked with grey. I remembered bending down and kissing his neck to comfort him, and I wanted to go back to that moment so badly and stay there for ever.

Then there was the guilt of the survivor. I felt guilty that

I was alive, guilty that I could see our boys every day, guilty that I still breathed air and saw daylight, when he didn't and never would. And guilt's companion was remorse. How could I have gone to John Lewis just days before he died, I asked myself. Why did I go to that spa with Tessa? Had I not known he was going to die? Had I spent enough time with him in those last weeks? I tried to remind myself of the things I *had* done, like stroking his tummy as I lay next to him to ease his discomfort, standing outside the door of the bedroom forcing my face into repose before entering, kissing his forehead time and again, rubbing moisturizing cream into his dry skin, massaging his foot, tending to his needs. But none of these memories gave me any comfort. I could still feel his vulnerability, the softness of his hair, the frailty of his limbs and of his spirit, and I was eaten up with self-reproach over what I hadn't done, what I might have done, and for every awful thing I had ever done to him during our entire time together, right down to my irritation at the traces of toothpaste he left on the towels. Night after night I'd end up rocking back and forth moaning, 'I'm sorry, my darling, I'm so sorry.' Sometimes I almost heard his voice whisper the words he'd said the day the cancer came back, when I said sorry for everything I had failed at, for everything I might have done but didn't ... for everything I regretted now that I no longer lived with the complacency of thinking he would be with me for ever. 'You know none of that matters ...' he had said. And I knew it to be true, even if it was of little comfort. I wanted to go back into the past, to re-do things, to make things better, be better. But the past was now cut off from me for ever, and my utter impotence, my inability to change things, fuelled my rage, a rage at myself and a rage at the world. For all I wanted to scream, 'Why me, why did this happen to *me*?' I also wondered why it hadn't been me who had left this earth and avoided this horror. Yet I couldn't have borne the idea that Nick would have had to endure this pain had it been I who had died.

Anger is one of the manifestations of grief. It is ugly. It can be all-consuming. But it is normal. In one of the major works written on the subject – Elizabeth Kübler-Ross's book *On Death and Dying* – I discovered that anger is identified as one of the five stages the bereaved go through. Anyone who knows, knows about the rage of loss.

When I wasn't raging at the parents at the school gates – sharing smiles with each other but averting their eyes from the woman crying by their side – I raged at friends whose silence howled loudly in my ears. There was one who 'reached out' by nothing more than a phone text on Christmas Day, another who called to ask how I was before terminating the call quickly when she heard my reply: 'I'm in a bad way.' I raged at the neighbour I spied at the Sainsbury's checkout and who, on seeing me, turned his back. At the woman from over the road who smiled and waved, yet never crossed. At the friend who did visit, but who cried – about her father, dead for eighteen years. 'I know how you feel,' she said, and I raged at her insensitivity in comparing her loss with mine. IT IS NOT THE SAME, I wanted to scream at her, and I wish I had done. Rage contained is rage untrammelled.

I've heard it said that in bereavement people confound you. The good friends you thought would be there for you in a time of crisis can disappear, while others, not so close, come up trumps. Some certainly did for me, like Jane Corbin, a former colleague from my *Panorama* days, back in the 1990s. She offered me unerring support, taking me out to dinner when

I was ready to start going out and inviting me and the boys over to lunch. Then there was Eddie Mair, to whom I'd instinctively turned when things were bad. All my instincts about him had been right: he kept up a steady stream of invitations, and we sat drinking coffee together as we had when Nick was ill; and I cried to him, just as I had before. Other people simply weighed in with unsolicited, practical help. My neighbour Liz started to pick the boys up from school once a week for me. Mark Damazer, Nick's old boss at Radio 4, visited and Zsuzsanna, the au pair who had accompanied us on that trip to France, took the boys swimming every Saturday. Tessa had even invited us for Christmas, but I felt I couldn't impose our misery on others.

The generosity of a handful of people who gave of their precious time was humbling. Perhaps what most obviously singled out the friends who 'came good' was that they talked *and* listened and didn't shy away from my pain. The awkwardness of others was so great, or their comments so insensitive, that I began to avoid a whole swathe of people in order to ease the discomfort – theirs and mine. Some came out with the words every bereaved person dreads: 'If there's anything I can do . . .' a phrase which places the responsibility firmly on the shoulders of the bereaved to ask for help at the very time when they're least capable of reaching out, of asking for anything, of even knowing what they need. Then there were those who never said anything, not a word, who carried on as if nothing had happened, as if Nick had never died, or indeed never lived, who seemed to feel that they could pick up where they had left off, who gave themselves permission to avoid the trouble of working out 'the right thing to say'. Try the word 'sorry', I wanted to shout at them. And of course there were those from whom I never heard a word. Ever.

Wounded and fragile, I withdrew from those who couldn't give me what I needed. It was self-protection. I felt let down by most, though I accept that the bereaved do not make good companions. Death's head at the feast, I suppose. Not that I was invited to many, or indeed any, feasts. The invitations – to dinners, functions, get-togethers – dried up overnight. I had two in the whole of that first year after Nick died, where once he and I had been out weekly, part of a large social circle of people in which I no longer fitted. In truth, I couldn't have accepted invitations anyway. I simply couldn't leave the house except when necessary, but it hurt that there were so few.

The letters of condolence still poured in. A few, from elderly Radio 4 listeners, included £5 notes 'for the boys', a gesture so touching I found the energy to reply, promising them that the money would be spent wisely. They were the only letters I answered. John Sergeant, Nick's friend and colleague, wrote of the day he'd met us walking along the street laughing as the boys ran riot around our feet: 'You seemed to have it all,' he said, and I wondered whether I'd been punished for having had it so good. But I couldn't get the words of one particular correspondent out of my mind: 'Remember the many friends who love you here at the BBC,' he said. Now I was seeing just how easy it was for people to write such words, and to believe them – and how rare it is to find someone who knows how to act on them.

Amidst the hundreds of letters I ploughed through, the few that did give me comfort were those that talked about me. I didn't need to hear what I already knew: that Nick had been a brilliant, charming and much-admired man whose loss was devastating. What I didn't know was how *I* was going to survive now, without him, and I wanted someone to tell me. My friend Anita provided, in the following words, exactly what I craved.

> Barbara ... I want you to know that you have been the most wonderful friend to me, from our very first conversation ... I appreciate your friendship so much more than you can imagine and I want to be there for you now, in your time of need. I need you to know that I am here for you, no matter what, and that you are foremost in my thoughts each day. I'm just a phone call away, Barbara, and I really do care for you and the boys deeply ...

And she stuck to her word.

Thoughts of death started to creep into mind, primarily of my own. I would take my life. When I contemplated the devastation of my world, or when I peered into the future and saw an empty space devoid of purpose and meaning, the response was obvious. To leave. To end my life at the point at which it had been ended for me. So logical was this thought, so alluring and so easy, that it petrified me, for I knew that abandoning the boys would be an act of unacceptable selfishness and callousness. I managed on every occasion to stop short of thinking how I would actually do it, before pushing the thoughts out of reach, for a while at least.

And then along with the suicidal came the murderous thoughts, which I spilled out to Sarah one day as she sat in my kitchen. 'I want some of my friends to die,' I said. And I could tell that she knew that I really, really meant it. It was only right. I truly wanted one, or two, or maybe several of them to die, to suffer for abandoning me so that their loved ones would realize how utterly devastating it was to lose your lover, partner, husband, wife. To ensure I wasn't the only person on the planet suffering such pain. And as I confessed these, my darkest thoughts, I looked her in the eye, fully expecting her to get up and leave the house there and then.

'I can quite understand that,' she said. 'In your situation, I think I'd feel that way too.' She helped me devise a strategy: I would write up on a board in the kitchen a list of the names of the people I felt had been there for me, and who therefore deserved mercy, and a list of those I felt should have been but hadn't – and who therefore deserved to die, preferably a slow and painful death. I added a third category: people who were neither on one list nor the other but who might either redeem themselves in the coming months – or be condemned if they didn't match up. I would then imagine armed assassins carrying out my wishes as and when and on whom I wanted them to. There were around twelve people in each list. The pleasure of the exercise wasn't confined to the list of the damned. It wasn't only about revenge. There really was comfort in seeing twelve names of people I had depended on and who had been there for me. That was more than I had allowed myself to imagine. It helped me get a perspective.

The list stayed up for many months, until one day someone in the condemned camp came round to see me. Reluctantly, minutes before she arrived, I wiped off her name, then the rest. Perhaps I was inching forward.

Realizing, as I did from Sarah, that the depth of my anger was 'normal' was the first step in being able to live with it rather than fight it, and probably the first step along my very long road to somewhere new. As was the awareness that the silence of others was also 'normal'. I learned this not just from Sarah but also from a Radio 4 listener called Kila Millidine. She had recently lost her partner Shaun to cancer when she wrote to me to share some of her experiences in the months following his death.

> Some friends, some acquaintances have been wonderful … but others, after the initial condolences, just haven't been there. The phone virtually stopped ringing, many people stopped dropping in, I've watched people 'not see' me because they've suddenly been too intent on studying a stack of baked beans.
>
> I've spoken to other bereaved people and I gather this is a common experience. Our fears, our social inadequacy, our lack of experience / imagination / confidence / time, causes us to effectively send the bereaved person to Coventry to a degree, at the very moment when they most need comfort, support and contact … I do think that our society deals with bereaved people very poorly.

I was not alone. I was not mad. I felt as if I had managed to raise my head and see daylight for the first time. And I began to realize that I had to learn to deal with, and come to accept, that my place in the world would never be the same again, and that there was no point wishing that it could be.

My answerphone was flashing when I got back from dropping the boys off at school one morning. The message was from a well-known actor whom Nick had much admired and with whom we had had a passing acquaintance, and just months after Nick died, he was inviting me and the boys for a weekend at his country house in Wiltshire. 'I'd like to do something to help,' he said when I called him back. The offer of something concrete, rather than the expression of platitudes, was an unexpected bonus. I jumped at the idea, not just for the chance of a weekend away, but because I still toyed with the hope that

I might one day be able to re-capture elements of the life I had lived with Nick, spending time in interesting places, in exalted company.

We arrived on a Friday evening after sitting for more than three hours in the heavy, slow-moving traffic which was heading out of London for what promised to be a hot weekend. Our host's house was enchanting and quintessentially English with its undulating red bricks covered with creeping ivy, over-looking a large sprawling garden. Inside, the low ceilings, sloping floors and rambling corridors made it feel comfortable and welcoming. We were given two large bedrooms with mustard-coloured carpets and creaking floorboards.

I soon realized I had made a terrible mistake. The boys were fractious and I couldn't settle them until late, by which time I was exhausted and dinner was long overdue. Conversation was a struggle. I felt exposed on my own, aware of a glaring gap at my side where Nick should have been, where we would have been the double act we always were. We would have talked, gossiped and laughed late into the night. But on my own I simply couldn't be what we used to be. I wasn't even half of the couple we had been: I was but a fraction and my self-confidence was crushed. My hosts looked embarrassed, bored.

The next day they took us to feed the horses in the paddock at the end of the garden and we walked along the lanes, but the awkwardness of our situation seemed to pursue us. It was more than just the gap at my side, it was the fact that any mention of Nick's name was greeted by an embarrassed silence, by a deft change of subject. The bereaved want to talk, need to talk, and too often, I'm afraid, have little else to talk about. I tried hard to find common ground with my hosts, but I couldn't help feeling I had become a one-trick pony, a woman preoccupied by loss, defined by widowhood.

A barbecue had been prepared for the Saturday evening. We sat on the terrace as the light dwindled and the air cooled. The struggle to converse, to be of interest, to be entertaining, became too much and I lapsed into tense silence, which was met by an echo of that silence. I was soon counting the hours, and couldn't wait to leave as soon as it was courteous to do so, early on the Sunday morning. I never heard from them again, nor they from me. But I drew a great lesson from the experience. I had to put my life with Nick behind me. I had to accept that it was gone. I couldn't cling on to bits of what we had, because they would never be the same without him and neither would I. As I had to build a new life, so I also had to build a new persona.

And to do so I would have to let go of many of the people I had known, as they had let go of me. Besides, I was in no state to share their joy, their zest for life, and – if I'm honest – I felt jealous that they were untainted by tragedy, that the wives still had husbands and the children still had dads and that their day-to-day worries seemed so trivial.

One incident crystallized for me how far removed I felt from the concerns of most people's daily lives. Just a few weeks after Nick's funeral the boys were invited to a school friend's party. As we arrived, the friend's father was showing another parent around his new house. It had five storeys and was nestled in a beautiful Victorian square on the fringes of central London. 'Yes, it's lovely, isn't it?' I heard him saying before adding ruefully, 'but it's not exactly Notting Hill.' It seemed to me that he had everything: a lovely wife, gorgeous children, a grand house, and yet he wished for more. It wasn't his fault that his passing comment had such a profound effect on me, but it seemed to underline the distance I now felt between myself and most of the rest of the world.

It might have passed me by that spring had arrived, or even that it was my first without Nick, were it not for the abundance of snowdrops that greeted us in the cool sun of late February when the boys and I went to Rose Cottage for half-term to clear up in anticipation of a tenant moving in, though none had yet been found.

The snowdrops reminded all three of us of a beautiful book we had discovered, called *Always and Forever* by Debi Gliori and which I read to the boys at night, although it often had me bursting into tears. In this children's tale, Fox, Hare, Otter and Mole live happily in a tree until one day Fox, who is the 'dad' of the family, goes out into the wood and dies. It is a cold, dark winter and the animals weep at his loss inside their little home. But then spring arrives in the animal world and along with the first sprinkling of snowdrops comes Squirrel, who tells the animals to stop being sad and to remember the happy times. Slowly they start to smile again as they recall, with affection, Fox's terrible cooking, his dreadful gardening and disastrous DIY. They learn that they can be happy again even though Fox has gone. Who he was and what he did, they tell each other, will be in their hearts 'always and forever'.

The snowdrops at the cottage had been transplanted from Nick's mother's house after she died and now, as in the boys' book, they burst through the grass and pushed up amongst the dead leaves at the foot of the beech hedge. And at the same time something began to shift in the swirling waters beneath me.

At first the shift frightened me. I didn't stop being sad, nor did I start to remember the happy times like the animals in the story, but I had occasional days where I cried just a few times, rather than incessantly. It ceased to be a struggle to don the mask I needed to face the world. My heart was still as heavy, my pain still as visceral, and my anger at the world still as raw, but I could park it in a safe place if I needed to and I seemed able to function, on the surface at least, as if I was normal. It was like seeing the sun's light at the top of the pit I was in and starting to feel its pale warmth on my face. Maybe, just maybe, this was the first rung up the ladder out of the depths.

We spent the whole of that half-term week in Somerset, sorting and clearing and storing. Joel and Benedict hared round the mossy lawn with a football while I packed away the myriad things Nick and I had bought together over the years – colourful old earthenware plates from our travels to the States, art deco mirrors from the nearby antiques shop, maps and pub guides, the wellington boots and outdoor coats we kept there, all the trappings of a life that was and that would never be again.

The fact that I managed some of the preparations without tears unnerved me. I needn't have worried. The change lasted just a few days before it ended, brutally, once we got back home and I fell right back to where I had been. But despite my return to the darkness of grief, I couldn't erase the knowledge that I had been out, briefly, in a place where I could see light, however dim and distant. I believed now that there was something worth fighting for, that there was a way through this horror, though I still didn't know what lay on the other side.

A week later, on a Saturday afternoon while I sat at home listlessly watching DVDs with the boys, I had a phone call from the letting agent. She had just shown someone round the cottage and he wanted to take it. Knowing that my finances were about to turn a corner was like another glimpse of sunlight coaxing me out of the shadows. What I didn't know at the time was how that phone call would transform the pattern of my journey through grief.

THIRTEEN

You killed Daddy, didn't you?

BENEDICT 5

M any years before he fell ill, and for no particular reason that I can remember, I teased Nick about what would happen if either of us died. 'There'd be a queue of women lining up to look after you if I went,' I said, 'and let's face it, they'd all be easier to live with than I am!' 'But I wouldn't want anyone else,' he replied. 'That's not the point,' I insisted, 'I'm just reassuring you that you wouldn't find yourself alone, because women would be falling over you. On the other hand, *no one* would ever take *me* on . . .' And I believed it. In the event of the great unthinkable, I couldn't imagine another man being interested in me. Besides, if I lost the man I loved more than life itself, would I ever want to be with anyone else? Would it even be possible to love again?

I never dreamed the day would come when such thoughts would be more than idle speculation.

By mid-March the paperwork for handing over Rose Cottage was almost complete and the letting agent asked if I would meet my prospective tenant at the cottage: we needed to make a final decision about how much of his furniture he could bring with him, and how much of mine I would be putting into store.

237

'He wants to move in by the end of the month, so it would be good if you could sort this quickly,' she said, before adding, 'You won't have any problems with him, he's a very respectable gentleman.'

And so, early one Saturday, the boys and I drove down to Somerset again and found new shoots speckling the trees with green, and daffodils littering the lawn. We wandered over to the small holding, next to the cottage, and sat with our friend Elly who, by extraordinary coincidence, had been widowed just weeks before Nick died. Only last summer Nick and I had sat with her and her husband in the very same kitchen drinking tea and discussing the effect on the crops of the long hot spell. Both her life and mine had been destroyed in the instant that is death and we understood each other's pain. She was running the farm down now, handing over the livestock to her son, clearing out the barn. In her late sixties, she no longer had the will to keep the business going on her own. The house seemed cold and desperately sad, and I felt bad that I would soon be leaving and would no longer see her.

In the afternoon a dark blue Volvo pulled up on the gravelled area at the end of the garden. A tall man strode across the grass and shook my hand. He was strikingly handsome, with chiselled features, swept-back brown hair and an easy charm. He followed me round the cottage, watching intently, listening with care. We talked about sofas, mirrors, curtains. When I realized I was showing him where the plug sockets were – and that he was showing an interest in finding out – I knew we were both taking longer than was absolutely necessary.

'We're sad to be losing this place,' I said as he headed back to his car.

'You're not losing it,' he replied. 'You can come down any time you want to. I'm on my own and I'd love the company.'

And so we returned just weeks later to Rose Cottage, this time as his guests. For lunch he cooked a tomato-and-cheese pasta and insisted he didn't mind when Joel declared it was 'disgusting'. In the garden he played football with the boys and as they fought, screamed and curtailed any semblance of conversation, he just laughed and said, 'They're great kids, aren't they!' And as we talked I started to acknowledge the absurd, the unthinkable, the ridiculous: there was a spark between us.

Courting in middle age and in the modern world was a new experience. You bring baggage. You bring children. You bring grey hairs and new technology.

We sent each other phone texts about the utility bills, the smell of silage, and our favourite songs. When the texts switched to emails I knew I'd made a decision: you don't email someone daily for no reason. And perhaps the reason was that one of the first things he ever said to me was, 'I'm so sorry about Nick.' In the cold and lonely world into which I'd been plunged, where most friends had found no words and where I felt shunned for being bereaved, he talked and listened and wanted to know. I later found out that he had once worked for the Samaritans.

I'll call him R.

Why did I do it? I asked myself the question many a time. And I'm sure others wondered too. Was it wise to embark on a relationship so soon after my husband had died? Was I in a fit state to know what I was doing? Was it fair on R., to allow him to engage with someone whose emotions were pulped, whose thinking was at times irrational?

And how – to be blunt – could I sleep with another man? Was not the act of sharing my body the ultimate betrayal of Nick?

There never was any pressure from R. I felt entirely in control of the way things unfolded: a hand was being held out to me in my loneliness and isolation and I could see no reason to turn it away. I knew without a shred of doubt that Nick would have approved of this, that he would have supported anything I did if it made life easier, less painful, more bearable for me in the pit of awfulness in which he had unintentionally left me. His last words to Daniel rang in my ears: 'Make sure she gets a lot of love.' Indeed, I wondered whether Nick had, from 'Beyond', contrived to make this happen.

Basic human instincts drove me too. I wanted to be cared for. I wanted to be held. And I badly wanted this man. My questions answered themselves with ease.

And so it was, after we'd met each other only three times, that R. and I made love one night in the cottage bedroom I had shared with Nick for nearly fourteen years, with its old Edwardian bed and art deco furniture, cocooned between caramel-coloured walls, a place Nick and I had created together and which was so familiar to me and yet, by the very act of what I was doing, was becoming part of another life and another time. I felt neither guilt nor sorrow that night and when our lovemaking was over I thought I would shed tears, but felt only wonderment at the ease of the act.

It was not that I had no tears: they had been shed earlier that day as I drove, light-hearted with anticipation, simultaneously heavy-hearted with grief, towards what I knew would be a tryst of enormous significance, destined to move me a small step further from my life with Nick and a small step closer towards the new life I would one day be forced to inhabit.

When it came to it, it was more wonderful than I had dared to hope. R.'s body had a comfortable familiarity: he was the same height and build as Nick, and I felt at ease being enveloped by it. His skin smelled different from Nick's, but was not unwelcoming, and although I couldn't get Nick out of my mind, I relished the discovery of new and different scents and touches. I had no nerves but was physically tense. R. was patient. 'I fully expected you wouldn't be able to do this when it came to it,' he whispered. 'And how would you have felt then?' I asked. 'I would have understood, of course I would.' I lay awake for hours afterwards, not daring to lose consciousness, the abandonment of sleep beside someone new seeming a more intimate act even than the sexual one.

The next day R. and I walked along the lane with the boys in sunshine that was warm and unexpected. Stopping to study bluebells and blow dandelion blossom into the still air, we sweated in the heat of one of the balmiest spring days on record. Later that evening, as the warmth of the day dispersed and the boys slept peacefully, we lay in front of the fire, the logs spitting and crackling in the tiny grate as they had done so often when Nick was there. To feel another's flesh next to mine, and to feel my own caressed, unearthed emotional and physical sensations I thought were buried for ever. I felt a heavy burden being released – the burden of fear. Maybe I could, one day, feel for someone again. Maybe the future I had lost could be replaced by another. It would never be the one I wanted or as good as the one that might have been, but a future of some sort was better than none at all. The terror of the blank canvas that I saw when I looked ahead receded slightly.

In the months that followed, and as spring drifted into

241

summer, Joel, Benedict and I spent many weekends at Rose Cottage. As the boys tore around happily, inhabiting every corner of the house and garden, R. and I sat on the wooden bench on the lawn watching, listening, talking. 'Tell me about your time here with Nick,' he would say, and I would recount how much Nick and I had loved Rose Cottage, what joy it had brought us to share it with those two small boys, and how we had planned to retire there one day. And as the weeks passed, the cottage ceased to feel like an albatross round my neck but somewhere that could still bring joy, albeit a joy that would for ever be tarnished. Thanks to R., I didn't lose it overnight, but was granted time to accept that it was now a different place from the one it had been, a place where I would always store some of my most precious memories.

R.'s visits to the house in London brought changes there too. 'It's dark in here,' he observed the first time he came, and in the sitting room he opened the curtains which had been closed since Nick died. He started the hall clock, which hadn't ticked for months. He dismantled and removed the stair lift, a reminder of Nick's terrible incapacity. He filled the kitchen with the sounds and smells of cooking again, and furnished many an evening with music, food, conversation and love.

It wasn't always easy to let R. enter that enclosed space at the core of my life, where only pain, anger, and sorrow had thrived. I wanted to open up, but needed compassion and understanding, which he gave me in abundance. So, slowly, patiently, he unfurled me from the foetal position in which I had braced myself against the world and gave me the strength to face it again. He took me out in the evenings and together we took the boys out at weekends. In May we celebrated his fiftieth birthday with a group of his friends at the Wimbledon

Greyhound Stadium. In June, on what would have been Nick's fifty-ninth birthday, we held a party in the garden, lit candles on a birthday cake, and set fire to the cards the boys had written to Nick. 'That way they can go up to Daddy,' they observed, watching the smoke drift skywards. In July it was the boys' turn and R. was there to help me organize a bouncy castle and party games for eighteen five-year-olds. In August we travelled to France for a week by the sea. I could never have managed these things alone.

I laughed more in those months than ever I would have done had R. not been in my life, but to my immense regret I never felt happiness even remotely close to what I had once known. My grief was still wretchedly raw. I still howled when it over-came me, at times so powerfully I retreated to bed, where I would curl up, shaking and inconsolable. R. would sit by me and stroke my head gently and reassuringly for as long as it took for me to calm. My rage, too, was never far away and at times it turned against R. himself. For all he gave me, he couldn't give me enough.

That summer I attended the annual MPs v. Fleet Street cricket match, an event Nick had always helped to organize and which this year was being held in his memory. The match was dedicated to 'Nick Clarke, journalist, cricketer, friend'. I was invited to address the assembled players and supporters. The Labour member Andrew Miller and his assistant Julie Spence coaxed several thousand pounds from MPs and various media outlets and asked me to nominate a charity to benefit. Without a moment's hesitation I suggested Winston's Wish, the charity for bereaved children, whose advice the boys' teacher Miss Keck and I had followed when talking to them about their dad.

Arriving at the cricket ground just outside London on the day of the match I realized that I was seeing for the first time the sights that Nick must have seen every time he came here – and should have been seeing now. I struggled to retain my composure. So tight was the grip on my chest, so laboured my breathing, I had to walk round the perimeter of the ground with Julie before I could face meeting anyone. It was all unbearably sad. I spoke briefly about the boys' grief for their dad and others spoke of Nick's passion for cricket and how they missed him. The Chief Executive of Winston's Wish, Julie Stokes, was there to receive the cheque and give me two cricket bats, signed by every player present, for the boys.

Driving home I was convulsed with sobs and when I arrived R. took me in his arms as I shook with sorrow. As he held me I began to shake with rage too, rage that he wasn't Nick, rage that he never would be Nick, and rage that he offered me so much yet couldn't protect me from the delirium of my grief. It was beginning to sink in that I would never re-capture any of what I had had before, that it really was gone for ever and that my journey through grief was going to be a long one, with very few hiding-places along the way.

There was only one place where my pain couldn't get me, and that was when we made love. I supposed this to be the animal nature of our most powerful drivers, food and sex. Afterwards my tears often fell, silently, as R. slept and I would close my eyes, listen to his steady breathing and imagine it was Nick lying beside me. For the briefest moment I flirted with bliss.

I still dreamed regularly of Nick – that same dream I always had where Nick appeared relaxed and well and only I knew that he was dying – but one night it was different. I found myself in a large dimly lit room looking across at Nick, who was sitting in the corner smiling contentedly at me. I knew I had to leave that room and I knew Nick realized I had no choice but to go and as our eyes locked we both knew our parting was inevitable. Strangely, it didn't even feel sad. Yet I couldn't leave because I didn't know how to get out, I didn't know how to take the first step, I didn't know where the door was. And as I looked around for help, I found R. He was there, at my side and he took my hand and gently led me from the room.

Given the questions that had coursed through my mind about the wisdom of entering a relationship with R., I waited several weeks before telling anyone other than Sarah, my bereavement counsellor. I thought she'd be shocked, or would assume I somehow needed her help less. 'Absolutely not!' she said. '*Anything* that helps you in this first awful year is wonderful and you should seize it.' I breathed again.

Then I told a girlfriend. She emailed: 'Wow, you're a quick mover,' to which I retorted indignantly, 'I didn't *do* anything. He walked into my garden.' Elly, at the farm, was thrilled. 'You're young, you *must* find someone,' she said. Another friend wasn't so sure. 'Do you think it's wise?' she asked coldly, to which I replied honestly, 'I have no idea.' Two acquaintances said it was 'disgusting' that it was so soon. Not to my face, though: I heard it second-hand.

Who is to say you should wait a day, a month, a year, before letting someone into your life after loss? The devastation of bereavement left me desperate for comfort, company and the human touch, and I was discovering that a new relationship in no way lessens the pain of grief, cushions the heartache nor changes any of the feelings you have for the loved one you have lost. At no stage did I stop yearning for Nick, did I stop wishing with every cell in my body that he could come back. Nick and my love for him, his death and my grief, were with me and would be for ever. They were part of who I had become. And they came with me into this new relationship, a constant subject of conversation. 'I feel I know him,' said R. time and again. Why deny myself the chance to find comfort when my life had been devastated? And what if this didn't equate with what I had before? If the life I had with Nick was like living in a palace, now destroyed for ever, then how foolish would I be to refuse a simple roof over my head in favour of staying in the gutter?

Looking back now, I can see I owe my very survival to R. He drip-fed me back into the real world, back into day-to-day life, back into a place I couldn't face alone – a place from which I was becoming dangerously isolated. I was calmer, better-fed, less lonely and, perhaps most importantly, a better mother when R. was around. And the boys knew it too.

From the moment they met him, they were hooked, but were uncertain how and where he fitted in. Their irritation at finding us lying in bed together the first time focused on the lack of space for themselves. 'Oh, bloody, bloody,' Joel muttered to himself in a corner while we tried to coax him out. He begged me to sleep in the spare room, so I did, for one night, and then asked his permission to return. 'He's my friend, guys,' I said, 'and it's like you having a sleepover for a mate, but if you don't like him you only have to say and I'll sleep on my own.' 'It's not that, Mum,' said Joel, 'he's a nice enough chap, but I'm worried you'll love him more than you love me.' I had under-estimated their understanding of the adult world. I reassured him that that would never happen and a deal was struck. I could share R.'s bed as long as I didn't kiss him. Our first 'public' kiss had made Benedict madly jealous and every time he saw us coming close he would rush over and squirm between us. I also told the boys they could tell me *anything* they wanted to about R., to which they replied, 'Yes, Mum, we *know*.' And I knew I couldn't force the issue when they weren't in the mood.

The day Bendy decided to speak his mind we were in the car, driving along a lane somewhere near Rose Cottage. He looked at me warily, and then, talking to the back of R.'s seat in front of him, said, 'You killed Daddy, didn't you?' He looked at me defiantly, waiting for a reaction. It was R. who spoke. 'I didn't kill your Daddy,' he said. 'I never knew him, but I wish I had. He sounds like a really lovely man.' 'I think he would have liked you,' Joel chipped in, 'because you like cricket.'

There never was a difficult moment again. And when August came and we all travelled to southern Brittany for a seaside holiday it seemed the most natural thing to do. We took the ferry from Portsmouth to Cherbourg, a five and a half hour journey during which the boys ran rings round us, demanding to be fed every thirty minutes, ducking and diving between people's seats, throwing their cuddly toys at each other and, inadvertently, at other passengers. I was bowled over by R.'s endless patience and humour, and it reminded me of the sheer joy of shared parenting, compared with the stress and anxiety of doing it alone. My heart thrilled, too, to see the boys excited and happy despite the shadow of their tragedy; they seemed totally at ease that R. was with us, when only a year ago we had been on a similar journey to France with Daddy.

R. never replaced, substituted for, or supplanted Nick in the boys' minds. I was beginning to understand that Nick was very much alive for them. He was still, and always would be, their father and they felt his presence vividly. When we finally arrived at the coast and Benedict spied pedal boats in the water, he shrieked, 'Look at those, Joel, they've got seats for four people. You and me can go in the back and we could get Daddy and R. in the front.' And we all agreed it was a great idea.

I needed that holiday badly. The exhaustion of grief, of being a single parent, of being woken every night by the boys, of creeping depression, of running a household alone, of my daily fight for survival, was catching up with me. 'Bereavement is like undergoing a massive operation,' Sarah reminded me time and again. 'It's exhausting and you have the added burden of looking after the boys. You need rest, rest, rest.' But when can you rest with small children? I could feel it bearing down on me: my head felt permanently fogged, I struggled to get up in the mornings and I had no physical energy. That week R. helped me to catch up on my sleep. He woke early with the boys and let me stay in bed, he did all the cooking and all the driving, and he played with the boys for hours on the beach and at the water's edge, while I looked on, just as I had a year earlier as Nick stood by the sea on the beach at Cromer watching his darling boys splashing about in the shallows.

One evening R. and I were by the water's edge again, but this time on our own, sitting in a restaurant in fading sunlight, looking out over the silver sand and listening to the push-me-pull-you of the waves, just a few feet away. And as I sat in this beautiful location with a kind and gorgeous man who cared for me deeply, with fine wine and fine food on my table, I cried.

I cried because I had everything at that moment and yet still I had nothing. I *felt* nothing, where I wanted to feel a sliver of happiness, a pang of emotion, maybe even a glimpse of love, but I couldn't. Neither could I see a time when happiness would no longer be tarnished by grief, joy contaminated by loss.

'When I say I love you, I know how hard you find that,' said R. sadly, 'but I can't bottle up my feelings.' And I envied him for having feelings at all. In the months since Nick died I knew I had made progress and that much of it I owed to R. I had become stronger, more capable of managing the daily load, less aggressive towards the boys, and more accustomed to the misery and isolation which had become part of my new normal. But I was struggling to feel, either for R. or for the boys, because I was still convulsed by grief. I was only a few steps into my journey and I was beginning to think I needed to take the next steps on my own. I realized I could offer R. nothing. I couldn't return what he gave. And all I could say was, 'I'm so sorry.'

I asked R. once what he thought of what I had done, entering into a relationship so soon, making love to another man within months of my husband dying. 'I think you were brave and I also think were making a choice,' he said. 'You were choosing life and turning away from death. Making love is life-affirming.'

But when I asked him how it had felt for him to be with a woman who was in love with someone else, he wouldn't be drawn. I think he showed enormous strength being alongside me, but I only realized the extent of it when he sent me the following words:

There is another man in my lover's life
I know of him
not from hushed phone-calls
nor the flush on her face
as their eyes meet across a room
but through her tears
that fall, softly and silent
in the darkness of the night

She sleeps exhausted in my arms
her naked body folded into mine
I watch her eyelids flicker and sense
her soul has gone again to him
my longing at times is immeasurable
yet I cannot follow her
into that lonely place
where her lover awaits
I hold her safe
hoping she will return

Then I understood.

In September it was my birthday. My mother came over and so did R., my neighbour Liz, and Nick's sister Suzie. There were presents and a cake and the boys' excitement filled the house. It ought to have been joyous, but all I could feel was utter loneliness, and the wretched agony of missing Nick.

As September gave way to October the memories of this time the previous year, when Nick had been fading before my very eyes, screamed round my head and stirred up waves of grief. The days began to gain enormous significance as the 'anniversary' of Nick's death approached. Each was given the currency of having a context, the context of a countdown to death. Today (a year ago) he took his last trip to the park. Today (a year ago) was a month before he died. Today (a year ago) he could still walk. Today (a year ago) he stopped eating. Today (a year ago) was the last time he . . .

At the beginning of November I hurtled towards a breakdown. I had felt it approaching for months now but couldn't muster the strength to hold it at bay. R. had left Rose Cottage and moved to London. But as I headed towards the crash I realized I couldn't sustain the relationship with him any longer. I wished I could have loved him deeply, but I couldn't; there was no space in my heart. Not yet, anyway. He could feel that I was moving away from him and that things were drawing to a close, and he reminded me of what he had often told me: 'I fear I'll teach you to fly again, and then you'll fly away.' I was about to fly, but not through new-found ease; rather I knew I had to fly to face alone the reality that I was widowed and was approaching the anniversary of Nick's death. Our parting was wretchedly tearful. I knew I was biting the hand that fed me, and I felt I was letting the boys down badly. But in my state of wretchedness I felt so bad I didn't want R. anywhere near me. I didn't want anyone near me except Nick, and I couldn't see a way out.

FOURTEEN

Mummy, please stop crying. Daddy died ages ago.

BENEDICT 5

If you can't smile, Mummy, just make a happy face.

JOEL 5

Slowly, during the course of that first year without Nick, the lengthy process of probate had come to a close, not without my having to answer a torrent of administrative inquiries, mostly by wading through boxes of documents – Nick's and mine. It was as time-consuming as it was painful. Every time I saw his name on a piece of paper it hurt – more so when I saw his actual handwriting. So immediate, so alive, so *him*. But eventually the various monies we were due came through and I started working out how much we had to live on. There was less than before, of course, but with careful expenditure I could see that we would survive. I could even afford some childcare – which I needed, because offers of work were slowly starting to come in.

Many of them were for me to advise the corporate sector on broadcasting matters. I still found myself operating through a thick fug, my head heavy with sleeplessness, my mind struggling to focus, my thoughts straying from the subject in front of me back to Nick, but over time it became easier. In May

I was invited on to Radio 2 to talk to Jeremy Vine about Nick's death and my grief and when, at the end, Jeremy said to me off-microphone, 'You're a great broadcaster,' a new thread in my life opened. I was invited back regularly to discuss terminal illness, bereavement and then broader family matters, and I absolutely loved it. They seemed to love me and I became their unofficial 'agony aunt'. How I wished I could share with Nick the irony that his death appeared to have given me a voice.

But the most important piece of work I had in front of me was this book. It had been commissioned when Nick was alive and was to be the story of his triumph over adversity: what it was like to get cancer, lose a leg, and recover. It was going to be called *Welcome Home, Pegleg* after the sign I had put in our window the day Nick returned home from hospital. Now of course it was a different story, with a different focus, without the happy ending, and the writing was down to me. What I wanted to impart more than anything was the raw and untrammelled horror of living with cancer, terminal illness and grief, a horror so awful that few people speak about it.

As I moved away from our old social circle, I started to find new friends. Kila — who had written me that moving and perceptive letter after Nick's death — became a confidante of immense importance, someone who understood the minutiae of grief. She understood what it was like to open the wardrobe and see Nick's clothes, understood why Nick's laundry basket remained untouched, knew that the trivia of everyday life takes on enormous significance in death. Only she could understand why I sat howling one day as I sorted through Nick's socks agonising about whether I should throw them away. Only she could understand why I scoured the obituary notices daily, comforted when I found news of other people who, like Nick, had died before their time. I needed people like her who really *knew*.

I visited her at her home on the Pembrokeshire coast, a stranger with whom I now had so much in common. In the cemetery high above St David's, washed by wild sea winds, we stood by her partner Shaun's grave. The boys, I noticed, were unfazed by this confrontation with death and ran round excitedly reading the names on all the headstones. I wandered on my own and came across a tribute to a woman who had lived to a great age. It brought me to my knees. 'She reached ninety-eight, Kila,' I sobbed, 'that's forty more years than Nick had. Why, why, why?' She understood perfectly. 'I resent every man who lives longer than Shaun,' she told me, 'and I resent the elderly couples I see in supermarkets. They are so *blessed* to be growing old together and sometimes I wonder whether they even realize how lucky they are.'

So I could make friends. And to my huge relief I realized as the months passed that I was rediscovering my true feelings for the boys and was able to experience again that surge of unconditional love that every parent knows and understands. I had never imagined how stressful it was to be the only person my children could turn to, to have to make every decision about their life alone, to be the only one who read to them night after night, settled them to sleep, woke in the small hours, planned their days, their weekends, their food, did their home-work. I grew to hate that casual Friday school-gate salutation, 'Have a great weekend!' when all I could see was the long hours stretching ahead as I sought to occupy them, amuse them, entertain them, on my own. But when they were happy and laughing – or sleeping peacefully with their hands around their favourite toys – I could still see what a blessed gift they were.

I gave them all I had, willingly, and that meant that there wasn't much left over for myself. It needed Sarah, on her weekly visits, to remind me to find time for me. One of her wisest pieces of advice was about the therapeutic power of massage. 'The human touch can be so healing,' she said. 'You may find you cry all the way through it, but let yourself go.' And I did.

I hadn't banked on what grief would do to me physically. If it's true that grief is the price you pay for love, I thought one day as I looked in the mirror when I was shopping for some new trousers, then a pale, aged and emaciated face is the price you pay for grief. Mired in middle age, I felt unattractive, spent. I had lost the man I wanted to grow old with, the man who would have carried the memories of my youth with him to sustain him as I became grey and weathered, and I dreaded growing old without him at my side.

I was ageing. No doubt about it. I had lost my appetite — and a lot of weight. My stomach hurt, like I imagined Nick's must have done as the cancer had spread around it. My left hip, on the same spot where Nick's cancer had grown, ached and twinged, causing me to limp slightly. I had other disturbing symptoms. My arms and fingers tingled numbly. I had heart palpitations off and on through the day and night. I had moments of mental blankness when I had no idea where I was or what I was doing. In the local ironmonger, buying some light-switches one day, I stood staring into space for the best part of a minute when I should have been paying, vaguely aware of the snorts of derision coming from the lads behind the counter. Strangest was the effect on my voice. Within days of Nick's death it developed a 'crack' which made me sound as if I was recovering from a cold. I had found a new GP now and she sent me to a consultant who told me that the shock of what I had gone through had been neuromuscular: it had affected my vocal cords and caused reflux, which in turn irritated the vocal cords further. He prescribed antacids and speech therapy to go with the anti-depressants my GP proposed.

But to look at me you might not have known. To others I probably looked 'normal', and I was beginning to understand that people suffering a great tragedy can learn to lead two lives that run alongside each other like parallel tracks. There's the 'real' life with all its sorrow and strain, and there's the life in which you just get on with things, learning to act as if you're normal, because that's the only way to fit in. You put on a face that doesn't put other people off, and when they ask, 'How are you?' you reply, 'Fine thanks.' And the sad truth is that you do, over time, begin to get *used* to your tragedy. I liken it to being sentenced to life imprisonment. It never gets less awful, but the day comes when it's no longer a shock to find yourself there; that's when you realize that you've learned to adapt.

It's not that 'time heals', a phrase so oft-used and so misconstrued. Healing doesn't begin, as people often assume, the moment a funeral is over. That's just the *beginning* of the grief, the first opening of a wound which, over time, will grow and become more painful as the true depth of your loss is revealed. There is, I think, a moment when finally, the wound stops growing. Two years on, as I write this, mine has. But I've yet to notice any sign that it is starting to heal.

For Mother's Day the year he died Nick had sent me flowers with a note that read, 'To the best single mum of three boys.' I had often joked that looking after him when he was ill was like having another child. This year the boys had painted cards at school, spattered with hearts and 'I love you's'. For Father's Day they made cards too: Miss Keck understood that, as far as they were concerned, they still had a dad.

The boys adapted well to our new and smaller family, yet as many bereaved children do, they tried to fill the gap they felt by reminding themselves of who else was now close to them. I drew a family tree with them one day; we included everyone we could think of, from Granny, to their cousins, half-brothers and sister, godparents and, at their insistence, all the dogs we knew. Godmother Cathy's dog Stella got pride of place. 'He's our God-dog,' said Benedict.

Nick was never far from their thoughts and they talked about him, or to him, daily. 'I can feel Daddy hugging me,' said Joel matter-of-factly at tea-time one day. 'He just reaches down from Heaven and hugs me. I can feel his arms around me.' 'He's sitting next to me,' said Benedict, pointing to the chair at his side. 'He's always around, you know, Mummy, and he knows everything we do.' Although Joel's rages of the early days grew fewer and less intense, when he was angry with me he would hide in a corner with a photo of Nick and whisper quietly to him. One day, after a particularly bad argument, he stormed into the garden, tilted his head to the sky and shouted, 'Only *you* really love me, Daddy.'

I understood that the boys would never 'move on' and forget him; Nick will always be their dad and they will probably feel his loss most keenly when they are grown men and yearn to know what he was like and to create a clearer picture from the shadows of their memories. But as small children their time-frames are on a different scale to mine. Only three months after Nick died, Benedict watched me dab away some tears and said, 'Mummy, please stop crying, Daddy died *ages* ago,' and in a life as small as his, I suppose it was. They still hated it when I cried. When I tried to explain how hard I found it not to, Joel told me he had 'a great idea'. 'Mummy, if you can't stop crying, just try to smile,' he beamed. 'But it's so hard, darling, to smile, when I feel sad about Daddy.' He thought for a moment. 'OK, if you can't smile, just make a happy face. That's what Daddy used to tell us.' And I promised to try.

Looking back, it was probably not surprising that I would eventually have that breakdown. It was the price I paid for surviving that dreadful first year, for coping, for putting on my brave face to the outside world, for holding things together for the boys, for living in near complete isolation and living with grinding pain.

In October the boys and I went to the Cheltenham Literature Festival, as we had done the year before with Nick, to attend a debate in his memory and support the launch – with the backing of the BBC – of an annual prize named after him for the best broadcast interview of the year. I managed to smile gracefully, quashing the tremors inside, but once the boys and I had retired to our hotel bedroom I drank a bottle and a half of wine in a very short time and went to bed fully clothed and miserably drunk.

I felt the crash coming for days and tried to turn my back on it. I found myself crying everywhere, caring nothing for what people thought, snapping at everyone. I couldn't focus for more than a few minutes and spent my days racing around trying to do things but achieving almost nothing in the process. Then one day I was standing in the reception area at the dentist with Joel with tears pouring down my face, shouting furiously about having to wait for his appointment. Joel was distraught, but I no longer cared.

Nearly a year had passed but all time had brought was a new clarity of vision as the anniversary of Nick's death approached. The immediate aftermath of loss can hold you in a haze of numbness. As that anaesthetic wears off, you see a whole new reality and feel a whole new pain.

I don't know what the clinical definition of a breakdown is, and in the days before I finally lost my grip I sat up late at night scouring the Internet, desperate to understand what was happening to me. I started to drink my way through a bottle of gin and then, one evening, unearthed my small stash of diazepam, which had been prescribed when Nick's cancer returned and I had pleaded with the doctor for something to keep me calm. Diazepam, anti-depressants and gin. A potent cocktail that would surely keep the world at bay. When I had swallowed the tranquillizers I hid the bottle in a secret place in case 'someone' tried to take it from me – although I had no inkling who that 'someone' might be. I did the same the next night, and the next, lurching into bed late and barely able to function the next day. But I did function, somehow, until my resistance ran dry.

In the end it was something mundane that tipped me over the edge. The Sainsbury's shopping list. I knew we were running out of food, yet again, and I had to write a shopping list, yet again. But I couldn't do it. I just looked at a blank piece of paper until it dissolved into a blur as my eyes filled with tears. Try as I could, nothing happened. So I stopped. Everything. I lay on the floor. I shook. I wished, wished, wished, I could be taken away to a dark, quiet room somewhere and be looked after, away from everyone and everything.

I phoned Sarah, barely able to speak, and she came round. She sent me to bed with instructions that I was to do nothing.

Suzie arrived later that day after requesting emergency compassionate leave at work and took over. After four days in bed I was ready to pick myself up and start again. It was a frightening experience.

I'd love to say that what happened never happened again. But it did. And again. I learned to see it coming and knew what to do and it was never as bad as that first time.

And I never told anyone about it apart from those who were there to help me get through it.

At the beginning of November, as the first anniversary of Nick's death approached, I phoned a company offering white dove releases for special occasions. 'Wedding or funeral?' were the woman's first words. 'Er, memorial I suppose.'

In anticipation of the day I asked the boys to think of prayers for the event. Benedict suggested, 'Dear God, I hope Daddy is having a *really* good time in Heaven,' and he drew a picture of Nick in a boat chasing another boat with a 'Baddie' in it. 'Are there Baddies in Heaven?' I asked him. 'Just one, Mum,' but he wouldn't tell me who it was.

I stayed awake until just before one on the morning of 23 November, the time at which Nick had died. I felt very close to him that night and I really think he might have been with me, by my side, holding my hand, or whispering in my heart.

In the morning we met Suzie and Alastair who came up to London for the day, and we took the boys for lunch at the Rainforest Café, a children's underground adventure with animated models of gorillas, elephants, and leopards, with all the sounds of the jungle. Later Father Gillean met us at St Mary Abbots Church and led us to a small chapel where a candle was burning in front of the altar. 'The light of this candle,' he said to the boys, 'is the light of Heaven. It's what Daddy sees every day, and it is a light that is more beautiful than any we will ever see on Earth.' Joel and Benedict read from cards they had written. 'I love you, Daddy, and I hope you're playing lots of cricket and that you're the umpire,' said Joel. They placed presents for Nick on the altar: a toy fire-boat from Joel and a half-empty (or was it half-full?) bottle of tomato ketchup from Benedict. Then I read from Genesis, where Noah sends a dove out from the ark and it doesn't return: a sign that there is land, there is hope, there is new life.

In the churchyard we found a sombre-looking man dressed in black standing by a large wicker basket. Inside were four white doves, one for each of the boys, one for Suzie and one for me. 'When you release that dove,' Father Gillean had asked me a few days earlier, 'will you be able to release some of your pain and some of your anger?' I pondered. I hoped.

The man placed the basket on a tomb, took the birds out and placed them gently in our hands. They were the purest white, soft as a baby's skin, and as I held mine I could feel its heart pounding, its wings pressing against my fingers, its delicate body bursting to be free. The day was bathed in watery sunlight. The steeple of St Mary Abbots reached to the brilliant blue above. One by one we let our doves go, throwing them into the air where they flapped frantically before soaring, circling above us and then flying away into a pale winter sky.

Then I took the boys to H&M and bought them a Spiderman belt each before going home, where it still felt empty without Nick, but where two small boys, like those tiny doves, were brimming over with energy and bursting to be free to move on with life.

Epilogue

A scene runs through my mind. I am standing with Joel and Benedict by the front gate on a warm summer's day. It is 2005, the year when the sun last shone on our lives. The boys are jittery with excitement, I am grounded with contentment. We wait several minutes before we spot him at the top of the road, crossing over to our side of the street and walking towards us, relaxed and easy on his way back from work. He is wearing a white shirt and an orange tie which flaps in the breeze. His step is bold, jaunty. One hand clasps the old black briefcase I bought him all those years ago and which he carries every day to the office. The boys start to scream, 'Daaaaaaddy, Daaaady's back!' and his face lights up with that wide open smile that lit up my life, our lives.

He's nearly here now: we can make out his features, hear him calling to us, see the sheer joy in his eyes as he approaches the place where he is happiest, where he is surrounded by those who love him as deeply as he loves them — his home.

I wish I could write a happy ending for this story. But the truth is that there *is* no ending with grief, let alone a happy one, though I know you would like one. Loss never diminishes and grief never ends. It will live with me for ever, along with my memories of, and love for, Nick. He will always be there, in those scenes that play and re-play in my mind, in the surroundings we once shared, and in every little thing that I now do in my life without him by my side, in the familiar and the unfamiliar, all of which feel meaningless to me now that I cannot share them with my soul mate. I see Nick every day in the big blue eyes of my children, and my heart will always be heavy with the knowledge that every breath they take, from this day on, will be taken without their father. That he cannot watch them live, breathe and grow up to be young men rips my heart to shreds.

Much time has passed now since Nick died. Yet in some ways so little. His suits still hang in the wardrobe, his sweaters lie folded in the drawers – all put away carefully in the expectation that they would be worn again. I cannot let them go. I haven't come to terms yet with what has happened, still can't believe he's not here, still wonder why this had to happen to him, why it had to happen to *me*.

When I started this journey I walked hand in hand with fear. I could see no future and had nothing to live for. But the fear *is* making way for hope, which breaks in like shards of light appearing from behind a dark curtain. It makes me think that in time there will be space again in my life for the emotions I used to live with. One of which – I hope – will be happiness. I just need to discover it, and then share it with the boys, who really and truly deserve it.

Sarah tells me this *will* happen. And I believe her now, where once I couldn't. And in my better moments I do think, Why *not* me? Why shouldn't I have a chance to live again, maybe even to love again? Somehow.

Grief, I now know, takes you to a different world, and you never really leave it. I wish we could 'get over' it, but I don't believe we do. You learn to incorporate it into your life, an unwanted travelling companion which stalks you day and night, invisible to others, but always by your side and never less than hateful.

If you ever see me you might think I've shed it along my way, as I've travelled the journey through grief. But look more closely and you will see, and understand, that it is still there, and will be there – always and for ever.

I miss him.

Acknowledgements

I have dedicated this book to Sarah Kershaw from Cruse Bereavement Care. Like thousands of Cruse volunteers around the country, she gives her time freely to help people who are experiencing the most painful time of their lives. I have only the words in this book to express my untold thanks to her for listening, understanding, encouraging and supporting me as she helped me to get back on my feet. I feel privileged to have met her, and privileged now to count her as a friend. There are so many things I would never have managed without her – not least finishing this.

Nor would this book have been completed without my editor, Alan Wilkinson, whose guidance, re-writing and all round incomparable brilliance turned my words from a muddled mishmash into something publishable. I also owe a huge thanks to Becky Swift at The Literary Consultancy for putting me in touch with Alan.

The other Alan to whom I owe thanks is Alan Samson at Orion for his belief in, and commitment to, this project – sometimes against the odds. Lucinda McNeile at Orion was meticulous with the text. My agent, David Miller, bought me loads of cups of (expensive) coffee and never lost faith in me, though many might have.

Anita Kidgell, Douglas Lee and Nick Sutton made helpful comments on the manuscript.

I'd like shamelessly to use this opportunity to thank the

people who in different ways were there for me – and the boys – through our difficult times. They are: Nick's sister Suzie Clark, who was a rock despite her own grief at the loss of her brother, her husband Alastair, Daniel Barry, Liz Brockmann, Jane Corbin, Mark Damazer, Gillean Craig, Lisa Jenkinson, Sally Keck, Anita Kidgell, Tessa Laws, Angela Levin, Eddie Mair, Zsuzsanna Mrena, Anna Roads, Gabby Osrin and my mum.

Thanks to Radio 4 listener and friend Kila Millidine and correspondent Fiona Newton.

Kate, Danny, Brett and many others at Winston's Wish have guided us with wisdom and compassion.

Thank you to everyone who wrote to Nick when he was ill and who wrote to me after his death: I'm so sorry we replied to so few. Every letter was read. And appreciated.

And no thanks at all to the wretched builders who never finished the bathroom adaptations for Nick. You know who you are.

I thank R. for holding my hand as I walked the treacherous journey that is grief and for opening new doors for me.

And of course I love and thank Benedict and Joel, who have shown incredible bravery for such small people. Thank you for putting up with my inadequacies as a single parent, thank you for sharing your zest for life, and thank you for giving me a reason to keep going. Your dad would be so very proud of you.

Finally . . . Nick. The other day I dreamed I met you in Heaven. We stood and stared at each other with smiles of utter joy. We didn't say a word. We didn't need to.

Thank you Nick for giving me the greatest gift: love.